"Good News" after Auschwitz?
Christian Faith within a Post-Holocaust World

*Soon afterward he [Jesus] went on through cities and villages,
preaching and bringing the good news of the kingdom of God.*
(Luke 8:1 RSV)

*The beginning, the end: all the world's roads, all the outcries of
mankind, lead to this accursed place. Here [Auschwitz] is the
kingdom of night, where God's face is hidden and a flaming sky
becomes a graveyard for a vanished people.*
(Elie Wiesel, *From the Kingdom of Memory*)

"Good News" after Auschwitz?

Christian Faith
within a Post-Holocaust World

edited and introduced by
Carol Rittner and John K. Roth

MERCER UNIVERSITY PRESS
June 2001

ISBN 0-86554-701-7   MUP/H520

"Good News" after Auschwitz?
Christian Faith within a Post-Holocaust World
Copyright ©2001
Mercer University Press, Macon, Georgia USA

The paper used in this publication meets the minimum requirements
of American National Standard for Information Sciences—
Permanence of Paper for Printed Library Materials, ANSI Z39.48-1984.

Library of Congress Cataloging-in-Publication Data

Good news after Auschwitz? :
Christian faith within a post-Holocaust world /
edited and introduced by Carol Rittner and John K. Roth.
p. cm.
Includes bibliographical references and index.
ISBN 0-86554-701-7 (alk. paper)
1. Holocaust (Christian theology).
I. Rittner, Carol Ann, 1943– . II. Roth, John K.
BT93.G66 2001
231.7'6—dc21

2001030303
CIP

Contents

To Harold Rosenn

May the LORD, maker of heaven and earth, bless you from Zion.
(Psalm 134:3)

Introduction

A Jarring Juxtaposition

Carol Rittner and John K. Roth

Two epigraphs introduce this book. One comes from the Gospel of Luke. It reports that Jesus brought "good news" about the kingdom of God. The other comes from Holocaust survivor Elie Wiesel. It speaks of Auschwitz, an accursed place at the center of "the kingdom of night, where God's face is hidden." The juxtaposition of these epigraphs creates dissonance. Especially for Christians, it should be jarring, because the "good news" that Jesus brought—at least as the Christian religion has often interpreted that news—turned out to be so hostile to Jews that it helped to produce the Holocaust's darkness.

After Auschwitz, can Christians still affirm that Jesus brings good news? The post-Holocaust Christians who have contributed to this book want to say *yes*. They know, however, that doing so is as complicated as it is important. Two documents—both issued too late for full consideration in this book—and some episodes related to them illustrate this point. A word about them may be helpful.

First, on 5 September 2000, the Roman Catholic Church's Congregation for the Doctrine of the Faith issued *Dominus Jesus*, a declaration "On the Unicity and Salvific Universality of Jesus Christ and the Church." At the time of this writing a month later, a firestorm of controversy showed few signs of abating despite claims from the Vatican and Pope John Paul II that the declaration has been misinterpreted and misunderstood.

Urging repeatedly that the Church's teachings in this declaration must be "firmly believed," *Dominus Jesus* contains at least two claims that are at the controversy's core. One claim is that "the salvation of all" comes uniquely, singularly, exclusively, universally, and absolutely through Jesus Christ. The other asserts that the Church is intended by God to be "the instrument for the salvation of *all* humanity," a condition entailing that "the followers of other religions," even if they may receive a kind of divine grace, remain "in a gravely deficient situation" compared to those who are fully within the Church.

Dominus Jesus claims that its absolutist teachings about Jesus Christ and the Church express no disrespect for "the religions of the world." Subsequent Vatican commentary urged that the declaration was intended primarily to guide the Catholic faithful. Nevertheless, *Dominus Jesus* affirms that the Vatican's version of Christianity should and does supersede every other religious tradition. In an increasingly pluralistic religious world, that stance is problematic to say the least. Adding fuel to the fires of controversy, the Vatican issued its declaration only two days after Pope John Paul II had beatified Pope Pius IX, the first step on that nineteenth-century pontiff's path to canonization as a saint. Not only did Pius IX reign longer than any other pope to date but his pronouncements and policies were frequently antisemitic.[1] His condoning of what has come to be known as the kidnapping of Edgardo Mortara—a six-year-old Jewish boy who was taken from his home by the Church after being baptized without the knowledge of his family—is only the most notorious example. Together, *Dominus Jesus* and the beatification of Pope Pius IX illustrate how little some Christians have learned from the Holocaust, which got support from attitudes and actions of the kind that found expression at the Vatican as the summer of the year 2000 drew to a close.

Overwhelmingly, the positions held by the Christians who have contributed to this book are at odds with the events just noted. For that reason, the contributors surely welcome a very different document that was also issued too late to be explicitly discussed in the essays that follow. This document does not have a Latin name but one in Hebrew: *Dabru Emet*, that is, "Speak Truth." While its contents were not greeted with complete approval within Jewish communities or elsewhere, it was endorsed by nearly 170 Jewish scholars and rabbis on 10 September 2000, just five days after *Dominus Jesus* appeared. *Dabru Emet* is a Jewish statement on Christians and Christianity. It certainly did not have *Dominus Jesus* and the beatification of Pope Pius IX in mind, but *Dabru Emet*

---

[1][Editors' note.] Except for some instances in quoted materials and titles, we use the terms "antisemitic" and "antisemitism" instead of "anti-Semitic" and "anti-Semitism." Particularly in the later decades of nineteenth-century European politics, the term "Semite" was exploited to set Jews apart from non-Jews, including even from other so-called Semitic peoples—Arabs, for example—and particularly to reinforce a negative, race-based perception of Jews and Judaism. The hyphenated and capitalized form "anti-Semitism" and its variations honor, however inadvertently, distinctions that are erroneous and misleading. Jews are not a race, nor is the category "Semite" a clear one. The forms "antisemitic" and "antisemitism" retain the prejudicial, anti-Jewish meaning, but also protest the harmful confusions that attend the hyphenated and capitalized forms of these terms.

warmly acknowledges that post-Holocaust Christianity embodies many changes for the good.

In particular, post-Holocaust Christianity has expressed remorse for "Christian mistreatment of Jews and Judaism" and considerably reformed its characterization and understanding of Jewish life and tradition. (Although Pope John Paul II's memorable visit to Israel in the spring of 2000 is not mentioned explicitly in the document, the pope's words and deeds in the Holy Land illustrate some of what *Dabru Emet* has in mind at this point.) As it states that Christianity's anti-Jewish teachings and policies helped make the Holocaust possible, and that too many Christians were implicated in the Holocaust, *Dabru Emet* also asserts unequivocally that "Nazism was not a Christian phenomenon," and it expresses profound gratitude for Christians who rescued Jews during those dark times.

The Jewish document also urges full recognition of the fact that there is a "humanly irreconcilable difference between Jews and Christians." Such recognition enjoins a deepening of fully mutual respect.

The essays here seek to affirm and to justify the proclamations made in *Dabru Emet*. Implicitly, if not explicitly, this book indicates that the paths taken by *Dominus Jesus* and the beatification of problematic popes are not the route to take, and it seeks to offer better alternatives. It does so with the awareness that especially the task of offering better alternatives requires precautions lest the Holocaust's full impact on Christianity be minimized and the unfortunate outcome of premature closure silences questions that should remain unsettled and unsettling. The Holocaust's impact on Christianity requires nothing less than a deepfelt reformation of Christian practices and a thorough rethinking of Christian proclamations. The essays found here advance those directions.

Often, reflections by Christian scholars of the Holocaust tend to dwell on guilt and shame about the Holocaust. While those moods have their place and must not be underestimated, let alone ignored, the contributors to *"Good News" after Auschwitz? Christian Faith within a Post-Holocaust World* believe the time has come for Christian Holocaust scholars to express a more affirmative Christian vision—not by downplaying the Holocaust and Christianity's part in it but by showing how Christianity has crucial affirmations to make *after* Auschwitz.

The thirteen contributors include laypersons and clergy from diverse Christian backgrounds, ranging from Roman Catholic and Southern Baptist to Jehovah's Witness and mainstream Protestant. Each is a seasoned Holocaust scholar who is well aware of Christianity's anti-Jewish tendencies and, in particular, its shortcomings during the Holocaust. Nevertheless, they also believe that Christianity—challenged, chastened, and changed by the Holocaust's tempering fire—does have "good news" to offer in a post-Holocaust world. The contributors have had free rein in putting together their essays, which vary in style, substance, and form, but in every case they clarify and focus that central theme.

For Christians, the idea of "good news" is closely connected with what the New Testament calls "the gospel of Jesus Christ" (Mark 1:1). The Christian gospel focuses on the life and teachings of Jesus, but it is not primarily a biography or a chronicle. Instead, the Christian gospel is a proclamation that bears witness to God's presence as it is revealed through the life, death, and resurrection of Jesus, the Jew from Nazareth.

The good news that Jesus preaches and brings is profoundly Jewish. When, for example, the Gospel of Luke describes Jesus' observance of the Sabbath in Nazareth, the writer identifies Jesus by having him read from the prophet Isaiah: "The Spirit of the Lord is upon me, because he has anointed me to preach good news to the poor. He has sent me to proclaim release to the captives and recovering of sight to the blind, to set at liberty those who are oppressed, to proclaim the acceptable year of the Lord" (Luke 4:18, Isaiah 61:1-2a). In the Gospel of Matthew, the writer has Jesus say, "Think not that I have come to abolish the law and the prophets" (Matthew 5:17a), and when the Gospel of Mark identifies God's most fundamental commandments, Jesus turns to the heart of his Jewish faith and says: "The first is, 'Hear, O Israel: The Lord our God, the Lord is one; and you shall love the Lord your God with all your heart, and with all your soul, and with all your mind, and with all your strength.' The second is this, 'You shall love your neighbor as yourself'" (Mark 12:29-31a).

The good news that Jesus preaches and brings is profoundly Jewish, but Christians believe Jesus delivers and reveals that good news in a distinctive way, which is summed up in the Christian teaching that Jesus is the incarnation of God. Jews and Christians strongly disagree on this point, and it must be acknowledged that the Holocaust is among the consequences of that disagreement. That fact, in turn, raises the motivating question for this book: How can the Christian phrase "good news" be paired in any way with an accursed place called Auschwitz? Striving to be committed post-Holocaust Christians, the contributors struggle with that difficult issue in ways illustrated by the book's three-part organization.

The first part contains essays about precautions. They stress problems that Auschwitz causes for any post-Holocaust proclamation of Christian good news. The second part contains essays about practices. They empha-

size actions that Christians need to take if any post-Holocaust proclamation of good news is to be credible. The third part contains essays about
proclamations. Sensitized by necessary precautions and reformed practices, they illustrate what Christianity's post-Holocaust good news could
credibly say. As the various essays complement, supplement, and at
times dispute one another, they are part of a process of post-Holocaust
Christian reflection that needs to be ongoing.

The development of this book reflects that process. At the 1998
meeting of the Annual Scholars' Conference on the Holocaust and the
Churches, which took place at the University of Washington in Seattle,
Vicki Barnett, Hank Knight, Carol Rittner, and John Roth found our
coffee-break conversation taking a Christian turn. For years, we have
been committed to Holocaust studies because of our Christian identities,
but on this occasion we wondered together what would happen if something took place that none of us had previously experienced, namely, that
Christian Holocaust scholars would meet to talk openly about the positive proclamations, if any, that Christianity could make after Auschwitz.

The four of us agreed to pursue the project. Soon, Carol Rittner had
secured resources and a venue at College Misericordia, Dallas, Pennsylvania, and John Roth joined her to convene the January 1999 consultation
that brought this book's diverse contributors together.

We asked people to bring questions to College Misericordia. There
were many. For example, the failure of Christianity in the mid-twentieth
century was monumental, but was it fatal? Is it appropriate for Christians
to speak about "good news" after Auschwitz? If there is no "good news,"
how do Christians retain their identity as Christians and remain faithful
to their God and loyal to their church? If Christianity moves beyond its
dependence on supersessionism and triumphalism to retain post-Holocaust integrity, what happens to the "good news" that Christians
proclaim? How does it change? What is retained? What guides our
governing work? Before, during, and after our deliberations at College
Misericordia, we have found that such questions are neither easy nor idle,
especially because the world contains some two billion confessed
Christians.

We also asked people to bring very brief working papers to College
Misericordia. Along with our many questions, these papers became the
focal points of discussion that informed the eventual elaboration of our
writing. Meanwhile, on two occasions—including the Annual Scholars'
Conference on the Holocaust and the Churches in 1999—members of our
group had the opportunity to make presentations to larger audiences. It
was particularly interesting and significant that large numbers of Jews

attended those sessions. They wanted to know what post-Holocaust Christians had to say about the future and the content of Christian faith. They encouraged our efforts.

It is fitting, then, that this book should be dedicated to Harold Rosenn, a good Jewish friend who has generously supported College Misericordia, its initiatives in Holocaust studies, and, in particular, the consultation that resulted in this book. We are also grateful to College Misericordia's president, Michael MacDowell, and his wife, Tina, who gave us warm encouragement and hospitality. We are indebted as well to Jason Stiffler at Claremont McKenna College, whose technical expertise facilitated production of the manuscript. Finally, Marc Jolley of Mercer University Press provided insightful guidance that enhanced our efforts in so many ways. To him and his excellent staff, especially Marketing Director Maggy Shannon, we offer heartfelt thanks. Writers, of course, always appreciate their readers, and the contributors to this book are no exception. Each and all, we hope you will find—whatever your religious persuasion—that the issues discussed in these pages are timely, significant, and worth the time that you invest in reflecting with us about them.

Part One

Precautions

Precautions are actions taken in advance to guard against danger or failure. Such circumspection is essential when Christians consider what they should—and should not—proclaim and practice after the Holocaust. One danger is that Christians will speak in haste; they will not confront deeply enough the credibility crisis that the Holocaust produced for Christian faith. Another danger is that Christians will simply reaffirm what they have long been professing; they will fail to realize sufficiently that the Holocaust raises questions that Christians can ill afford to ignore. Unless Christians recognize these dangers, failure will stalk their efforts to present "good news" after Auschwitz. Such failure will reveal blindness and arrogance that further damage a Christian tradition already badly wounded by the Holocaust.

The following contributions by Stephen Haynes, Stephen Smith, Bev. Allen Asbury, and Hubert Locke are cautionary essays. Haynes identifies "fallacies and false promises that bedevil the path toward genuine post-Holocaust Christianity." Smith warns that post-Holocaust Christianity must reckon with "a crisis of moral, spiritual, and theological credibility." Asbury sees that Christians need to wrestle profoundly with a fundamental question: Can one still be a Christian after Auschwitz? Locke observes that the Holocaust makes problematic Christianity's basic theological premise that God works in history.

These post-Holocaust Christians rightly bring skepticism, even suspicion, to the exploration of "good news" after Auschwitz. Their motive for doing so is not to undermine Christianity, although some versions of that tradition richly deserve it, but instead to chasten, recover, and restore what can and should be practiced and proclaimed by post-Holocaust Christians. They all write in the service of what Locke calls "Christian integrity after Auschwitz."

Chapter 1

Beware Good News:
Faith and Fallacy
in Post-Holocaust Christianity

Stephen R. Haynes

This book is about the possibility of good news after Auschwitz. While I am anxious to hear that good news and let it sink into a soul that has become weary, I am also suspicious of Christians—including myself—who want to preach good news before fully comprehending the bad news of the Holocaust. Perhaps this attitude reflects my Calvinist background and temperament, which make me suspicious of theological reflection that is overly positive. Whatever the reason, I offer my contribution to this book as a way of ensuring that post-Holocaust Christians will not engage in premature self-congratulation. Because considerable patience and acuity are required to navigate among the fallacies and false promises that bedevil the path toward a genuine post-Holocaust Christianity, I will focus on the temptations that can seduce Christians who want desperately to hear good news in the wake of Auschwitz.

Fallacies of Continuity, Discontinuity, and Authenticity

The axiom that religion was a "necessary" but not a "sufficient" condition for the Holocaust is a reliable starting point for assessing the problem of Christianity's implication in Nazi genocide.[1] But between the parameters outlined by these philosophical concepts lies a wide and treacherous territory that must be navigated by the post-Holocaust Christian.

---

[1]Richard L. Rubenstein and John K. Roth, *Approaches to Auschwitz* (Atlanta: John Knox Press, 1987) 290. The principle may be applied to Christian faith in this way: Christianity was a *necessary condition* for the Holocaust inasmuch as the statement "if there had been no Christianity, there would have been no Holocaust" is true. Christian faith was not a *sufficient condition* for the Holocaust inasmuch as the statement "since there was Christianity, there would eventually be a Holocaust" is not true.

On one edge is the *discontinuity fallacy*. Calculated to distance Christian faith from the horrors of the Holocaust, the discontinuity fallacy eschews Christian responsibility for the Shoah[2] by claiming that Nazism was anti-Christian, that true Christians do not participate in murder, or that "authentic Christianity" is not anti-Jewish. While these statements may be true in themselves, each can be used to sustain the fallacy of discontinuity in a way that falsifies history and evades moral responsibility. While the discontinuity fallacy is an attractive refuge for post-Holocaust Christians when the moral credibility of the faith is threatened, history and faith alike compel them to avoid it.

Ironically, attempts to elude the discontinuity fallacy can push Christians toward the equally false fallacy of *continuity*. Advocates of this fallacy argue or imply that Christianity is *the* reason for the Holocaust—because Christians have always hated Jews, because Christianity has always sought to replace Judaism, or because the Nazis only did to Jews what Christians had desired to do for centuries. While there is truth in each of these statements, they can be used to falsify history by creating the appearance of a substantive identity between Christian and Nazi forms of Jew-hatred. This presumed continuity ignores important dimensions of the Christian understanding of the Jew, including its reliance upon religious rather than racial identity to define "Jews," and its preservationist notion that God wills for the Jewish people to remain until the consummation of history.

When considering their faith's implication in the Holocaust, Christians often careen back and forth between the fallacies of continuity and discontinuity. But even when these fallacies have been acknowledged and avoided, the *authenticity fallacy* can exercise a strong attraction for post-Holocaust Christians. This fallacy affirms that Christians contributed to the presence of antisemitism and aided the annihilation of Jews during the Holocaust, but contends that a remedy for these problems lies in a recovery of authentic Christian faith. Like the other fallacies, this one contains some truth, but it encourages Christians in the dangerous belief that the legacy of Christian anti-Judaism can be ended through personal

---

[2][Editors' note.] *Shoah*, from שׁוֹאָה or שֹׁאָה, is a Hebrew term for "tempest," "storm," and by extension of the resulting "devastation" or "desolation." Apparently, Shoah has become the preferred term for the Holocaust by, especially, Jewish scholars who feel "Holocaust" has lost much of its significance through overuse. Often italicized, Shoah is here considered adopted into English—although it has yet to be listed in many current dictionaries—and thus occurs simply as (roman) Shoah.

repudiations of antisemitic prejudice rather than serious analysis of the church's textual and historical traditions.[3]

Scholars, clergy, and laypersons responding to the church's moral failure during the Nazi era often invoke "authentic Christianity" to emphasize the breakdown of Christian values under Hitler. But if "authentic Christianity" remains undefined and disembodied, this project can become the means for a flight from history and tradition. Like other obstacles to genuine post-Holocaust faith, the authenticity fallacy can be found throughout the contemporary church. In my experience, church groups that study the Holocaust almost instinctively deflect the moral burden of Christian complicity in the Shoah upon someone else. If they are liberals, responsibility for the faith's corruption falls upon "conservatives"; if they are conservatives, "liberals" were to blame. The lesson seems to be that "inauthentic Christianity" is always easier to recognize when it appears in someone else's institutions or traditions.

The authenticity fallacy can also enter Christian discourse when stories of rescue and resistance are told. As important as these stories are, they can be used to obscure the church's larger failures. Christians are naturally attracted to stories that confirm the purity of Christianity and the faithfulness of at least some practitioners. But can we be trusted to keep these compelling stories in perspective? In 1974 American Lutherans acknowledged the temptation these stories represent when they wrote that, "the kindness of Scandinavian Lutherans towards Jews cannot alter

---

[3]See Stephen T. Davis, "Evangelicals and Holocaust Theology," *American Journal of Theology and Philosophy* 2/3 (September 1981): 121-29. For a more subtle form of the fallacy, see Jack Forstman, *Christian Faith in Dark Times: Theological Conflicts in the Shadow of Hitler* (Louisville: Westminster/John Knox Press, 1992). Forstman analyzes the theological conflicts among German theological heavyweights of the 1920s and 1930s with an eye toward identifying resources in Christian faith that can enable us to recognize evil before it shows itself and, if necessary, respond with a loud "No." But, strangely, Forstman never defines "Christian faith," nor does he defend the assumption that authentic Christian belief contains no foothold for antisemitism. The real question facing post-Holocaust Christianity—whether Christian faith is essentially anti-Jewish or only historically so—is bypassed in Forstman's otherwise insightful study. See my review of Forstman's *Christian Faith in Dark Times*: "Anti-Judaism among the Bad Guys and the Good," *Cross Currents* (Fall 1994): 413-15. For another example of this phenomenon, see William Foxwell Albright, "Gerhard Kittel and the Jewish Question in Antiquity," in *History, Archeology, and Christian Humanism* (New York: McGraw-Hill, 1964) 229-40, where Kittel's entire career is understood as an aberration from true Christianity.

the ugly facts of forced labor and concentration camps in Hitler's Germany."[4]

The Fallacy of Superficial Engagement

The fallacy of superficial engagement is closely related to the fallacies of continuity, discontinuity, and authenticity. It tempts Christians to conclude, without serious analysis, that Christian antisemitism *is* an oxymoron because it *ought to be*. The logic seems to go like this: Jew-hatred is a blight on Christianity that is foreign to the Bible and to the church's best theology and doctrine. Through a lamentable historical irony, Christianity became tainted with anti-Judaism. The Holocaust has revealed this problem and its evil consequences, and the church must now remove this taint and return to the purity of New Testament faith.

In the years following the Holocaust, the fallacy of superficial engagement was perpetuated by scholars of antisemitism who miscalculated its connection to biblical Christianity. This "reformist"[5] view of the relationship between Christian faith and antisemitism actually evolved in the first two-thirds of this century. It was forged by historians who sought to document the tragic history of Jewish life in Christendom. While not hesitating to assign Christendom responsibility for the existence of antisemitism, these reformists considered Jew-hatred a tragic corruption of Christian faith in its essence. Whether they detected the source of this corruption in "the conflict of the church and the synagogue" (James Parkes), the credulity of popular Christianity in the Middle Ages (Joshua Trachtenberg), or the innate human need to condemn what is strange or threatening, reformists were (and are) guided by the conviction that Christian Jew-hatred has historical roots that can be identified and extirpated.

In the 1970s a new model for understanding Christianity's relation to *Judenhass* began to take shape with the publication Rosemary R. Ruether's *Faith and Fratricide*. Ruether's book generated considerable debate, and by the end of the 1970s a "radical" paradigm for interpreting the relationship

---

[4]"The American Lutheran Church and the Jewish Community" (1974) in *The Theology of the Churches and the Jewish People: Statements by the World Council of Churches and Its Member Churches,* ed. Allan Brockway, Paul van Buren, Rolf Rendtorff, and Simon Schoon (Geneva: WCC Publications, 1988) 69.

[5]For a fuller development of my argument, see Stephen R. Haynes, "Changing Paradigms: Reformist, Radical, and Rejectionist Approaches to the Relationship of Christianity and Anti-Semitism," *Journal of Ecumenical Studies* 32/1 (Winter 1995): 63-88.

of Christianity and antisemitism became widely accepted in scholarly circles. Ruether contended that anti-Judaism was fundamental to the early Christian movement's self-understanding as the "true Israel," and of its Lord as the Jewish Messiah. In a memorable formulation of the problem, she maintained that within two decades of Jesus' death anti-Judaism had become "the left hand of Christology." On the other hand, Ruether claimed that this anti-Jewish trajectory in the early church was not faithful to the life and teaching of Jesus, whom she located squarely in the world of first-century Jewish sectarianism.

Following Ruether, radical interpreters of the relationship between Christianity and Jew-hatred acknowledge that anti-Judaism is woven into the very fabric of the Christian story; but they believe that critical scholarship can extricate authentic Christian faith from the New Testament *kerygma* ("proclamation"). Thus, even if anti-Judaism is detectable in some of the earliest expressions of Christian theology, it is not essential to saving faith in Jesus. This caveat is pivotal, since it allows radicals to admit deep flaws in Christianity's very heart without relinquishing the life of faith itself.

More recently, scholars such as Gavin I. Langmuir of Stanford University, Hyam Maccoby of Leo Baeck College (London), and Joel Carmichael, editor of the journal *Midstream*, have begun to raise a "rejectionist" challenge to the reformist and radical views outlined above. These "rejectionists" assail the supposed discontinuity of religious anti-Judaism and modern antisemitism in which Christian scholars have sought refuge from the burden of responsibility for Nazi racism, and they are suspicious of unproven assertions that the religiosity which paved the way for Nazism was a tragic distortion of authentic Christian faith. More crucially, they cast doubt upon all attempts to defend Christianity by positing a pristine gospel essence that is free of anti-Judaism. In these ways, they problematize the assumption shared by reformists and radicals alike that antisemitism is a corruption of authentic Christian faith.

Most Christian scholars with an interest in the problem of antisemitism have moved from the reformist to the radical camp, but they are reluctant to go further. In fact, the rejectionist challenge has not been widely acknowledged—let alone welcomed—in the Christian community. Resistance seems to be the result of several factors.

First, the desire to believe that Jew-hatred does not affect Christian institutions, texts, or convictions—that it is "a contradiction and an affront to the Gospel," as the Evangelical Lutheran Church put it in 1994[6]—is quite strong. Second, since most churches have responded to the Shoah with strong condemnations of antisemitism, it is not clear why the relationship of Christianity and Jew-hatred should remain an issue. As long ago as 1948, the World Council of Churches Assembly called upon Christians "to denounce antisemitism, no matter what its origin, as absolutely irreconcilable with the profession and practice of the Christian faith."[7] With a multitude of statements denouncing Jew-hatred as "sin against God and human life," many Christians have come to believe the church has done its part to rid the world of this evil. Third, many of the scholars most vitally concerned with the problem of Christian anti-Judaism are emissaries of the institutional church, which remains the object of their loyalty and identity.[8] For them to consider the rejectionist challenge seriously might create serious personal and professional conflicts. Fourth, the most significant post-Holocaust Christian theology to emerge in the last few decades is firmly rooted in "radical" assumptions regarding the connection between faith and Jew-hatred.[9]

Finally, reformist views are popularized by church statements that confidently regard antisemitism as a corruption of authentic Christian belief whose origins are identifiable. A chief example is Vatican II's *Nostra Aetate*, which states that "all should take pains, . . . lest in catechetical instruction and in the preaching of God's Word they teach anything out of harmony with the truth of the gospel and the spirit of Christ." This statement follows a rather superficial treatment of Christian anti-Judaism and its biblical roots. A similar assertion was made in 1972 by the General Conference of the United Methodist Church, which stressed that "there is no valid biblical or theological basis for antisemitism," but did not address how the church's traditions had provided such a basis in the past.[10] Finally, the Presbyterian Church (USA)'s "A Theological Understanding of the Relationship between Christians and Jews" (1987) observed that "sometime during the second century of the Common Era, a view called 'supersessionism,' based on the reading of

---

[6]"The Declaration of the Evangelical Lutheran Church in America to the Jewish Community," in Frank E. Eakin, Jr., *What Price Prejudice?: Christian Antisemitism in America* (New York: Paulist Press and the Stimulus Foundation, 1998) 163.

[7]Cited in Eakin, *What Price Prejudice?*, 157.

[8]This source of resistance is evident in Wesley J. Fisher's "Response to Stephen R. Haynes," *Journal of Ecumenical Studies* 33/1 (Winter 1996): 93-96.

[9]For a sustained argument of this point, see Haynes, "Changing Paradigms."

[10]In Brockway et al., eds., *The Theology of the Churches and the Jewish People*, 63.

some biblical texts and nurtured in controversy, began to take shape."[11] Christian supersessionism, in other words, can be rooted out without reevaluating the message of Scripture.

Such church statements bolster the popular perception that there is nothing in Christian belief in which antisemitism can find a foothold. Because thoughtful Christians deplore hatred and prejudice, they believe that when church bodies officially condemn antisemitism as unchristian, the innocence of their faith, if not historic Christian behavior, has been vindicated. Though reformism seems to represent the most efficient method for responding to the tradition of Christian anti-Judaism, it only perpetuates the fallacy of superficial engagement. For the characteristic of reformism that accounts for its popularity—the belief that contempt for Jews is related to Christian belief only superficially through historical circumstance—is also its chief limitation. For the more we learn about antisemitism, the more unlikely it appears that it is the simple result of failure to fulfill the demands of Christian charity or Enlightenment values.

The Fallacy of Theological Retrieval

The fallacy of theological retrieval is a post-Holocaust pitfall that has proven particularly alluring for theologians and church bodies wishing to set a new tone for Jewish-Christian relations. Intimately related to the temptations discussed above, this fallacy assumes that the positive elements of traditional church teaching concerning the Jews can create a solid basis for post-Holocaust Jewish-Christian relations. This is a natural Christian response to the Holocaust, of course. As the Texas Council of Churches noted in 1982, the Shoah summons the churches "to re-examine (and reform) their traditional understanding of Judaism and the Jewish people."[12] This reexamination typically begins with references to the "spiritual ties" binding Jews and Christians, ties that are crucial to Christian self-identity and that can encourage Christians to support Jews under threat. For instance, in 1943 the Lutheran bishops of Denmark resisted a Nazi request for action against Danish Jews by pointing out that "we will never forget that the Lord Jesus Christ was born in

---

[11]"A Theological Understanding of the Relationship between Christians and Jews" (1987), in Eakin, *What Price Prejudice?*, 140.

[12]"Dialogue: A Contemporary Alternative to Proselytization" (1982), in Brockway et al., eds., *The Theology of the Churches and the Jewish People*, 96.

Bethlehem of the Virgin Mary, according to God's promise to the Chosen People of Israel."[13]

However, there are reasons to beware the good news represented by the spiritual ties that bind church and synagogue. First, as Arthur Cohen argued in the 1950s, the notion of the "Judeo-Christian tradition" is a myth, and remains an illusion in the post-Holocaust world, despite the desire of both Jews and Christians that it be otherwise. As Cohen pointed out, the intimate connection between Judaism and Christianity was actually forged in the minds of Enlightenment *philosophes* who regarded both as enemies of reason.[14] Second, post-Holocaust theological reflection that begins with a recognition of common spiritual paternity almost inevitably issues in a reiteration of Christian mythology regarding the Jews.

While this is not the intent, it is often the result. In many cases the mythological Jew enters the picture when post-Holocaust theology returns to the first Christian understanding of the Jew articulated by Paul in Romans 9–11. This is the case, for instance, in the World Council of Churches' 1957 statement on "Attitudes in Relation to the Jewish People" and in Vatican II's *Nostra Aetate* (1965).[15] Paul's confirmation of Jewish election *post christum* is a natural place for post-Holocaust theology to commence. However, because the Pauline conception of the Jew is a theological construction,[16] one that by the fourth century CE gave rise to an elaborate myth of the Jews as witness people, it is a dangerous starting place for post-Shoah theology. For centuries the witness-people myth has animated the Christian imagination with the notion that Jews witness to God's grace and judgment in the vicissitudes of their history.

Of course, the Pauline/Augustinian understanding of Jewish existence is retrieved precisely to counteract Christian anti-Judaism. The problem is that both "positive" and "negative" dimensions of traditional Christian teaching are lenses in a larger mythological camera through

---

[13]"Letter from Danish Lutheran Bishops to German Occupation Officials (October 3, 1943)," in Alexis P. Rubin, *Scattered among the Nations: Documents Affecting Jewish History 49 to 1975* (Northvale NJ: Jason Aronson, 1995) 246.

[14]Arthur A. Cohen, *The Myth of the Judeo-Christian Tradition* (New York: Harper & Row, 1963) xviii.

[15]"Report of the Ecumenical Institute to the Executive Committee of the World Council of Churches," and "Declaration of the Relation of the Church to Non-Christian Religions," in Rubin, *Scattered among the Nations*, 296 and 302.

[16]As Arthur Cohen has said, "Pauline theology is a dialogue with the Gentiles in which the Jew is assumed and is silent" (*The Myth of the Judeo-Christian Tradition*, 75).

which Jews are perceived as unique witnesses of divine action in the world. Though well-intentioned, then, the effort to develop a post-Holocaust theological understanding of the Jew that is "biblical" or anchored in "salvation history" makes the Jew vulnerable once again to the fantasies and projections of non-Jews. Historically, the church's "positive" theology of Judaism has encouraged preservation of the Jews based on their role in "the last things." But what happens when Jews do not fulfill the role set for them in the Christian mind? The result is Christian post-Holocaust theological reflection in which reverence for mysterious Israel is accompanied by "pious indignation at Jewish stubbornness."[17]

Thus, even if it succeeds in eschewing all taint of Christian anti-Judaism, post-Holocaust theological retrieval risks reiterating mythological notions that militate against Christians perceiving Jews in "normal" terms. In fact, once the salvation-historical view of Jewish existence has been recovered, even the Holocaust can be incorporated into the "mystery" of Israel. Thus, the authors of the 1957 World Council of Churches (WCC) statement, who regard as definitive the Pauline understanding of Jewish life articulated in Romans 9–11, "must ask whether the centuries-long preservation of the Jews as an ethnic as well as religious group . . . is not intended by God to teach both us and them new lessons concerning the problems of race and nationality, which so gravely vex the world."[18]

Statements on Jewish-Christian relations published by church bodies over the last three decades include numerous examples of theological retrieval that inadvertently remythologize Jews and Jewish existence. This tendency has been particularly visible in European statements, which refer to Jews as unique signs and witnesses of divine truth. At a WCC Commission on Faith and Order meeting at Bristol in 1967 the Committee on the Church and the Jewish People declared that the Jewish people are to be a "living revelation to others." It is by virtue of their miraculous persistence that Jews become a "living and visible sign of God's faithfulness to men."[19] "Israel: People, Land, and State," a paper adopted in 1970 by the Netherlands Reformed Church, emphasized that Israel is "a people unlike all other peoples," a people with a "unique destiny," whose irrevocable election as God's covenant-people places upon it a "visible

---

[17]Cohen, *The Myth of the Judeo-Christian Tradition*, 118. The reference is to the Roman Catholic publication *The Bridge*.

[18]"Report of the Ecumenical Institute to the Executive Committee of the World Council of Churches," in Rubin, *Scattered among the Nations*, 297.

[19]In Brockway et al., *The Theology of the Churches and the Jewish People*, 17ff.

mark," and whose very existence constitutes a "visible sign of [God's] electing faithfulness." The Old Testament, according to "Israel: People, Land, and State," is both a "sign of Israel's identity" and a "sign of Israel's vocation to be a blessing to all nations," while Israel's faithlessness "mirrors our own alienation from God." Finally, the return of the Jews to their land reminds the church of the "special significance of this people in the midst of the nations," and is "a sign for us." The "Statement by the French Bishops' Committee for Relations with Jews" (1973) argued that "the Church, speaking in the name of Jesus Christ and, through Him, linked to the Jewish people since her beginnings and for all time, perceives in the uninterrupted existence of this people through the centuries a sign that she would wish fully to comprehend."[20] Finally, the statement by the Synod of the Protestant Church of the Rhineland in 1980[21] stressed "the insight that the continuing existence of the Jewish people, its return to the Land of Promise, and also the creation of the state of Israel, are signs of the faithfulness of God toward his people."[22]

All this suggests that in the post-Holocaust world the church's interpretation of God's way with the Jew is once again being animated by the oldest and most permanent traditions regarding the Jewish people. Much has been made of the post-Holocaust "turning point" in Christian thinking about Jews and Judaism and the way this watershed is represented in the official church pronouncements published during the past four decades. But under careful examination these statements testify that the theological grid through which Christian theologians view the Jewish people has in fact not been shattered by the Holocaust. Even though the church's attitude has changed "from dismay to solicitude, the Jew is still

---

[20]In Helga B. Croner, ed., *Stepping Stones to Further Jewish-Christian Relations: An Unabridged Collection of Christian Documents*, Studies in Judaism and Christianity (New York: Paulist Press/Stimulus Books, 1977) 60.

[21]"Toward Renovation of the Relationship of Christians and Jews," in Helga B. Croner, ed., *More Stepping Stones to Jewish-Christian Relations: An Unabridged Collection of Christian Documents 1975-1983*, Studies in Judaism and Christianity (New York: Paulist Press/Stimulus Books, 1985) 207-209.

[22]Ibid., 207. American statements contain similar notions, though they are usually overshadowed by issues of practical coexistence. In "A Theological Understanding of the Relationship between Christians and Jews" (1987), the Presbyterian Church (USA) spoke of the continued existence of the Jewish people (and of the church) as a "mystery" (Romans 11:25), and averred that God's reign in the world was "signified by . . . the continuing existence of and faithfulness within the Jewish people."

the *object* of an action—a mere object."[23] The Jew as incomplete, inadequate, and awaiting conversion has been replaced by the Jew who is already in covenant with God, but this image has not given way to the Jew as normal human being.

At least one church statement has assiduously avoided the pitfall of theological retrieval. The Episcopal Church's "Guidelines for Christian-Jewish Relations" (1988) notes that

> In the process of defining itself, the Church produced its own definition of God's acts of salvation. It should not be surprising that Jews resent those scriptural and theological interpretations in which they are assigned negative roles. . . .
>
> Many Christians are convinced that they understand Judaism since they have the Hebrew Scriptures as part of their Bible. This attitude is often reinforced by a lack of knowledge about the history of Jewish life and thought through the 1900 years since Christianity and Judaism parted ways.
>
> There is, therefore, a special urgency for Christians to listen, through study and dialogue, to ways in which Jews understand their own history, their Scriptures, their traditions, their faith, and their practice.[24]

However, this approach to comprehending the meaning of Jewish existence should be accompanied by the realization that some Jewish thinking actually confirms the mythologizing tendencies in Christian theology.[25]

How shall Christians proceed, then, if they wish to reflect anew on the meaning of Jewish existence but avoid the fallacy of theological retrieval? If Arthur Cohen is correct that "Christian and Jew cannot avoid mythologizing each other because each can only know the external function the other performs within the closed system of his truth,"[26] then how

---

[23]Cohen, *Myth of the Judeo-Christian Tradition*, 70. Cohen also writes that "Christianity does not really consider Judaism to have survived. As such, the survival of Israel is made a sign and a witness, a testimony to historical guilt, a mystery. Israel is a theological device, a *ficelle* of Christian history—but she is not alive and independent" (125).

[24]"Guidelines for Christian-Jewish Relations (For Use in the Episcopal Church)," in Eakin, *What Price Prejudice?*, 153.

[25]See Stephen R. Haynes, *Reluctant Witnesses: Jews and the Christian Imagination* (Louisville: Westminster/John Knox Press, 1995) 179-81.

[26]Cohen, *The Myth of the Judeo-Christian Tradition*, 48.

do post-Holocaust Christians speak as Christians about Jews? Perhaps the safest approach would be to balance the doctrine of election—with its focus on the theological uniqueness of Israel as witness—with the doctrine of creation and its corollary that all "are equally God's children, and equally precious in his sight." This will lead naturally to a recognition of Jews' "intrinsic worth and import,"[27] quite apart from their success in living up to Christians' expectations. Interestingly, this is precisely the balance we find in the Danish bishops' response to the German occupying forces, cited above. Immediately after affirming the Jewishness of Jesus and the election of the Jewish people, the bishops write that "persecution of the Jews conflicts with the humanitarian conception of the love of neighbors and the message which Christ's church set out to preach. Christ taught us that every man has a value in the eyes of God."[28]

"We Remember": A Case Study

Is the illusory attraction of good news evident in contemporary Christian reflection on the Holocaust? As a test case, we shall review the recent Roman Catholic Church document "We Remember: A Reflection on the Shoah," published in March 1998.[29] "We Remember" immediately became a target of criticism from Jewish groups—mainly for failing to blame the Church for traditional anti-Jewish teachings, and for defending Pope Pius XII from charges that he failed to speak out against Nazi persecution of the Jews.[30] As we shall see, the statement also contains much that should

---

[27]"The American Lutheran Church and the Jewish Community" (1974) and "Statement of Inter-Religious Dialogue: Jews and Christians" (General Conference of the United Methodist Church, 1972), in Brockway et al, eds., *The Theology of the Churches and the Jewish People*, 67 and 65.

[28]"Letter from Danish Lutheran Bishops to German Occupation Officials (October 3, 1943)" in Rubin, *Scattered among the Nations*, 247. Cf. "Resolution on Anti-Semitism," from the WCC Third Assembly in New Delhi: "Only as we give convincing evidence to our Jewish neighbors that we seek for them the common rights and dignities which God wills for his children can we come to such a meeting with them as would make it possible to share with them the best which God has given us in Christ" (in Rubin, *Scattered among the Nations*, 298).

[29]The text of "We Remember: A Reflection on the Shoah" can be found on the worldwide web at <http://www.vatican.va/roman_curia/pontifical_councils/chrstuni/documents/rc_pc_chrstuni_doc_16031998_shoah_en.html>. All references are to that electronic version of the text.

[30]Anton La Guardia, "Jews Cool on Apology," *The Age* (18 March 1998), posted at <http://www.theage.com.au/daily/980318/news/news19.html>. In a

concern post-Holocaust Christians, since it encourages the fallacies of authenticity, superficial engagement, and theological retrieval.

The fallacy of superficial engagement is detectable throughout the document's discussion of Christian contributions to antisemitism. "We Remember" defines the Shoah as "the attempt by the Nazi regime to exterminate the Jewish people, with the consequent killing of millions of Jews." But while the Holocaust is called a major fact of history that "still concerns us today," it is not clear just how this "us" is implicated in the tragedy. If it is "the Nazi regime" which bears responsibility for the fact that Jewish women and men, children and infants, were persecuted and deported, degraded, ill-treated, tortured, and murdered, then in what sense is the Church in particular or Christianity in general implicated in these crimes and in need of forgiveness? "We Remember" does acknowledge that the Shoah took place in "countries of long-standing Christian civilization." And this "raises the question of the relation between the Nazi persecution and the attitudes down the centuries of Christians towards Jews." The history of relations between Jews and Christians is characterized as "quite negative," but the explanation for this problem is superficial. Emphasis is placed on disputes between Christians and "Jewish leaders and people who, in their devotion to the Law, on occasion violently opposed the preachers of the Gospel and the first Christians." While Christians soon "incurred the persecution of the State," Jews were "legally protected by the privileges granted by the Emperor and the authorities." Under the influence of "certain interpretations of the New Testament regarding the Jewish people as a whole," the document

---

press release dated 18 March 1998, National ADL Director Abraham L. Foxman said that "the document rings hollow. It is an apologia full of rationalization for Pope Pius XII and the Church. It takes very little moral and historical responsibility for the Church's historic teaching for the contempt of Jews. It talks about the past in question marks rather than providing answers." The same week the Canadian Jewish Congress announced: "[W]e are disappointed that the declaration defends the inaction of Pope Pius XII. It is inconsistent to admit the failures of ordinary Christians to speak out against the Holocaust, but to ignore the deafening silence of the pope." According to B'nai B'rith President Tommy P. Baer, the document fell "short of expectations and sadly attempts to varnish the controversial wartime conduct of Pope Pius XII in his failure to speak out against the genocide of European Jewry" ("B'nai B'rith President Meets with Pope in Rome; Calls New Vatican Holocaust Document 'Important but Short of Expectations,' " press release dated 25 March 1998, posted at <http://www.bnaibrith. org/pr/baerrome.html>.

admits, Christian mobs sometimes attacked synagogues. But how were these interpretations disseminated?

> "In the Christian world—I do not say on the part of the Church as such—erroneous and unjust interpretations of the New Testament regarding the Jewish people and their alleged culpability have circulated for too long, engendering feelings of hostility towards this people." Such interpretations of the New Testament have been totally and definitively rejected by the Second Vatican Council.
>
> Despite the Christian preaching of love for all, even for one's enemies, the prevailing mentality down the centuries penalized minorities and those who were in any way "different."[31]

Christian anti-Judaism, then, "circulates" and Jews are denigrated by a "prevailing mentality." But no Christian persons or institutions are held responsible for these things. With its preference for the passive voice and its reluctance to assign responsibility for reigning anti-Jewish attitudes, "We Remember" gives implicit support to the fallacies of authenticity and superficial engagement.

Concerning European Christendom, the document acknowledges briefly that "sentiments of anti-Judaism in some Christian quarters" (though anti-Judaism is undefined) led to "generalized discrimination, . . . expulsions or attempts at forced conversions." But "We Remember" quickly places distance between the (Roman Catholic) Church and antisemitism by referring to the "Christian" world in quotation marks. Here the document once again assumes the passive voice: Jews were "looked upon with a certain suspicion and mistrust. In times of crisis such as famine, war, pestilence, or social tensions, the Jewish minority was sometimes taken as a scapegoat and became the victim of violence, looting, even massacres." But the subjects of these actions—members of the Church hierarchy, Christians, or perhaps "Christians"—is left unclear.

When in the nineteenth century the Jews' position deteriorated through the effects of "a false . . . nationalism," the result was "an anti-Judaism that was essentially more sociological and political than religious." The Jewish situation was exacerbated by social theories that denied the unity of the human race, among which was German National Socialism. "We Remember" laments that "many saw in National

---

[31]Footnotes refer the reader to Pope John Paul II, "Speech to Symposium on the Roots of Anti-Judaism," 31 October 1997, 1; *L'Osservatore Romano*, 1 November 1997, 6; and Second Vatican Ecumenical Council, *Nostra Aetate*, #4.

Socialism a solution to their country's problems and cooperated politically," but does not allude to those whose political cooperation stemmed from a sense of religious duty. Not surprisingly, the document renders the story of the Church's relationship to National Socialism in rather rosy terms.

"The Church in Germany replied [to Nazism] by condemning racism," this section of the document begins. "The condemnation first appeared in the preaching of some the clergy, in the public teaching of the Catholic Bishops, and in the writings of lay Catholic journalists." Several examples of Catholic resistance to German fascism are given—including Cardinal Faulhaber's Advent sermons of 1933, and papal statements that "condemned Nazi racism" and "deification of the State."

The following section of "We Remember," "Nazi Anti-Semitism and the Shoah," carefully distinguishes between "anti-Semitism based on theories contrary to the constant teaching of the Church on the unity of the human race and on the equal dignity of all races and peoples, and the longstanding sentiments of mistrust and hostility that we call anti-Judaism, of which unfortunately, Christians also have been guilty." Many Nazis hated God, the document observes, and this attitude "led to a rejection of Christianity, and a desire to see the Church destroyed or at least subjected to the interests of the Nazi state." In conclusion, "We Remember" regards the Shoah as "the work of a thoroughly modern neopagan regime. Its anti-Semitism had its roots outside Christianity and, in pursuing its aims, it did not hesitate to oppose the Church and persecute her members also."

The document criticizes the behavior of "the governments of some Western countries of Christian tradition" who did not open their borders to the persecuted Jews. But to the matter of whether Nazi persecution was enabled by anti-Jewish prejudice among Christians—sentiments that may have made them less sensitive, or even indifferent, to Nazi persecution—"We Remember" evasively states that a response would need to be given case by case. On the question of possible resistance—did Christians lend every possible assistance to persecuted Jews?—the document states equivocally that "many did, but others did not." Pius XII is credited with saving "hundreds of thousands of Jewish lives"; it is observed that many bishops, priests, religious, and laity have been honored as rescuers by the state of Israel; and the lack of "spiritual resistance and concrete action" on the part of other Christians is called a "heavy burden of conscience." But the document reminds us that we cannot know how many Christians were horrified at the disappearance of their Jewish neighbors but "were not strong enough to raise their voices in protest."

Thus, while the Church "desires to express her deep sorrow for the failures of her sons and daughters in every age," "We Remember" does not sufficiently clarify these failures in the case of the Holocaust. The emphasis is not on serious engagement with the past, but in moving forward: "We pray that our sorrow for the tragedy which the Jewish people has suffered in our century will lead to a new relationship" based on mutual respect. As evidence of the Church's bold response to the Holocaust, the document cites occasions on which Church representatives have deplored "the hatred, persecutions, and displays of anti-Semitism directed against the Jews at any time and from any source." It also contends that antisemitism and racism "are opposed to the principles of Christianity."[32] But these are not conclusions drawn from a sober exploration of the Church's implication in anti-Jewish thought and action, but the very premises on which a superficial analysis of Jewish-Christian relations has been based.

If "We Remember" is plagued by the fallacies of authenticity and superficial engagement, we should not be surprised if it is also affected by the fallacy of theological retrieval. Indeed, traces of this fallacy are evident throughout. The document states that "by reason of her very close bonds of spiritual kinship with the Jewish people and her remembrance of the injustices of the past," the Church cannot remain indifferent before the Shoah. And in a section titled "Looking Together to a Common Future" stress is placed on renewing awareness of the Christian faith's Hebrew roots, namely, that Jesus was a descendant of David; that the Virgin Mary and the apostles belonged to the Jewish people; that the church draws sustenance from the root of the Pauline olive tree (cf. Romans 11); and that the Jews are "our elder brothers."

As important as it is for Christians to recall these connections, these invocations of the myth of the Judeo-Christian tradition have the effect of smoothing over the problems that have been so insufficiently plumbed elsewhere in the document. Even more worrisome is the use of witness-people language to describe the meaning of Jewish existence in the past and future: "While bearing their unique witness to the Holy One of Israel and to the Torah, the Jewish people have suffered much at different times and in many places." The "terrible fate" of the Jews, the document continues, "has become a symbol of the aberrations of which man is capable

---

[32]The document here quotes from Pope John Paul II's address to the leaders of the Jewish community in Strasbourg in 1988.

when he turns against God."[33] In another place, the Jewish people are referred to as "a people called to witness to the one God and the Law of the Covenant."

The document's inattention to the pitfalls of theological retrieval is also evident in its reference to "the well-known Advent sermons of Cardinal Faulhaber in 1933, [which] . . . clearly expressed rejection of the Nazi anti-Semitic propaganda." It is quite true that in these sermons Cardinal Michael Faulhaber denied the religious significance of racial thinking, reaffirmed Jesus' Jewishness, and defended the Old Testament. However, Faulhaber's homilies were characterized by the same ambivalence toward Jews that is reflected in the early anti-Nazi writings of Dietrich Bonhoeffer.[34] For instance, Faulhaber makes clear that though the church "has stretched forth her protecting hand over the Scriptures of the Old Testament," Christianity does not thereby "become a Jewish religion. These books were not composed by Jews; they are inspired by the Holy Ghost. . . . "[35] Faulhaber is especially careful to distinguish between the people of Israel before the death of Christ and after, when "Israel was dismissed from the service of Revelation":

> She had not known the time of her visitation. She had repudiated and rejected the Lord's Anointed, had driven Him out of the city and nailed Him to the Cross. Then the veil of the Temple was rent, and with it the covenant between the Lord and His people. The daughters of Sion received the bill of divorce, and from that time forth Ahasuerus wanders, forever restless, over the face of the earth. Even after the death of Christ the Jews are still a "mystery," as St. Paul says (Rom. xi, 25); and one day, at the end of time, for them too the hour of grace will strike (Rom xi, 26).[36]

---

[33]This sentence is quoted from Pope John Paul II, "Encyclical Letter *Centesimus Annus*," 1 May 1991, 17: *Acta apostolicae sedis* 83 (1991): 814-15.

[34]Also like Bonhoeffer, Faulhaber accuses his opponents of repeating Jewish sins. Ironically, rejecting Jesus' Jewishness reenacts the Gospel scene in which Jesus is attacked by the (Jewish) crowds. In a similar comment, Faulhaber belittles Nazi racism by noting its "Jewish" character: "No nation ever insisted more on race and ties of blood," writes Faulhaber, "than the Israelites of the Old Testament." George Mosse, *Nazi Culture: A Documentary History* (New York: Random House, 1966) 260.

[35]Ibid., 258.

[36]Ibid. Commenting on these sermons, Mosse says "these remarks, though they may be well founded from the standpoint of Christian theology, must be read against the accelerating policy of excluding Jews from German life" (239).

While Faulhaber's sermons included a "rejection of the Nazi anti-Semitic propaganda" at a crucial juncture in the National Socialist revolution, they also trafficked in religious propaganda that played into Nazi hands by highlighting Jewish perfidy and normalizing Jewish suffering and dispersion. This sort of mythologizing of Jewish existence actually endangered Jews in 1933; for this reason it ought to be regarded very cautiously in the post-Holocaust world.

Conclusion: Fallacy-Free Faith?

Is there good news for Christians after Auschwitz? How this question is answered depends on how well Christians do their homework. Given the susceptibility of official Christianity to the fallacies described here, individual believers and congregations must take it upon themselves to make genuine post-Holocaust theological revision a priority. Attention to the fallacies of authenticity, superficial engagement, and theological retrieval will cause post-Holocaust Christians to proceed carefully. No longer will they glibly affirm that "authentic Christianity" is sufficient to restore Christian credibility in the shadow of Auschwitz. No longer will they assume that anti-Judaism represents an irruption into Christian faith of an external contagion that is easily removed once identified. And no longer will they suppose that a new basis for Jewish-Christian relations can be forged from the church's unalloyed biblical and theological traditions.

If fallacy-free faith is the goal, Christians will speak of the Holocaust and Jewish-Christian relations only in fear and humility. But with this attitude comes a lifting of the shame that we bear for the Holocaust and the long history of Western antisemitism that it represents.

Chapter 2

The Failure of Goodness:
In Search of the *christian* Christian

Stephen D. Smith

A Personal Preface

At Auschwitz, I confronted myself.
At Treblinka, I learned how little I understand the human condition.
At Belzec, how incapable I am of ever understanding the divine.

I approached the Shoah as an individual who "knew" the means of salvation and who boasted "faith." Then, faced with the mass destruction of European Jewry, faith, as I had formerly understood it, lost its meaning. How do you blithely believe in goodness, when children, no older than my own toddlers, were summarily executed? How do you justify the virtue of hope, when millions were plunged into despair? Faced with this reality, no longer could I define my own faith by religious practice, by theology, by institutions, or by emulating great men and women. Faith in the face of the soul-destroying reality of mass death, became the strength to believe in anything, when everything suggested one should not. Faith, though more than actions alone, became something that could only be measured by them. Faced with oblivion I discovered that faith is when you realize that you cannot define that which you believe in, but still have hope for the future. Faith, in the shadow of the Shoah, is to embark on the search for truth, but never to claim to have found it, never to impose it, never to enforce it upon another.

This is my story. This is what I believe.

Preliminary Questions

In attempting to respond to the question "What is the good news of Christianity after Auschwitz?" a number of further queries present themselves. Does such a question assume that the good news of Christianity is *different* in some way after Auschwitz than it was before? If so, how does Auschwitz specifically or the Shoah more generally alter the message? What happened at Auschwitz that may lead Christians to ask such a question? Does a question of this nature assume that all Christians everywhere are subject to its demands; that is, does this change the nature of Christianity itself?

To ask what the good news of Christianity might be after the Holocaust does not assume the good news is different, but does ask whether it can remain the same in view of all that has happened. The way in which the Shoah might have altered that particular message is *not* because six million Jews were murdered, but that six million Jews were murdered in the context of a so-called Christian environment, and with the complicity of certain Christian individuals and bodies. What happened at Auschwitz not only calls into question the Christian belief and practice, but all believers. Jews who were sent to their deaths either prayed in vain for God's intervention or felt abandoned by God in the lonely act of dying en masse. Whoever, or whatever the God of the Jews is, Christians must enter into the same struggle, because God is the God of Jews and Christians alike. In this regard, if the "good news" is in any way altered by the impact of the Shoah, then it not only alters what Christians say about the Christian message, but alters the nature of Christianity itself. Both belief and practice are called into question.

The good news of Christianity as traditionally understood by Christians is that Jesus of Nazareth is the Son of God who has come to take away the sins of the world and that through his death and resurrection anyone who believes in him shall be granted salvation and, by extension, eternal life. Christendom has thus preached a message of redemption from sin through Jesus Christ. As a result of this salvation, the "good news" in a world ridden with evil has been that Christianity, and with it Christian people, might be "salt" and "light" in a presumably "tasteless" and "dark" society. Thus, the Christian message should have resulted in Christians behaving in a better way than those around them through the redemptive power of Christ's salvation. That Christians on the whole failed to do so casts doubt upon the credibility of their Christian practice. Furthermore, the almost universal nature of Christian response raises questions about the validity of Christian good news itself as it calls into question the ability of Christian belief to transform the person and actions of the believer. If the "good news" of the Christian message did not result in Christian behavior, might it not be assumed that it is no longer appropriate to talk of the good news since, clearly, its results did not bear witness to its goodness?

The Problem of Christian Complicity

Lisl Beck's grandparents on her mother's side owned the world's largest toy factory in Nuremberg—that is, until the Nazis came to power. They were forced to sell their hard-earned empire for a pittance, the family was roundly ostracized and the thirteen-year-old Lisl discovered that to be considered Jewish was a fearful thing. As her father was "Aryan," Lisl decided to attempt to merge into her own German environment by converting to Christianity and enrolled for confirmation classes. She was taught Bible, the sacraments, and Nazi ideology. Finally the day of her confirmation came; now she would become a true Christian. Officiating at the altar were two SS officers, who conducted the ceremony under the banner of the swastika. As she was confirmed, Lisl, like the other young people in the church that day, swore her allegiance over the body and the blood of the Führer. To become a member of the church was for Lisl to become a Nazi, too. Four years later she fled for her life, reaching Holland just two days before the outbreak of war. For Jews, even a Nazi-style conversion did not count.

The story of Lisl Beck serves as but one illustration of the mixed relationship Jews had with the church during the Nazi period. Lisl went to the church in part to distance herself from her newly assumed Jewish identity and simultaneously to become somewhat closer to the Nazi environment. Not that she wanted to be a Nazi, quite the contrary, but she assumed that the affiliation to the church would bring her sufficiently close to the Nazi regime so as to afford her greater safety as a Jew. It was this assumed association of church and state in Germany that led many Jews to disparage church leadership, often with good reason. From time to time, there were robust denunciations of National Socialism, or during the Shoah itself, pleas on behalf of the Jews. However, these shining examples of Christian practice were so few and far between that the vast majority of murdered Jews went to their deaths entirely convinced that no Christian, anywhere, at any time, had either said or done anything to relieve the burden of their predicament. Not only did few of the victims ever experience Christian help or words of support, but the vast majority did not even have the comfort of knowing that there were indeed some brave Christians who did do something at some time, so intangible was the reaction of the church as a whole.

Images of war-torn cities and columns of ragged refugees and the procession of victims lined up alongside mass graves might cause one to believe that the sun stood still and life on earth was all but suspended during those merciless times of human barbarity. The sun did not stand still, and life on earth, though severely disrupted, went on regardless. Surely, these were trying times, painful times, difficult times, but people went about their lives because they had to. They loved, they laughed, they cried, and they prayed. In the confused melee of human interaction, hardship, and suffering, people needed that which they knew: their family, their friends, their politics and their religion. Amongst a foray of new and troubling experiences, people needed guidance and support, and they looked to those around them to make sense of the senseless and to provide a means to navigate the overpowering circumstances. At this moment in time, when the demand for Christian leadership, for decisive moral conduct and spiritual fortitude might have been there to guide the faithful—and indeed the faithless too—all too often, all too frequently, church leaders failed to exercise their Christian duty beyond that of their own self-preservation. While church leaders either collaborated, or denied their obligation to intervene in what was happening, thousands and millions of Jews were hauled from their homes in parishes right across the European continent, and Christendom faced its greatest test ever.

At Auschwitz, Belzec, Chelmno, Majdanek, Sobibor, and Treblinka, not to mention hundreds of other sites of mass execution, Jews from all sectors of society, all walks of life, and every country in Europe were murdered without reprieve. The Christian church itself did not organize, conduct, or openly condone such activity. However, that it could happen at all, without a *concerted* effort to halt it from the Christian environment, questions the validity of the good news of the gospel of Jesus. Christian people were there, they saw it and did not act, as they did not see it as their Christian (or even human) duty so to do. The majority of Christians did not perceive the antivalues of National Socialism as being something for Christians to challenge, but instead attempted to synthesize their religious practice with Nazi acceptability. Neither did they understand that the fate of the Jews was in part their responsibility.

Therefore the dilemma facing Christians following the mass destruction of European Jewry is most easily understood as a crisis of moral, spiritual, and theological credibility. Jews were murdered simply because they were Jews, and this in the context of a nominally or even actively Christian environment. But there are questions that are more troubling still. To highlight the shortcomings and question the credibility of the Christian world during the Holocaust might suggest that, prior to the Shoah, there was some kind of moral high ground, real or perceived. Unfortunately, the crisis of credibility during the Nazi period may actually be more accurately understood as a symptom of a longstanding, fundamental problem that preceded it. Did Christianity lose credibility *because* of its failure to act, or was its theology and ecclesiastical structure such that failure was *inevitable* and hence its assumed moral credibility already nonexistent? In so many words, was the Christian environment in some way causal, creating the context in which antisemitism could thrive and hence providing the Nazis with a basis on which to build their anti-Jewish policies?

The *christian* Christian

The credibility crisis hinges on asking why so few Christians demonstrated *christian* behavior in their actions during the Nazi period. Conversely, one also observes that many non-Christian individuals were entirely *christian* in what they were prepared to do. The irony is disturbingly clear: the very religion that lent its name to the virtues of moral humanitarianism was unable to demonstrate such virtue consistently—certainly not as an institution. As the church was unable to give clear guidance on how Christians should behave, the *christian* Christians (those who did demonstrate acts of support for the Jews) did not demonstrate the credibility of their Christianity, so much as their humanity. In this way, we can only gauge the individual's goodness by what she or he was prepared to do, not because of his or her affiliation to Christianity. That goodness required saving someone, helping to hide someone, or risking one's life to oppose injustice in some way. It meant doing what was not required of anyone, but doing it anyway.

Of course, to "act" means different things for different people. For a peasant in the Ukrainian countryside, to take in a Jewish family, to feed, clothe, and maybe hide them, was an act of enormous heroism as the chance of denunciation and hence of death was very high. For church leaders, acts were limited to making statements to encourage members to act accordingly. Some ecclesiastical institutions did make vocal, public, and official stands against Nazi policy. The vast majority did not. That some did demonstrates all could have done so. Therefore, the lack of understanding, leadership, or care with respect to the persecution of the Jews during this period amounts to negligence on the part of the church. Negligence implies that a clearly defined and understood responsibility was overlooked with reckless disregard for the consequences. Whether such a duty was clearly defined in relation to the Jews is a moot point, not least because of the antipathy generated by the Christian church over many centuries. However, the Christian duty of charity and care for those who are suffering required no explanation, and yet the response was still muted. Such negligence implies that the Christian Church cared neither about the Jews as people nor about what happened to them as a community.

The causes of this indifference are not difficult to find in Christian historical precedent, but they are difficult to reconcile with the supposed nature of Christian virtue. The failure to understand the relationship between Judaism and Christianity—except in terms of longstanding enmity—ensured that Christian clergy were not equipped to evaluate their moral and fraternal responsibility, and furthermore often justified the persecution of the Jews as a divine retribution. The Jews were the "other," and that "otherness" was often sufficient to salve the Christian conscience of any personal liability.

If Christian individuals could justify their (in)action through their theology, clearly that theology requires reassessment. If Christian individuals could *not* justify their actions through their theology, how did they feel at liberty to behave in such a way and still feel able to call themselves Christians? In either case, the failure of professing Christians to act on behalf of the Jews demonstrates the abject failure of Christianity as a theological tradition and Christian people as its representatives.

The bravery of the "Righteous among the Nations," those who rescued Jews during the Shoah, stands in counterpoint as a powerful example of human behavior. Their actions must be included in our considerations, not least because they showed what could be done. That many among them were practicing Christians, including priests, pastors, and bishops who spoke out against the Nazis or assisted Jews, illustrates the possibilities. Many will point to the example they set as being the type of example that all Christian believers should follow, for that exemplary behavior is worthy of both honor and emulation. Such individuals set very high standards; indeed they should rightly be identified as role models for *christian* conduct. It is nevertheless important to address the question of their relatively small numbers. The danger is that in emphasizing the significance of their actions it becomes too easy to suggest that "it was not so bad after all." In some way, it may be thought, their goodness compensates for the evil and the apathy of the others. Unfortunately, this is not so. On the whole, the righteous ones took great personal risks in a very hostile environment. Not even the sympathy of their own family, friends, and coreligionists was guaranteed. But from the perspective of the victims, while any individual who did help was surely appreciated, they did not represent a concerted effort from the Christian community. Why were these few righteous people of Christian persuasion so often acting on their own? Why did some see it as their duty to take great risks on behalf of condemned individuals in an all-but-hopeless situation? Whatever their motivations, perhaps their actions do demonstrate that Christianity can lead to altruism of the highest order. But then maybe they also demonstrate that this pattern is likely to be found in only a small number of cases.

What Christians Must Admit

The failure of Christians to understand their obligation toward the Jews demonstrates the lack of historical understanding Christians had of the Jewish origins of their Christianity. It indicts Christian theological thought for its contempt of both Judaism and the Jewish people over many centuries, and simultaneously it reveals the inhumane behavior that Christians were prepared to accept while still professing their Christian identity.

The glaring hiatus in the relationship between Jews and Christians was present centuries before the Shoah, and it still remains a troubling reality today. The Shoah brings into sharp focus the fact that Christians have long ignored their duty to address the historical development of Christian theological thought and practice. During the Shoah, enmity toward the Jews became more than a matter of contempt. During the Shoah, that enmity took a much more destructive turn in blatant negligence and complicity to murder. Examining how Christians could align themselves with such a force is essential to a reevaluation of Christian values after the Shoah.

Christians still need to face the fact that the metamorphosis of Christian theology and practice was nothing short of the *rejection* of Jesus as a practicing Jew. Every time Christianity misconstrued or poured contempt on Judaism or the Jewish people, so too it poured contempt on Jesus, its source. There are few religions that revere their figurehead as highly and yet misconstrue the life and teachings of that figurehead as wholly as Christianity. The message of Jesus of Nazareth was entirely bound up within the Jewish tradition, with Halakhah, with Jewish messianism, and with the politics of the Judea of the time. Take away the theosophical and Christological assumptions of the developing Greco-Roman church and what is left is Judaism. So why cannot Christians simply state and even emphasize—without its sounding like an admission of defeat—that Jesus was Jewish, that he was a practicing Jew? To those within the tradition, his ideas were revolutionary; to those on the outside, they were revelatory. Jesus' disciples could declare him a messianic figure to usher in a new kingdom, wholly and completely *within* the context of the Jewish tradition of the time. To those outside the Jewish tradition, such a statement creates a universal message within an entirely different context. Unfortunately, in the transfer the message of Jesus became a rod with which to beat his own people. Admitting this and ensuring its reversal, even at this late stage, is crucial, not only to restore historical propriety but to create the conditions in which Christian complicity with the Shoah itself can be admitted and addressed.

Humility in the Face of Suffering

Before one can even begin to think about the gospel of Christ after the Shoah, soul searching and humility should be the watchwords of all Christians. How can one reformulate a message of "good news" when the news is so bad? The bad news is that Christianity has *not* sufficiently admitted its own failings with respect to the Jewish people for far too long. The bad news is that a religious community, which gave to Christianity its God, its ethical code, and most of its scriptures, cannot with any justification support the idea of a credible Christianity. The bad news is that Christians have brought the message of Christianity into disrepute through persistent *unchristian* conduct, particularly in relation to the Jews. All of this calls for Christians to step back and take stock. It is not good enough to say "Never Again!" and pray that genocide does not repeat. Christians must make it an active part of Christian conduct to avoid being accessory to anything like it again.

In the shadow of the destruction of European Jewry, an understanding needs to be reached between Jews and Christians, allowing Christianity to reform its role while readdressing its relationship to the Jews. Repentance (*teshuvah*) plays a key part in this work. Christianity needs to surrender its supersessionist triumphalism in which the "new" is said to supersede the "old" and accept that the more recent springs from what came before. If Judaism preceded Christianity, then for Christians to proceed toward an appreciation of Judaism is not to regress, but, under the circumstances we have experienced recently, is surely to make progress.

At this time, a search for "good news" may not be completely appropriate. That is, the search will not be sound unless Christians are prepared to be honest about their history, to learn to be *christian* as well as Christian, and to be the defenders of the preciousness of human life. Otherwise the chances are that the same mistakes will be repeated, and more bad news will surely follow.

The news will be truly good only when it is clear that Christians have learned to resist forces of the kind that targeted the Jews for destruction during the Shoah. Except for that, there cannot be much Christian "good news" after Auschwitz. But if Christians follow with honesty, repentance, and humility the example of Jesus, their Jewish teacher, then "good news" will not have to be proclaimed or preached. It will simply be the outcome.

Chapter 3

Can I Still Be a Christian after Auschwitz?

Bev. Allen Asbury

The question is addressed to me. Personally. To me. To my intellect. To my beliefs. To my faith. To my being. The question is unavoidably personal. And so must be the reply. It involves thought, feeling, reflection on experience, decision, and the acceptance of responsibility for it and the consequences arising from it.

I write this in my seventy-first year, and I think back to the beginning of the question for me fifty years ago, when I was twenty-one. Traveling in Europe in the summer of 1950 under the auspices of the World Student Christian Federation, establishing postwar contacts between North American and European students, paired with an older Jewish student from Cornell, we visited a Nazi concentration camp. We were there on the day that Stars of David and crosses were being erected over mass graves for the first time and that gave occasion for my roommate to observe and accuse: "These are the graves of my people, and your people put them there." Something to that effect. Personal. Historical. Confrontational. Challenging. It set my quest.

"Can I still be a Christian after Auschwitz?" is the way the question got stated later on, but I can see that it began to form my life from that moment on. And, to jump ahead, Yes, I am inescapably a "Christian" but, unavoidably, an "agnostic Christian," a post-Auschwitz Christian, one for whom skepticism, doubt, and uncertainty about the "truth claims" of Christian faith and tradition are ineradicably present.

At a meeting of the Education Committee of the United States Holocaust Memorial Museum, a distinguished retired rabbi, Dr. Herman E. Schaalman of Chicago, responded to a religious statement made by a Christian member of the Committee by declaring that conventional theology was suspect, that statements made about God pre-Auschwitz cannot be made or considered valid post-Auschwitz. He expressed perplexity at the uncritical use of religious language and propositions about God today that remain oblivious to the Shoah's having taken place.

He was asserting that a Jew could never be the same post-Auschwitz as a Jew had been pre-Auschwitz, just as I have come to know that about being a Christian. Since the rabbi and I seem to be in a minority of clergy who believe, feel, and know that, I have to wonder if such conviction is a matter of age and experience. But I continue to hope not, lest the resurgence of religious fundamentalism and literalism blot out the insistent question.

Recently, I moved from the mid-South to a sea island on the South Atlantic Coast, and the move gave this post-Auschwitz Christian an opportunity to "shop" again for a church; really, more than that, to see if it were possible again and any longer to be a practicing, worshipping Christian. So, after many years of not having attended worship services regularly, I set out to try anew and to gauge what had changed.

What I have discovered is the fulfillment of H. Richard Niebuhr's prediction of forty years ago: the emergence of the pastoral director who begins "worship" with greetings of "good morning" followed by the "concerns" of church programs. And what I have found is language of religion and faith unaware of and uninformed by Rabbi Schaalman's dictum. However the liturgy has been reformed and informed by events of the twentieth century, it still seems to me to be oblivious of the challenges posed to it by the intellectual revolutions of modern times, to wit (loosely phrased), the Darwinian, Freudian, Marxist, Einsteinian. Moreover, the contemporary life of most American churches seems to be totally devoid of consciousness of social issues except those involving sexuality, and even they go largely unmentioned in worship. And this void or silence takes place in a community riven with class and race divisions and issues of development that will determine identity for generations to come. The "scriptural preaching" takes place as if the preachers never attended a theological seminary, and it always manages to edit out "the violent legacy of monotheism," collapsing the "Good News" into psychological categories, unwittingly undercutting the very piety it celebrates.

Needless to say, it hasn't been easy for me to find a home, and I have been tempted to forgo the search. After all, I *know* that my experience and my agenda are not typical, any more than is Annie Dillard's as expressed in *For the Time Being*. Our questions may be unanswerable, but we cannot give up on them. In my case, I may be incurably religious. That is, I may be infected by the disease of religion, but it promises and promotes a cure of souls. And I cannot forgo that search for a cure from within it.

In any case, I began to alternate attending a racially integrated Episcopal parish with its historical liturgical tradition and an African-American Missionary Baptist church with its sectarian free worship being increasingly influenced by an MTV style and music with Pentecostal overtones. And I go to them hoping that one or both can and will learn to transcend Sinclair Lewis's wry observation that only bars and churches have stained glass and that both are escapes from reality.

That hope was inspired by a story told over and again by Henry Myers, formerly the Episcopal chaplain at Vanderbilt University and previously a professor at Sewanee's School of Theology. Myers told about a colleague there, a professor of "Old Testament," now deceased. It seems that this Yale-educated professor learned rather late in life about the Shoah, but that when he did, he studied relentlessly about the Christian complicity in it. As he began to fathom the history of the Christian teaching of contempt for the Jewish people, he arrived at the decision as an Episcopal priest never again to celebrate the Eucharist. He continued to receive it but never again to celebrate it—his protest against the continuing libel present in the scriptures and liturgy of the church *and* his inability to forsake his faith along with a commitment to address its problems. His story strikes me as one of a righteousness-seeking Gentile, one who took the Shoah personally and responded within the context of the church.

I draw hope too from the story of a law professor and his wife—he a former dean of the law school at Southern Methodist University—both devout and sensitive Roman Catholics. They shared their excitement a decade ago with an interfaith group about their planned trip to Germany to see the Oberammergau Passion Play. The group, with great respect for this couple, gently broke the news about the anti-Judaic elements of that play and the negotiations proceeding to have the text amended. Reservations were expressed about this play and its Bavarian connections to antisemitism. Peggy and Charles were distressed to learn what they had not known, and it sensitized them to the anti-Judaic elements still present in their lectionary and liturgical tradition. Charles, being a scholar of law, resolved to become involved in his church's efforts to remove prejudicial readings of the texts from the church's life.

I have told these stories to give reason to hope that churches, the ones I attend and thousands of others, can face the reality of the Shoah and feel and respond to the accusation that "Here are the graves of my people, and your people put them there." Nevertheless, the hope is continually undercut. On Palm Sunday 1999, at the Episcopal church, a major portion of the service consisted of a responsive reading drawn from the Passion Story in the Gospel of Matthew. As in all the Gospel accounts, it is "the Jews" who crucify Jesus but only here do "the people shout 'His blood be on us and on our children.' " Not a word of explanation was offered about the libel against "the Jews" or "the blood libel" that has

promoted Christian hatred of and pogroms against Jews for all these centuries. Perhaps the priests planning the service had never heard of Bill
Griffin, the Sewanee professor, or never studied under him or others who
tried to free the Christian liturgy from the teaching of contempt for Jews
and Judaism. At the very least, their putting the words, "His blood be on
us and on our children," into this Passion "play" as a congregational
shout of "the Jews" came close to ending my resolve to continue to hope.

Then, a day or two later, a prominent Presbyterian minister wrote his
weekly column in the local newspaper to mark "Easter's eternal
example." After quoting the Apostle Paul's epistle to the Corinthians,
"Where, O death, is your victory? Where, O death, is your sting?" he
wrote:

> My friends, whatever struggles you face today, whatever
> temptations you fight or fears from which you run, take just a
> moment to lift them to God in prayer and rejoice in the good
> news that sin in our lives and in our world has been defeated.
>
> There is no longer any reason to dread life or fear death, for
> their sting is gone! Christ literally took the sting of death and the
> grave upon himself, on the cross, and now we live in light of the
> resurrection.

I fairly wanted to cry out, "In what world do *you* live?" The atrocities, the
"ethnic cleansing," the genocide in Kosovo put the lie to such pieties as
"there is no longer any reason to dread life or fear death, for their sting
is gone." The pastor never examined his language enough to question if
the Serbian Christians were living "in the light of the resurrection." He
provided me once again with the knowledge that the Holocaust's
challenge to Christianity has not been heard or, if heard, not heeded.

These experiences of hearing and reading brought me to acknowledge
that my stories of hope do not express all that I feel and think as I
personally address the question of being a Christian after Auschwitz. The
question has put me into a more radical place of questioning God, one
that is not alleviated by the example of "righteous Gentiles" or "Christian
rescuers." I am not persuaded that whatever it was that led the one
percent of Christians to rescue or resist in the Shoah can be replicated
widely in a tradition so deeply flawed. I recognize my position to be
profoundly pessimistic, but it is what pushes me beyond the examples of
hope that I have framed here to another level of personal response.

I am drawn increasingly to such books as Franco Ferrucci's *The Life
of God (as Told by Himself)* (1996) which portray God as a troubled,
imperfect, still-developing deity who unintentionally becomes the father

of Jesus. Ferrucci's God grows to feel uncomfortable with the world he has made and prepares to leave it. I am drawn also to David Blumenthal's *Facing the Abusing God: A Theology of Protest* (1993), and to Regina Schwartz's *The Curse of Cain: The Violent Legacy of Monotheism* (1997), both of which focus on the genocidal tendencies in the nature of God "himself" as portrayed in scripture and embraced in the three great monotheistic traditions.

These books speak powerfully of monotheism's propensity to see history as One God revealing Oneself in the world by the choice of One People. And this One People gets defined over against the Other (people or peoples) who is (are) inferior, and the consequences are predictably violent. The movement is from Totalism to Victimization to Violence. Scripture-sanctioned history produces brutality. However, this is not to claim that monotheism or religion alone lies at the root of genocidal tendencies; there are many other culprits in history that offered transcendental rationales for their killing ways. Still, monotheistic traditions serve as a post-hoc justification for humanity's violent tendencies. Each one has exclusivist claims, and the two younger traditions of Christianity and Islam aim to supersede Judaism and one another. Each has triumphalist views that negate the scriptural injunctions to love and respect the other as "neighbor" or "People of the Book." Not one has escaped the cycle of victimization and violence. It remains unbroken.

In José Saramago's novel, *The Gospel according to Jesus Christ* (1994), Jesus asks God what the future will be like once he has died on a cross. Saramago puts eloquent but heretical words in God's mouth as God describes to Jesus the establishment of the church, the persecution of the martyrs, the violence and murder of the Crusades, the barbarities of the Inquisition, the wars of schism, the horrible cruelties arising from exclusivism, supersessionism, and triumphalism. Jesus asks God to remove him from this, to spare him, to prevent this awful sequence of events, which is to follow his death. God refuses. How could God even consider Jesus' plea?

James Wood, in a review-article on Saramago's work in *The New Republic*, does an excellent job of stating the case made in *The Gospel according to Jesus Christ*:

> The story winds outward from Herod's massacre of the children. God, the supposed Father, did not save the little children. Joseph, Jesus' father, did not save them either. God condemns Joseph to death for this sin, and the sins of the fathers pass to Jesus, who is crucified like his father. Thus, in Saramago's reading, Jesus went to the cross not as our savior but as one of

us, condemned by a form of Original Sin. We are Jesus's inheritors, condemned like him to crucify each other, generation after generation. We are the victims of an original sin, and our sentence is to be human. But "Father murdered the children of Bethlehem," says Jesus, and Saramago, of course, intends us to note the irony. It was God, the original Father, who killed the children, and therefore God must have condemned himself, and therefore God is not only the inventor of original sin, but its first practitioner, and thus its first victim. The sins of the fathers are in fact the sins of the Father's. God is condemned by the evil that He Himself allows. As Satan cannily tells Jesus, "Your God is the only warden of a prison where the only prisoner is your God."

Saramago adds almost nothing to the Gospel story. What he does, rather like Milton but more emphatically, is activate the ancient heretical cruxes, above all the familiar one that a God who originates evil must Himself be evil. In addition, he turns on its head the New Testament idea of Jesus as the sacrificial lamb, slaughtered to cleanse humans of their sin. No, says Saramago, Jesus was slaughtered for his Father's sins, both Joseph's and God's. Here Saramago is the splendid heir, in force and in idea, of Nietzsche in *The Anti-Christ*, who rails against the "paganism" of Jesus's "sacrifice." And Saramago makes resonant the implicit blasphemy at the heart of the incarnation. For if Jesus was truly human, then he inherited Adam's sin; but if he was also truly divine, then the sin he inherited was not Adam's but God's—not his father's, but his Father's.

Saramago professes a-theism. He uses literalism both to affirm and to subvert. He enunciates old, simple truths, but he states them literally, because literalism leads to skepticism about belief and to a protest against the abusive God.

Something akin to such skepticism, doubt, and uncertainty about belief itself while holding onto, reexamining, and retelling the story, permits me to give a positive answer to my question, "Can I still be a Christian?"

Yes, that is a part of who I am. But I repent of it. More radically, more skeptically than the "Old Testament" professor who gave up celebrating the Eucharist but not receiving it. More alienated, distrustful, and pessimistic than the law professor and his wife who were optimistic about the chances for reform. I repent of monotheism and embrace a pluralism in religious traditions, even if that risks a theological relativism. I repent of the unbroken cycle of victimization and violence by affirming a theology of protest. I repent of surrendering the traditions of Christianity to the literalists and fundamentalists, even if that means being unchurched. I repent of seeking closure on the questions posed by the Holocaust by refusing to embrace either traditional theism or a-theism, by accepting that Mystery lies behind all the mysteries of human existence.

To repent is to turn back. I turn away and then turn back, post-Auschwitz—wary, vigilant, cautious, skeptical; conscious, informed, sensible, affirming. I turn back to life out of a confrontation with death with a passion remaining to seek a renewal and reordering of human life and society. I turn back to a cosmic optimism out of looking in the face of genocide and atrocities to a hope and belief that life and not death will prevail and that life itself is our best clue to meaning in the universe and to human meaning. Despite all the evidence to the contrary.

Chapter 4

Christian Integrity after Auschwitz

Hubert G. Locke

In the light (or shadow) of the Shoah—the annihilation of almost six million Jews by the Nazi regime of Germany between 1939 and 1945—what do we understand to be the "good news" in the Christian message?

Several preliminary observations about the nature of this question may be raised. At issue is the core matter that Harry James Cargas of blessed memory has always put to his colleagues and, by extension, to Christians everywhere: How can we call ourselves Christians in the light of what we know to be the complicity of an untold number of people, who also considered themselves as Christians, in the destruction of the Jews? In a sense, it is a Christian version of the ancient lament of the Jewish exiles in Babylon: "How can we sing the Lord's song in a strange land?" (Psalm 137:4). For Christians, it is the question of how we can advance any serious or meaningful claims about redemption, atonement, compassion, or justice, given the fact that the murder of the Jews occurred in what Franklin Littell has so aptly termed "the heart of Christian Europe."

The Shoah has cast both Jews and Christians into alien territory, but it is Christians especially who find ourselves forced to ask new and disquieting questions about our faith. Early on, however, Christians need to decide whether these are historical or theological or ethical or practical inquiries we are undertaking. Not only will our answers be conditioned by the kinds of questions we raise, some forms of the questions—so I have come to believe—are far more useful or significant than others.

For example, I am never quite certain what to make of or do with the oft-repeated question that on occasion takes the form of an accusation: Why were the churches silent or why did the Christians do nothing to stop the Holocaust? If this is an ethical question, it hangs heavy over the Christian community. But if it is a historical query, it requires a great many qualifiers. The record of the German churches, for the most part, is less than praiseworthy; the leadership of the Bulgarian Orthodox Church was, on the other hand, quite remarkable and courageous, while that of the Anglican and Roman Catholic prelates in England was forthright and exemplary. The blanket condemnation of the churches for having been bystanders to the Shoah, therefore, does not hold up under scrutiny.

Similarly, when I am asked to account for the fact that those who conceived, planned, and implemented the so-called "Final Solution of the Jewish Question" considered themselves to be Christians, I confess being not quite certain how to respond. Again, if the question is a historical one it, too, needs serious modification: most of the hard-core Nazi leadership considered Christian belief and church membership to be antithetical to Nazi ideology. One has to reach into the ranks of the Nazi bureaucracy and into the right-wing, fanatical sector of the churches to find persons who were both devout churchgoers and ardent Nazis. But what are we to make of this discovery? Does the fact that there were committed Nazis who were also earnest church members provide the basis for a wholesale condemnation of Christianity? There were ardent Nazis who were also distinguished university professors or lovers of classical music or holders of doctoral degrees or renowned research scientists. Does this mean we should consider devotees of classical music, scientists, and doctoral-degree recipients to be ideologically tainted or suspect as well?

Some post-Shoah reflection, accusation, and recrimination simply cuts too wide and undiscriminating a swath to be either analytically or morally useful. As we enter a new millennium I want to raise a small but fervent voice for a more accurate and temperate examination of what remains the most important issue confronting Western societies. Our task should be to search for the harsh facts and let them speak for themselves, acknowledging the church's failures where they appear, with a determination to learn from those failures but without the spiritual self-flagellation that is mistaken for genuine repentance.

A.

What is the (Christian) "Good News" after Auschwitz? In one of his last essays before his death—the "Introduction" to *Holocaust Scholars Write to the Vatican*—Harry James Cargas asserted that "the whole question of scriptural interpretation requires study" ([Westport CT: Greenwood Press, 1998] 19). That study might usefully begin with the term "good news" or what we know in the English-speaking churches as the "Gospel." *Euaggelion* is predominantly a Pauline term; in the letters of Paul, it occurs seventy-two times while it appears in all four of the books that carry the title of Gospel a grand total of seventeen times; five times in Matthew, eight in Mark, four in Luke and, curiously, none at all in John. Of the seventeen uses of the term in the first four books of the Christian Scriptures, the Greek term *euaggelion* appears in sayings attributed to Jesus a total of nine times, one of which is in a widely disputed text. Biblical writers other than Paul may have had a far more chastened view of Jesus' message than the contemporary use of the term "good news" conveys.

In what is perhaps the most well-known and cited of the uses of the term by Jesus, that in Luke 4:18, he is recorded as reading in synagogue from the Isaiah scroll: "The spirit of the Lord is upon me, because he has anointed me to preach good news to the poor." Auschwitz, in my humble opinion, has not altered the spiritual truth of that proclamation; the good news remains a message which is today, as it has been from the beginning, primarily for the poor, the oppressed, and the brokenhearted. It is this proclamation which has inspired the poor and dispossessed down through the ages to struggle against their oppression. When it has touched the hearts of those who have possessions—either power or other resources—this proclamation has moved them to abolish oppressive institutions, to reform the structures and processes of society that harm those who are marginal to its interests, and to share the goods of this world more equitably. The grim reality of Auschwitz, it seems to me, does not eclipse this wider reality.

What Auschwitz does fundamentally alter, if not thoroughly repudiate, is the widespread and popular theological idea of a God whose sovereign activity occurs in human history—an idea on which I was nurtured in seminary forty years ago. As an American of African descent, I found this concept, on one hand, to be ennobling and inspiring and, on the other, deeply troubling. It struck me at the time that the idea of a God who steps into history to raise up a leader or rescue people from bondage or execute some other saving act is a comforting idea for the generation that happens to be around when God finally decides to act and that consequently becomes the beneficiary of God's saving effort. But it is hardly a matter of great comfort or satisfaction to the generations who lived and died in bondage or slavery before God decides to act! What redemption is there for those ancestors of either the ancient Israelites or mine who did not live to see the Exodus or Emancipation? The idea of the God of history leaves one with a somewhat capricious God to whom some generations can be grateful, with their forebears left to wonder about the Divine Goodness.

Auschwitz is the reality that cannot be reconciled with a God who is active in human history. Auschwitz would not pose the theological problems for Christians—and for Jews for that matter—were we not so insistent on the idea of Scripture—as one renowned biblical scholar subtitles his book on the Bible—as "the unfolding drama of God's dealings with men." That phraseology is now politically incorrect; Richard

Rubenstein has made abundantly clear how theologically flawed a concept it is, as well.

In *After Auschwitz* (New York: Bobbs-Merrill, 1966), Rubenstein recounts his interview with Probst Heinrich Grüber, one of the legendary figures in the German church's encounter with the Nazi regime. Grüber risked his life to save Jews from Nazi persecution. A staunch opponent of Hitler and a colleague of Martin Niemöller in the Confessing Church, Grüber established an organization shortly after the Nazis came to power that initially had the objective of aiding Christians of Jewish descent, but he subsequently broadened his efforts to assist Jewish organizations in their efforts to get Jews out of Germany. When war broke out in 1939, Grüber was the target of frequent harassment by the Gestapo, was finally arrested in 1940, sent to Sachsenhausen and subsequently to Dachau. Grüber survived the war and was the sole German witness to testify against Adolf Eichmann at his trial in 1961.

Grüber, then, was no ordinary German. But in spite of his heroic efforts, Grüber firmly believed, as he stated to Rubenstein, that "it was part of God's plan that the Jews died" (p. 54). It was a logical and inevitable consequence of his belief in a God who acts in history! Little wonder that Rubenstein concluded: "After the experiences of our times, we can neither affirm the myth of the omnipotent God of History nor can we maintain its corollary, the Election of Israel" (p. 69).

B.

If "the God of the Bible is the God who acts" (Bernhard Anderson, *Rediscovering the Bible* [New York: Association Press, 1951] 24), then one faces the painful question of why God did not act to save millions of Jews from mass murder. If history is the arena of God's activity, then one is left to wonder why, in the midst of one of history's worst moments, God chose not to intervene. It could be argued that the biblical record of the people of Israel is one in which they were subject to continual trauma and tragedy—from the years of slavery in Egypt to the wars with various foes and finally the conquest and period of exile in Babylon. And if we extend beyond the period which the Hebrew Scriptures encompass, there is the occupation of the land of Israel by the Romans and their destruction of the Jewish temple, with the subsequent scattering of the Jewish people to other lands and nations.

The Hebrew prophets treated all the disasters that occurred during the biblical period as judgments of God on a people that had not remained faithful to the Covenant. It is the extension of this interpretation of the meaning of Israel's tragedies that Probst Grüber horridly makes.

But can one seriously believe in a God who purposely allows young children, along with their mothers and grandparents, to be led into gas chambers because of some unfathomable Divine Plan? Least of all, if such a horrendous judgment is to be made or interpretation offered, has a Christian any business whatsoever doing so? And yet, the uncomfortable truth is that such is the unavoidable conclusion to which one must come if the God-in-History view is maintained. Either that, or one is left with a God who breaks the covenant He established with His people. There are Christians of the supersessionist variety who would make precisely this claim, but they leave us with a God who not only breaks His word but acquiesces in the annihilation of those who were, in the eyes of the supersessionists, once His People. It is not blasphemy to state that such a God is not worthy of adoration by anyone.

The traditional posture of Christian theology is that Jesus is the supreme manifestation of God's action in human history. The doctrine of the Incarnation and nearly everything else that flows from it is predicated on this assumption or understanding of the divine drama. It is a theological position hallowed by the fact that it is one of the earliest Christological interpretations on record. The same questions that agonize Jews from a God-in-History perspective are an agony for Christians as well. But Christians may find some solace in the fact that the Incarnation is not the only interpretation of the meaning and significance of the life and death of Jesus. In fact, an older Christology saw Jesus not as God-Incarnate but as a Jew who ran afoul of both Jewish tradition and Roman politics, whose death was at the hands of "lawless men" but whose resurrection was proof that the sovereignty of God cannot be thwarted by the evil of humans. This is the essence of the sermon of Peter at Pentecost. It is the oldest kerygma we have on record. And it accords much more closely with the attempt to place Jesus in the context of Jewish messianic belief than in the later Greco-Roman philosophical milieu where Paul placed Jesus with such brilliance and effectiveness.

C.

If the idea of a God who works in history is no longer tenable after Auschwitz, what is there to take its place? In 1943, during the battle of Stalingrad, Helmut Thielicke, who was preacher at St. Michael's Church in Hamburg and later rector of the Universities of Tübingen and Hamburg, delivered a sermon on "The Silence of God." The sermon is interesting for its historical as well as its theological content; it is the latter that I find of particular interest. Taking as his text the story, recounted in Matthew 15:21-28, of the woman of Canaan who beseeches

Jesus to heal her daughter, Thielicke says at one point: "How many meaningless blows of fate there seem to be!—life, suffering, injustice, death, massacres, destruction; and all under a silent heaven which apparently has nothing to say."

Thielicke was preaching to a confused and dispirited congregation of German churchgoers who were just coming to terms with the fact that the tide of the war in which Germany had been so victorious in its first few years was now turning against the nation and its people. Within months, Allied bombs would begin to rain down on Hamburg and other German cities. Thielicke's congregants were likely hoping that the God of history would intervene on behalf of their nation and, shortly, on their own personal behalf, to save them from a destruction that, in 1943, appeared to be inevitable. Instead of offering such a hope, Thielicke simply speaks of heaven's silence.

We moderns of the twenty-first century and the third millennium live in a world of instant communication and unending words—advertising commercials, talk shows, political debates, mindless chatter and the ubiquitous ritual of "sharing." Because we prize doing and are ourselves engaged in ceaseless activity, we are exceptionally comfortable with the notion of a God who is worthy of our attention as One who also acts, in our world and on our behalf.

Rather than the God who is active in human history—leading, redeeming, judging, saving, proclaiming—perhaps we for whom conversation and communication are almost constants have instead to confront and learn to grapple with a God who is silent when we most expect God to speak and act, and thus—in the moments of God's silence—leaves us to come to terms with the consequences of our own human failings.

Part Two

Practices

According to the Gospel of Matthew, Jesus said: "Every tree that does not bear good fruit is cut down and thrown into the fire. Thus you will know them by their fruits" (Matthew 7:19-20).

In their relation to Jews, Christian practices have often failed to bear good fruit. To the contrary, they have, for example, falsely indicted Jews as "Christ killers," and they have falsely denigrated Judaism as a tradition that has been superseded by Christianity. Such attitudes provided fertile soil in which the Holocaust's seeds were planted.

Two of the essayists in this book's second part—Eloise Rosenblatt and Robert Bullock—identify practices that remain problematic within their Roman Catholic tradition, but not only there. Rosenblatt uses the controversial canonization of Edith Stein to explore what she calls "the power of residual antisemitism in Catholicism." Exploring what he calls "the ways we worship," Bullock shows that Christian liturgy still needs substantial revision after Auschwitz. Both of these scholars recognize that many positive steps have been taken to rid Christianity of anti-Jewish elements. Both also recognize that much remains to be done.

Jolene Chu, James Pellechia, Henry Knight, and Carol Rittner join Rosenblatt and Bullock in expressing what Christians need to do. Chu and Pellechia speak as Jehovah's Witnesses. Their tradition had no Christian rival when it came to overt resistance against the Third Reich and its virulent, racist antisemitism. Its record during the Holocaust sets an example that can be beneficial for post-Holocaust Christians. Drawing deeply on Jewish sources and traditions, Knight develops a Christian theology of hospitality. Had it been practiced by Christians, the Holocaust would not have happened. Rittner takes up a controversial post-Holocaust topic—forgiveness—and assesses the strengths and weaknesses contained in that much-emphasized aspect of Christian faith.

Each and all, these writers show what Christians need to do to make credible that Christianity does possess "good news" in spite of the Holocaust.

Chapter 5

Canonizing Edith Stein and Recognizing Catholic Antisemitism

Eloise Rosenblatt

Professor David Noel Freedman, noted biblical scholar and editor of the Anchor Bible commentary series, talked with me in May 1997 about the theological and political contradictions raised by the prospect of Edith Stein's canonization to sainthood by Rome.[1] He said there was uncertainty about why Edith Stein was not able to escape from Echt in Holland in the last months of her life and, despite all the efforts on her behalf, cross the border into Switzerland. He proposed that I submit a prospectus for a book about her.[2]

I found myself haunted by the question of what forces were at work in blocking her escape. Did they come from within Catholic circles? Was there antisemitic feeling among Catholics that interfered with her escape and left her to her fate as a woman of Jewish ethnicity? I also quickly became aware of the difficulties of writing a biography about this woman to whom the Catholic Church was laying claim as a saint.[3] How would

---

[1]This conversation took place about the time that articles about Edith Stein appeared in the Los Angeles archdiocese Catholic newspaper *The Tidings*: "Pope says cure of U.S. girl is miracle for Edith Stein" (18 April 1997) and "Pope formally declares Blessed Edith Stein will become saint" (30 May 1997). See the discussion, just prior to the canonization, of the cure of Benedicta McCarthy by Eleanor Michael in her anecdotally rich "The Convenient Saint," *The Guardian Weekend*, 26 September 1998, 28-31.

[2]There are a number of English-language publications between the 1960s and more recent studies, for example, Harry James Cargas, ed., *The Unnecessary Problem of Edith Stein. Studies in the Shoah*, vol. 4 (Lanham MD: University Press of America, 1994). See Waltraud Herbstrith, O.C.D., ed., *Never Forget: Christian and Jewish Perspectives on Edith Stein*, trans. Susanne Batzdorff (Washington DC: Institute of Carmelite Studies, 1998).

[3]See Eloise Rosenblatt, "Edith Stein's Canonization: Acknowledging Objections from Jews and Catholics," in Carol Rittner et al., eds., *The Holocaust and the*

an analysis of Edith Stein be different from the hagiographical, meditative genre characteristic of some writing from the period 1950–1980?[4]

I was not alone in my considerations. Professor Dana Greene had already suggested that "the hagiographic tradition with its didactic purpose and ahistorical interpretation" may not be adequate to the questions of contemporary readers."[5] She proposed, "Her life can be more appropriately examined through a thoroughly secular biography which would emphasize development and contextualization and would honor complexity and ambiguity"[6] as well as address "ordinary themes of family and student life, love of country and loss of opportunity."[7]

Greene proposed adding new material to biographies of Edith Stein, examining her contribution to philosophy, theology, education, and feminism:

> Is her work on empathy and her attempted integration of phenomenology and Thomism of enduring significance? Does she have original insight into women's condition as distinct from men? Is there merit in her understanding of the function of the state? What is the literary value of her autobiographical memoir of her Jewish family and how is it connected to her philosophical work on empathy.[8]

Christian World (London: Kuperard, 2000).

[4]Henry Bordeaux, *Edith Stein: Thoughts on Her Life and Times,* trans. Donald and Idella Gallagher (Milwaukee: Bruce Pub. Co., 1959). See the bibliography for early editions of primary sources and English language articles from 1952 to 1958 in Catholic religious journals and magazines. The introduction by the Gallaghers invites readers to seek "information concerning her cause for beatification and the movement for the conversion of Jews to Catholicism" from the Edith Stein Guild in New York.

[5]Dana Greene, "In Search of Edith Stein," unpublished paper, 4. I am grateful to Victoria Barnett who called my attention to this author and her scholarship and forwarded a copy of the paper to me. Dana Greene is professor of History at St. Mary's College of Maryland and author of *Evelyn Underhill: Artist of the Infinite Life* and *The Living of Maisie Ward,* both published by the University of Notre Dame Press.

[6]Greene, "In Search of Edith Stein," 2.

[7]Ibid., 5.

[8]Ibid., 2.

Multiple Identities of a Catholic Saint

Edith Stein represents multiple identities, and there are several approaches researchers have undertaken. Some focus on her as a European philosopher represented by her writings as the academic Dr. Stein, phenomenologist and disciple of Edmund Husserl.[9] Carmelites claim her as Sister Teresa Benedicta of the Cross, representative of the order's spirituality, whose attraction to Teresa of Avila and John of the Cross places her within the mystical tradition of spiritual writers and theologians. Devotionally minded Catholics approach her life as the story of a heroic woman who died for the faith, and whose life was marked by Christian virtues. Related to this approach are those who study her spirituality as an occasion of the mysterious dynamic of conversion. Jewish scholars place her within the context of Jewish intellectual life. Some list her with the voices of other women associated with the Holocaust, such as Anne Frank, Simone Weil, and Etty Hillesum. For feminists, Stein's writings and lectures from 1923 to 1933 belong to the social and political feminist movement vibrant in Europe that initiated a feminist consciousness which, by the 1990s, became a global movement.

A necessary but neglected scholarly approach, noted by Edith Stein's niece, Susanne Batzdorff, has been to approach the sources in light of her identity as Aunt Edith, a woman related to a large and loving Jewish family, which lost many of its members in the Holocaust, together with Edith. A balanced approach to any study of Edith Stein must take into account her family relations. The scholar should attend the contextualization provided by surviving family members who knew their aunt personally, and who both support some perceptions and disagree significantly with other portraits of family members recorded by Edith Stein in her autobiography.[10]

---

[9]Pope John Paul II read the writings of Edith Stein as Karol Wotyla, university student, when his professor was Roman Ingarden, a colleague of Edith Stein. See Stein's correspondence with Ingarden in letters numbered 6, 7, 8, 9, 10, 11, 12, 13, 14, 15, 16, 17, 18, 19, and 20, in L. Gelber and Romaeus Leuven, O.C.D., eds., *Edith Stein: Self Portrait in Letters: 1916-1942*, trans, Josephine Koeppel, O.C.D. (Washington DC: ICS Publications, 1993) 6-24. This correspondence was first published in *Philosophy and Phenomenological Research* 23 (1962).

[10]The autobiography is Edith Stein, *Life in a Jewish Family: Her Unfinished Autobiographical Account*, ed. L. Gelber and Romaeus Leuven, O.C.D., trans. Josephine Koeppel, O.C.D. (Washington DC: ICS Publications, 1986). On 2

The Distracting Question:
Why Couldn't She Escape from Holland?

Amidst all the possible approaches to a study of Edith Stein, the single question that dominated my thoughts concerned her failed efforts to escape Holland. Why hadn't Edith Stein been saved from arrest by the Nazis? Within six weeks of *Kristallnacht* in early November 1938, her prioress in Germany had successfully negotiated Edith Stein's transfer from the Carmel of Cologne to the Dutch Carmel of Echt, Netherlands, a trip that took place the night of 31 December 1938. Over several months, Edith Stein made concerted efforts to move from Echt to the Carmel in Switzerland, but that effort was delayed for months by a variety of factors.

One was the fact that Germany was at war with the Allies, declaration of war on Germany by Great Britain and France having been made on 3 September 1939. By May 1940, Germany had invaded and occupied Holland, Belgium, and France.

The most complete provisional answer lies in the urgent letter of 31 December 1941, written by Edith Stein to Hilde Verene Borsinger, Stein's laywoman friend who was both an academic and lawyer.[11] The

---

February 2000, I was graciously received on a visit by the niece of Edith Stein, Susanne Biberstein Batzdorff and her husband Alfred Batzdorff in Santa Rosa, California. Susanne is the daughter of Erna Stein Biberstein, older sister of Edith. She sailed from Bremmerhaven to the United States with her husband, daughter (Susanne), and son (Ernst) on 16 February 1939. See letter 294, letter to Mother Petra Bruning, OSU, Dorsten, written by Edith Stein from Echt on 17 February 1939, in L. Gelber and Romaeus Leuven, O.C.D., eds., *Edith Stein, Self-Portrait in Letters 1916–1942* (Washington DC: Institute of Carmelite Studies, 193) 302-303. Continuing the legacy of her mother, Susanne Batzdorff presently maintains the family archives concerning "Aunt Edith," and is an author, translator, and editor in her own right. See the valuable biographical material on the family, most of whom remained Jewish, in *Aunt Edith: The Jewish Heritage of a Catholic Saint* (Springfield IL: Templegate, 1998). The essays complement, explain, and in some cases qualify Edith Stein's own perspective in her autobiography *Life in a Jewish Family*. See also Susanne Batzdorff-Biberstein, "Erinnerungen an meine Tante Edith Stein," *Edith Stein: Ein neues Lebensbild in Zeugnissen und Selbstzeugnissen*, ed. Waltraud Herbstrith (Freiburg im Breisgau, Basel, Wien: Herder, 1983) 69-76.

[11]The annotation on Hilde Verene Borsinger after letter 331 provides data that she was born in Baden/Aargau, Switzerland in 1897, and died in Luzern in 1986. A jurist, she completed her studies at the University of Zurich with a thesis on

letter requested Borsinger's help in getting Edith Stein and her blood sister Rosa to Switzerland. Edith said her superior at Echt wanted to place her and her sister with the Carmelites who had a convent in Switzerland. Edith was unsure whether they would be accepted by such a convent.

> From you, on the other hand, I would like to find out whether, provided we are accepted by a convent, we could obtain an entry permit and visa, and to whom we ought to apply for it. I do know that Switzerland is strictly closed to immigrants, but I could imagine that under these particular circumstances an exception would be made.[12]

Borsinger, writing from Basel in 1945 after the war, recalled her arduous efforts to obtain clearances for Edith and her sister, and notes that there were several causes of delay: the German Occupation Authority in Holland had informed Edith Stein in April 1942 that emigration was out of the question until the end of the War. The prioresses at the Carmelite convent of Le Paquier and the convent of Seedorf originally accepted the refugees, but later raised objections which Borsinger had to defuse by assuring the superiors based on her knowledge of the good character of Edith Stein.

The Swiss Immigration Service demanded additional lay sponsors, besides the guarantee by the monasteries. The Congregation for Religious in Rome cited Canon Law as creating a requirement that the bishop of Freiburg had to give official certification to have the Stein sisters in his diocese. The two sponsoring monasteries had to submit decisions from a chapter, representing the formal consent of all the nuns. Finally, there had to be an "assertion de Rome," whose vagueness was never defined. It is uncertain that this document ever arrived from Rome.

Eventually the Swiss Immigration Service told Borsinger it could give Stein an entry permit, but not her sister Rosa. Borsinger wrote again on behalf of the two sisters, since she knew Edith would not leave without Rosa. Yet, Borsinger later would write, "Despite all these efforts, on August 2, 1942, the very day on which Sr. Teresia Benedicta a Cruce and

---

the "Legal Status of Woman in the Catholic Church." Dr. Borsinger was editor of *Schweizerin* ("The Swiss Woman"), was founder and head of an educational authority for youth who were learning disabled. She met Edith Stein in 1930 at Beuron, the Benedictine monastery, through Erich Przywara, S.J.

[12]Letter 331, to Hilde Verene Borsinger, Bern, Switzerland, Echt, 31 December 1941 in *Edith Stein: Self Portrait in Letters: 1916–1942*, 341–43.

her sister were deported, I received the reply from the Swiss Immigration Office that the application for an entry permit from the two sisters had been denied."[13]

There are several unanswered questions about what took so long for the Carmel of Switzerland and what questions occasioned the nuns' ambivalence after they had given their consent. The discomfiting implications of these questions have not received extensive treatment in biographies of Edith Stein. According to the 1980 summary of her biography by Di Muzio, the Carmelite prioress announced the clearance for passage to Switzerland to the SS officers in the presence of Edith and her sister while the women were being arrested in the front parlor of the monastery.

> The prioress then came in to say that by now all the documents for the transfer to Switzerland were ready. The reply of the officers was peremptory: "All that can be taken care of later; Sister Stein must come along now."[14]

The representation of the question in the German-produced docudrama, *Edith Stein*, gives a rather long opening reenactment which portrays the prioress at Echt devoted to assisting Edith Stein, and emphasizing her attentiveness and approval of Sr. Teresa Benedicta's efforts to be transferred to Switzerland.[15]

The film represents Edith Stein's Jewish background in an idealized way, through a formal seder, around the family table. The explanation of her scholarly work as a phenomenologist is focused and clear. The orien-

---

[13]Hilde Verene Borsinger, "Attempt to Bring Edith Stein to Safety in Switzerland in 1942," in Herbstrith, ed., *Never Forget: Christian and Jewish Perspectives on Edith Stein*, 268-71. The essay was originally published in a collection of Dutch tributes to Catholics of Jewish ethnicity, many clergy and nuns, as well as laity, who were rounded up by the Nazis on 2 August 1942, among them Edith and Rosa Stein, and deported to death camps. See *Als een brandende toorts* (Echt, 1967). A description of Dr. Borsinger's efforts is also acknowledged by Beatrice Eichmann-Leutenegger, "Edith Stein—Leuchtschrift und Sternverdunkelung" in Waltraud Herbstrith, ed., *Ein neues Lebensbild in Zeugnissen und Selbstzeugnissen*, 143-50.

[14]Fr. Louis Charles Di Muzio, O.C.D. "Edith Stein: Truth and Calvary," *Messenger of the Holy Infant of Prague*, special edition (4 April 1980): 18.

[15]*Edith Stein*. German version: Maran Film, Stuttgart; English version: EWTN, Birmingham AL, 1996. Distributed by EWTN, 5817 Old Leeds Road, Birmingham AL 35210. VHS copies available by calling 205-951-2194.

tation of the film emphasizes her character as a Catholic martyr, prior to her actual canonization.

> Probe the heart and soul of Edith Stein, the exemplary Jewish convert and philosopher, great intellectual and worthy daughter of Saint Teresa of Avila. Stein, a Carmelite beatified on German soil by Pope John Paul II, is a precious example of holiness and heroic virtue facing down a culture of death.[16]

Edith Stein and Unsettled Feelings between Catholics and Jews

In the period after Edith Stein's canonization, I wonder about the timing of the public honor, and what must be acknowledged of ecclesiastical politics and the urgency to "repent" of centuries-long abuse of Jews and Judaism. The Vatican's statement "We Remember: A Reflection on the Shoah" was not well received in many quarters. For example, on the eve of her canonization, several of Edith Stein's relatives wrote an open letter to Pope John Paul II affirming his many steps toward reconciliation. He had branded antisemitism a sin, visited the synagogue of Rome, established diplomatic relations between the Vatican and state of Israel, and changed the climate for conversation from fearful relations to one inviting mutual interaction. In the same letter, Stein's relatives regretted that "We Remember" failed to indict Catholic leadership for its lack of moral guidance during World War II, and to condemn Catholic leaders for promoting antisemitism.[17]

The canonization was meant to be "good news," but its effect has been blunted in interfaith dialogue. In noting reactions of some Catholics toward Jews on this controversial matter, I wonder whether feelings released by the canonization are linked to the unfinished business of redeeming residual antisemitism in the post-World War II Catholic community.

---

[16]Video jacket blurb on *Edith Stein*, English edition, 1996.

[17]"Open Letter to John Paul: Speak the Whole Truth about Christians and the Holocaust," *National Catholic Reporter* (23 October 1998): 22. The four members of the family of Edith Stein who published the letter included her nephew, Ernst Ludwig Biberstein, and his wife Hannah, of Davis, California; his son Michael and his daughter-in-law Debra Biberstein, living in San Diego. They attended the canonization in Rome and wrote the letter in advance of their trip.

As one example of the sort of resentment that manifests the power of residual antisemitism in Catholicism, I noted a strong reaction against Jewish reservations about Stein's canonization. It came from well-known Benedictine archeologist Bar-Gil Pixner, expressed in the *Jerusalem Post* in 1998. I was alerted because I had been one of many researchers and students who profited from his scholarship and attended his excavation-site lectures in Jerusalem in the 1980s:

> Why should many Jews resent that this believer in Jesus is being declared a woman of extraordinary faith? That's all that canonization really means. Would Jews rather have her an atheist than one who through the Jew Jesus came to believe and love the God of Israel?[18]

To this complicated question of Edith Stein's relationship to Judaism and her self-understanding as Jew, some qualifications should be noted. Pixner assumes that Edith Stein was atheistic and that this alienated her from her family's faith. However, her letters show that Edith Stein always loved "the God of Israel," and was not alienated from Judaism, even though she chose to locate her spiritual path within Roman Catholic tradition. For example, she respected the religious devotion of her mother and spoke of her death in 1936 as an example of fidelity, countering a rumor that her mother had converted from Judaism:

> The news of her conversion was a totally unfounded rumor. I have no idea who made it up. My mother held to her faith to the very last. The faith and firm confidence she had in her God from her earliest childhood until her eighty-seventh year remained steadfast, and were the last things that stayed alive in her during the final difficult agony. Therefore, I have the firm belief that she found a very merciful judge and is now my most faithful helper on my way, so that I, too, may reach my goal.[19]

---

[18]Bar-Gil Pixner, O.S.B, "Why Resent Canonization?" in "Letters," *Jerusalem Post International Edition*, 2 November 1998, 11. Pixner is a monk of the Dormition Abbey near Zion Gate in Jerusalem. Susanne Batzdorff proposes that Pixner may be referring to Edith Stein's statement that she had stopped praying at age fourteen. "She is thus often described as an atheist, and some people consider her as having converted not from Judaism but from atheism to Catholicism." If this is true of Pixner's view, he is mistaken.

[19]Letter 227. To Sr. Callista Kopf, O.P., Speyer, 4 October 1936, in *Edith Stein: Self-Portrait in Letters*, 238.

Pixner's recognition of Jesus' ethnicity (the Jew Jesus) does nothing to soften his perception of Jews as resentful enemies of faithful believers in God such as the Catholic Edith Stein. Pixner offers Jews troubled by the canonization only two choices: celebrate Edith Stein's faith in God, or profess their own atheism. The tone of Pixner's remarks exposes long-standing antipathies of Catholic clergy and religious orders. It is a deeply conditioned reflex, unaffected by Vatican II and ameliorative statements from Pope John Paul II. Jews have, in the eyes of many within Catholic religious orders, no right to protest against the choices made by Catholics or to interfere with Catholic belief and practice, since they are outsiders, and persons who do not have "true faith."[20]

A less offensive variant of this rhetorical posture which expresses the problematic "we versus them" relationship appears, ironically, in an article by Eric Zuckerman, S.J., in a Jesuit newsletter published twice yearly in Berkeley, California.[21] Born Jewish, Zuckerman converted to Catholicism at age twenty-six, and later entered the Jesuits. In an optimistic first-person essay, he describes his conversion, and outlines the various reactions his Catholicism now evokes in Jewish colleagues, from cautious interest to understandable mistrust.

> Instances such as these have inculcated within me a profound sense of how truly complex and potentially volatile the vocation of being a Jesuit of Jewish background can be, especially when relating to Jewish persons, and how deftly one must tread in this regard. And when I find myself being me with some cautious initial reactions from Jewish individuals I encounter, I see this as a highly graced and privileged opportunity to help break down some long-fostered and deeply felt notions toward both the Church and the Jesuits that were formed before Vatican II and

---

[20]Religious communities need to undertake an examination of their internalized theology and spirituality to identify forms of anti-Jewish bias, typically encoded by a silent agreement to exclude certain topics. Like the taboo subjects of domestic violence and incest, which are not addressed in homilies, antisemitism does not appear on annual agendas of religious communities because it is regarded as "not an issue" and "outside" the concerns of Catholic nuns, brothers, and priests. This dichotomy remains the norm even though all religious communities ground their lives in the reading of Scripture and theology, with a spirituality informed by this tradition.

[21]Eric Zuckerman, S.J., "Twice Blessed," *JSTB Bridge* (Jesuit School of Theology at Berkeley) 15/1 (Fall 1998): 1, 3, 15.

that have had little exposure to changes brought about since then.[22]

Zuckerman also hints at day-to-day, unspoken and spontaneous expressions of suspicion directed at him by Jesuits inside community houses. The notation implies that among his fellow Jesuits he senses an instinct that divides "Catholic" responses to Middle East politics from "Jewish" responses.

> [W]hen conversations regarding the politics of Israel come around in Jesuit rec[reation] rooms, eyes still flicker toward me despite my twenty years of being Catholic.[23]

The statement is intriguing as an analogy with Edith Stein's situation. Zuckerman's brother Jesuits do not, apparently, forget he is ethnically Jewish. Either he or they seem to expect that if he is truly Catholic, he will react to criticisms of Israel in accord with what non-Jewish Jesuits feel. He senses that their eyes "still flicker" toward him to detect whether he will have a "Jewish" reaction twenty years after his baptism. The inference is that a Jewish reaction, or one sympathetic to Israel on political issues, is alien to a truly Catholic perspective, and to Jesuit values in particular.

Reexamining the Culture of Antisemitism in Catholic Religious Orders

As a consequence of Edith Stein's canonization, members of Catholic religious orders have new occasion to reflect on the impact interreligious dialogue may have on their corporate spirituality and internal social culture. Pro-Nazi sympathies and antisemitic feelings survive(d) long after World War II in Europe. Cargas calls attention to the collusion of Catholic religious orders in assisting Nazis to escape after World War II.

> [M]any Catholics, particularly clergy, participated in an under-ground railroad system that assisted Nazis to hide and flee after the war was lost for them. Some of the most notorious names were rescued that way. The most recent proof of this came to light in May 1994 when Paul Touvier, a pro-Nazi French militiaman, was arrested after having been hidden by right-wing Catholics. He was seized in Nice, in St. Francis Priory, after

---

[22]Ibid., 15.
[23]Ibid.

having been on the run for forty-four years. He sometimes dressed as a priest in public. He had been condemned to death in absentia in 1945 for murder, torture, and collaboration with the Nazis. The Catholic abbot from whose monastery Touvier was captured said that he was only doing his charitable duty as a Catholic priest in granting asylum.[24]

There is ample evidence that members of the Catholic clergy in Rome were involved in fabricating documents and new postwar identities, thus assisting Germans and their supporters to emigrate from Europe after their defeat in World War II. The names of personnel and location of Vatican embassies in Rome are documented in a declassified "top secret" report to the U.S. Department of State, compiled in 1947 by Vincent La Vista: "Illegal Emigration Movements in and through Italy." The agent lists twenty-two Vatican relief and welfare organizations in Rome, representing various nations such as Austria, Hungary, and Germany, which were engaging in or suspected of engaging in illegal emigration. The directors of all these agencies were Catholic clerics.[25]

The report provides evidence that Catholic clergy representing the Vatican used the International Red Cross (IRC) as part of the chain of documentation to enable legal and illegal refugees to emigrate from Europe. Vatican representatives would provide and verify identities of persons of a certain national group. These persons would then be provided passports by the IRC. Little supervision or checking was done to prevent fraud.[26] The agent noted that many persons in the IRC were pro-German, and that persons of nations formerly allied with the German army were successful in obtaining documents. Padre Don Carlos, a Vatican representative with connections in South America, was part of the

---

[24]Harry James Cargas, introduction to *Holocaust Scholars Write to the Vatican*, ed. Harry James Cargas, Contributions to the Study of Religion 58, John K. Roth and Carol Rittner, series editors (Westport CT and London: Greenwood Press, 1998) 16.

[25]The report by Vincent La Vista, "Illegal Emigration Movements in and through Italy" is addressed to Herbert J. Cummings. Dated 15 May 1947, it is date-stamped 14 July 1947 by the Department of State, Office of American Republic Affairs. One copy was originally sent to the American Legation in Vienna. Declassification no. NND760050. The twenty-two Catholic agencies and sixteen committees are listed in appendix A, 1-2. I am grateful for assistance in obtaining this document through advice from Peninah Rothenburg. It was sent to me by Bonnie Gurewitsch, archivist at the Museum of Jewish Heritage, New York.

[26]Ibid., appendix B, 6.

chain of contacts by which German nationals were funneled through the IRC, then through Barcelona, Spain, and from there to South America.[27]

James Reites, S.J., and Antisemitism in the History of the Society of Jesus

In an article distilling his dissertation, James Reites, a Jesuit, chronicles the history of antisemitism in the Society of Jesus.[28] Ignatius of Loyola founded the Jesuits in 1540. In his 1979 dissertation, Reites attempted to show that Loyola's relations with Jews and Christians of Jewish heritage was benign and should be revived in the post-Vatican II church as an example of the founder's toleration. Reites argues that since Ignatius himself did not exclude persons of Jewish lineage ("New Christians") from membership in the Jesuits, he was enlightened. Reites claimed Ignatius's spiritual vision distinguished him from his contemporaries who held to the practice of excluding from Catholic religious orders persons of Jewish ancestry. Others, not Ignatius, demanded and soon restored the "blood purity" requirement. Reites admits that for 400 years the Jesuit constitutions excluded or made it difficult for men with Jewish ancestry to enter the Society.

However, in a well-intentioned, but naive effort to make Ignatius a model for post-Vatican II interfaith relations, Reites misreads the evidence that Ignatius was tolerant of Jews. The facts cited by Reites indicate that Ignatius welcomed Jews who had converted to Christianity but, reflecting the bias of his century, he had no use for Jews who remained Jewish. Moreover, if he had prohibited persons of Jewish heritage from the Society, he would have excluded from the initial foundation his close friend Laynez who was a third generation "New Christian." As distinguished from "Old Christians," the New Christians were persons whose families had not always been Catholic, that is, had been ethnically or religiously Jewish, or in some cases Muslim. On this general distinction between racial and theological antisemitism, Harry James Cargas notes:

---

[27]Ibid., appendix B, 5.

[28]James W. Reites, S.J., "Ignatius and the Jews," *Studies in the Spirituality of the Jesuits* 13/4 (September 1981). Reites taught in the religious studies department at Santa Clara University in northern California, and is presently assistant director of novices in Los Angeles. Paul Locatelli, S.J., president of Santa Clara University, serves on the board of trustees at the Jesuit School in Berkeley. JSTB published the issue of *Bridge* with the autobiographical piece by Zuckerman, who received his M.Div. from JSTB in 1998.

In an important sense, racial anti-Semitism was more totally destructive than theological anti-Semitism because, according to the latter, Jews could theoretically be accepted through conversion to Christianity. However, according to the racial theory, Jewish blood is corrupt; therefore there is no possibility for approval.[29]

Reites attempts to mitigate the conclusion that Ignatius shared the anti-Judaic sentiments of his day, calling him a "humble apostle to the Jews of Rome." It would be more honest to admit that Ignatius shared the triumphal attitude of Christians in his day that Jews should be spiritually conquered, submit to conversion, join the true faith, and reject the blindness of unenlightened Judaism. Ignatius worked for the conversion of Jews in Rome. He saw converted Jews as attracting other Jews to Christianity. Reites judges Ignatius's zeal to convert Jews as an expression of personal holiness and dedication to God, not his social prejudice or theological supersessionism.

Reites's own evidence undercuts his attempt to portray Ignatius as a hero of interfaith relations. Hardly ten years after the foundation of the Society, Ignatius capitulated to the demands of Siliceo, archbishop of Spain, that the *limpieza de sangre* (purity of blood) restriction be imposed, and that New Christians be excluded from membership in the Society in Spain (1551). Ignatius made the political choice to restrict membership to non-Jews so the greater good of Jesuit apostolate in Spain could be carried out.

There was resistance against the norm for a couple of decades, but by 1592, the *limpieza de sangre* restriction was formally enacted and no New Christian could be accepted into the Society. In 1608, the "impediment of origin" was defined as Christian identity which could not be traced back five generations. Such an impediment blocked a man's ability to enter the Society.

Reites acknowledges that Ignatius actively supported the promulgation in 1555 of the papal directive (bull) of *Cum Nimis Absurdum*, which restricted the Jews of Rome to a ghetto, stated they did not have equal rights of citizenship with Christians, and imposed restrictions on Jews' economic life and mobility. His narration of this harrowing attack on Jews does not analyze the logical irreconcilability of two assertions: Ignatius was a model of toleration toward Jews in general, but Ignatius

---

[29]Cargas, introduction to *Holocaust Scholars Write to the Vatican*, 11.

promulgated papal racism toward the Jews of Rome.[30] It is difficult to avoid the assumption that a series of papal directives against Jews in the 1500s shaped the theological and social culture of the Jesuits, since they were specially dedicated to the service of the pope.

Ignatius and the Jesuits after him accepted the prevailing prejudice that Jewish religion and race denoted bad blood (*mala sangre*), as opposed to purity of blood (*limpieza de sangre*); that Christians with Jewish lineage were mixed-race (*mezclados*); that there was a distinction between New Christians and Old Christians when it came to applicants to the Society; that such lineage was a handicap, an imperfection (*la falta*), a defect or characteristic (*la nota*) that might be overcome and compensated for by extra hard work, dedication, good example, and mortification. Nevertheless, there were some places such persons could not be sent. Their origin (genus) was offensive to people and could thus hinder the fruitfulness of the apostolate.

Belatedly, in 1946, the Jesuits rescinded the antisemitic provision in their religious constitutions. Jesuit history, however, is interrelated with the history and cultural context of many religious orders, both those of European origin, and those which emerged in other parts of the world. A culture of racial discrimination nurtured throughout a 500-year-old history, with many collateral effects on the Church's preaching tradition, educational institutions, religious formation, and spiritual outlook is not easily displaced in the fifty years since World War II, or thirty-five years since Vatican II.

Jesuits have had steady intellectual, spiritual, and theological influence over both women's and men's religious orders. Jesuits have served

---

[30]A similar expression of logical inconsistency regarding the antisemitism charge against Pope Pius XII was manifest by Peter Gumpel, S.J. During a television interview in 2000, Fr. Gumpel insisted Pius XII assisted Jews during World War II, but excused the Pope's nonintervention by word or conduct to defend the Jews of Rome when they were being rounded up by the Nazi occupiers starting 16 October 1943, and then driven in trucks within yards of the papal residence. The incident is reported by John Cornwell in the controversial *Hitler's Pope: The Secret History of Pius XII* (New York: Viking, 1999). See "The Jews of Rome," 298-312. There was also a plot to kidnap the pope so that his ability to interact with the Allies would be suppressed, but this was abandoned by Hitler when he was apprised of the revolt against the Nazi occupation likely to erupt from the Italian population if harm came to the pope. See "Hitler's Plan to Kidnap Pacelli," 313-15. Cornwell suggests that Pius XII ignored his own strength, and did not take advantage of the social and political power of the church at large to disrupt Nazi policies.

as diocesan authorities, pastors, chaplains, retreat directors, confessors, spiritual directors, theologians, teachers, canon lawyers, and episcopal and papal representatives. In the life of Edith Stein, Fr. Erich Przywara, S.J., was an occasional adviser. Johannes Hirschmann, S.J., member of the Jesuit community at Valkenburg (Limburg, Netherlands) wrote a letter of opinion in 1941 on the directions a canonical process of Edith Stein's incorporation into a new Carmel might take after her transfer from Cologne to Echt.[31]

Many Jesuit churches, houses, and schools in Poland and Germany were seized by the Nazis during the war. Jesuits were arrested, and ninety-six were imprisoned at Dachau between 1940 and 1945, which was the major prison camp for priests. Of this number, seventeen Jesuit priests, nine scholastics, and five brothers died, with the Jesuits "having the ironic distinction of having the largest number among the members of religious orders and congregations imprisoned." There were, by one count, 2,600 priests from 134 dioceses and twenty-four nations at Dachau.[32]

A Polish priest, Mizgalski Gerard, arrested in December 1939, remained at Dachau until 29 April 1945, until the liberation by American forces. He provided statistical data on the number of religious (members of a religious order) who died there: 846 priests and monks who were members of the Polish clergy perished in Dachau; 305 abbots were sent to gas chambers; and eighty-four priests were transferred to other concentration camps where they perished without a trace. Gerard testified that the administration, staff, and guards of the camp at Dachau were

---

[31]See letter 330 to Mother Ambrosia Antonia Engelmann, O.C.D., at Echt (presumably December 1941), in *Edith Stein, Self-Portrait in Letters 1916–1942*, 341. Here, Edith Stein writes to her prioress at Echt and refers to having received a letter from Johannes Hirschmann, S.J., in the midst of decisions being made about her canonical status at Echt. She does not know who will make the final decision about whether or not she will be granted permanent status—the sisters at Echt, the father provincial, or the diocesan bishop. Nor does she know what her intermediate status will be if she is to go to another Carmel. She describes the uncertainty and leaves it in the hands of the prioress. See the essay written as a tribute to Edith Stein by Johannes Hirschmann, S.J., "Schwester Teresia Benedicta vom heiligen Kreuz," in Herbstrith, ed., *Edith Stein: Ein neues Lebensbild*, 151-55.

[32]Vincent A. Lapomarda, S.J., "The Jesuits and the Holocaust," *Journal of Church and State* 23 (1981): 244.

exclusively members of the SS. This evidence was included in documentation compiled for the trials of Nazis at Nuremberg.[33]

Peter Gumpel, S.J., and the Cause of Pius XII

The record indicates that members of Catholic orders suffered under Nazi persecution along with Jews. Yet, in spite of their share in the oppression of World War II, followed by Vatican II's *Nostra Aetate*, with many subsequent official statements of the correct way to teach about Jews and Judaism, an undercurrent of intolerance towards Jews persists in the culture of religious orders.

A particularly regrettable example was provided by a Jesuit's televised statements in March 2000 during the CBS News program, "60 Minutes." Peter Gumpel, seventy-six, a Jesuit historian, is postulator for the cause of canonizing Pope Pius XII. In response to Ed Bradley's interview, Fr. Gumpel asserted that Pius XII deserved to be canonized in spite of questions that had persisted for decades about the pope's public silence and failure to explicitly condemn Nazi persecution of Jews, despite the power the Church wielded throughout Europe. Fr. Gumpel could reconcile his concept of sainthood with an admission that Pius XII would not risk his personal safety to intervene when Jews were being rounded up by Nazis in 1943 within yards of the papal residence. Fr. Gumpel's assertion of papal holiness was also not affected by evidence that Pius XII voiced racial prejudice against black American soldiers, asking that they not enter Rome with troops liberating the city after the war.[34]

---

[33]See "Statement of Rs. Mizgalski Gerard, Paris, 1.7.1946," copy of Document 4043-P, in *Nazi Conspiracy and Aggression, Supplement A: A Collection of Documentary Evidence and Guide Materials Prepared by the American and British Prosecution Staffs for Presentation before the International Military Tribunal at Nurnberg, Germany*, Office of United States Chief of Counsel for Prosecution of Axis Criminality (Washington DC: U.S. Government Printing Office, 1947) 804.

[34]See transcript of "CBS News: 60 Minutes," Sunday, 19 March 2000: "Pope Pius XII: Hitler's Pope?" by Ed Bradley. Copyright Federal Document Clearing House. 2000WL 4212866. Bradley interviewed John Cornwell, author of the controversial *Hitler's Pope: The Secret History of Pius XII* (Viking Press, 1999), and Father Peter Gumpel, S.J., on their assessment of why Pius XII never publicly condemned the Nazis for persecuting Jews, and whether his reticence effectively abandoned them to their fate. See also Allesandra Stanley, "Book Revives Issue of Pius XII and Holocaust," *New York Times*, 3 November 1999. Other Jesuits engaged in the defense of Pius XII include Pierre Blet, S.J., *Pius XII and the Second World War* (New York: Paulist Press, 1999). This is a one-volume summary of

Fr. Gumpel's admission of racial bias in his subject's character, yet dismissal of its significance, is analogous to the conceptual frame of James Reites, S.J., in relation to Ignatius. Reites admitted that Ignatius actively promulgated a papal decree ghettoizing the unconverted Jews of Rome, but then did not analyze its inconsistency with his theory that Ignatius should be emulated because of his toleration of Jews. In proposing the exemplary character of their candidates, both proponents downplayed the significance of antisemitic sentiments and behavior. One conclusion that can be drawn from this pattern is that Catholic tradition itself can anesthetize members of religious orders, those who live the tradition most expressly, from recognizing and reforming their antisemitic reflexes.

Edith Stein herself was aware of the possibility of anti-Judaism within Catholic religious orders. In a letter to Fr. Laurentius Siemer, a Dominican of Cologne, who had appraised her translation of Thomas Aquinas's *Disputed Questions* from Latin into German, she thanks him. She does not assume he would wish to be mentioned in her acknowledgments.

> I felt the need to mention, with thanks, your gracious assistance and I would be very happy if you would give me permission to do so. But I do want to inquire first whether for any reason whatsoever you find it unwelcome. The editor annotates this request, "Presumably because of her Jewish descent." This was in 1934.[35]

Antisemitism in the Benedictines

Eleanor Michael's article, "The Convenient Saint," includes exploration of the question why Edith Stein was unsuccessful in her efforts in 1936 to be transferred to the Carmelite convent in Bethlehem, a community of Arab Christian sisters.[36] Edith Stein, after her baptism as a Catholic and

---

previously published historical research on the years of Pius XII. Blet and three other Jesuits gathered material from the Vatican archives and, between 1965 and 1981, published them in twelve volumes as *Actes et Documents du Saint-Siège Relatifs à la Seconde Guerre mondiale* (Vatican City: Libreria Editrice Vaticana, 1965–1981). See "Vatican Presents Fr. Blet's Book Defending Pius XII," *The Wanderer* (21 October 1999): 6.

[35]Letter 184 to P. Laurentius Siemer, O.P., Cologne, 4 November 1934, in *Edith Stein, Self-Portrait in Letters 1916–1942,* 189-90.

[36]Eleanor Michael "The Convenient Saint," *The Guardian Weekend* (26 September 1998): 28. I am grateful to Ms. Michael for a copy of this article on

prior to her entrance into the Carmelites, spent many liturgical seasons on retreat at the Benedictine Abbey of Beuron. Her spiritual advisor and friend during these years was the young, dynamic superior of the Beuron monastery, Archabbot Raphael Walzer. Hermann Keller was the prior of the Benedictine monks in residence at Beuron, and in charge when Archabbot Walzer was absent. Because of Edith Stein's relationship with Walzer, Keller was knowledgeable about her since she was a regular visitor to Beuron.

Keller joined the Nazi party and offered his services to the Nazi secret intelligence service under Reinhard Heydrich. Walzer was anti-Nazi. On one occasion when Walzer was returning from a missionary trip to Japan, where he had founded a monastery, Keller denounced Walzer to the Gestapo. Walzer, warned by some monks, resigned his office at Beuron, and Keller took over as acting Archabbot. When Keller's machinations were discovered by the head abbot of the Benedictines, he was sent to Dormition Abbey in Jerusalem. There, according to Michael's sources, Keller spied for Egypt. Later, when Keller returned to Germany, he was reinstated as prior at Beuron, and the new archabbot, Benedict Bauer, authorized Keller's continued work for the Nazis.[37]

Eleanor Michael surmises that there is a relationship between the pro-Nazi Keller's presence at Dormition Abbey in Jerusalem and Edith Stein's failure to get permission to transfer to the convent in Bethlehem, only a few kilometers from Jerusalem. Michael proposes that the Latin Patriarch would have naturally relied on a German cleric's advice regarding the transfer of a Carmelite from Germany to a Carmelite convent in Bethlehem, a convent under the Patriarch's jurisdiction. Having lived at Beuron, Keller knew that Stein was a convert from Judaism. The fact that he denounced his superior, Walzer, to the Nazis, implies not only his ambition, but his support of Nazi racial policies, and his resentment of persons of Jewish ethnicity connected with Walzer, in keeping with the Nazi racial ethos. That Archabbot Bauer himself endorsed Keller's Nazi party activities suggests that antisemitic sentiments were promoted under the umbrella of patriotism.

---

which this discussion of antisemitism in the Benedictines depends. She has engaged in research for more than a decade, and I have benefitted from several exchanges with her in which she has alerted me to details in the original sources, and provided a fresh context for my pursuit of these discomfiting questions about antisemitism in Catholic religious orders.

[37]Ibid., 30-31.

Greene proposes that a significant issue in a biography of Edith Stein should deal with the relationship between Judaism and Christianity, not merely as a personal and internal issue, but as a tension which "profoundly influenced" Stein's relationships, not only with her family, but with Carmelites who were biased against Jews:

> Reconciliation between Judaism and Christianity was not merely personal and internal for Stein, it profoundly influenced her relationships. It had consequences for her family, particularly her mother, for her attitude toward the German state, which she loved but which became increasingly anti-Semitic after 1933, and even for members of the Carmelite order who reflected that same prejudice.[38]

Professor Ingrid Rosa Kitzberger, writing from Germany, suggests:

> When Edith Stein was in the Carmel in Cologne already and elections were held, it was noticed that not all sisters had given their vote. At this occasion the prioress gave away Edith Stein's Jewish identity when she told the men who were missing a vote that she is Jewish and therefore does not, or cannot vote. So the authorities knew about the Jewish woman in the convent. Whether this was anti-Semitism or just stupidness I do not know. But how different Edith's life might have developed without that incident.[39]

Susanne Batzdorff, however, qualifies the ability of Edith Stein, ultimately, to have concealed her Jewish identity, even behind the convent walls:

> The whereabouts of "Non-Aryans" were known to the authorities. Germany had a thorough system of registration for all its inhabitants. They had to register with the police wherever they took up residence anywhere in the country. The same system was established in countries occupied by the Germans. This system existed prior to Hitler and was accepted and taken for granted.[40]

---

[38]Greene, "In Search of Edith Stein," 7.

[39]Ingrid Rosa Kitzberger, University of Munster, Germany, personal correspondence by e-mail, 2 Febrary 1999. Kitzberger is a noted New Testament biblicist, and has, besides producing many articles, edited two anthologies representing an international slate of scholars. See *The Personal Voice in Biblical Interpretation* (London and New York: Routledge, 1999) and *Transformative Encounters: Jesus and Women Re-viewed* (Leiden/Boston/Koln: Brill, 2000).

[40]Annotations of Susanne Batzdorff to the original draft of this manuscript, 3

Biographical Summary

Edith Stein (1891–1942) was born into a Jewish family in Breslau in Silesia on Yom Kippur, 12 October 1891. Her family owned a lumber business, and her mother, widowed when Edith was two years old, raised her as the youngest of seven siblings. Though her mother was observant, Edith described her own religious identity as agnostic from age fourteen on. She trained as a philosopher, and prepared for an academic career as a university professor. She pursued doctoral studies at Göttingen (1913–1916) under the phenomenologist Husserl and followed him to the University of Freiburg where she received her doctorate in 1917, having defended her dissertation, "Zum Problem der Einfühlung," in 1916.[41] She converted to Roman Catholicism in 1922 when she was thirty.

Denied a university teaching post because of her Jewish heritage, she taught women students at a Dominican-sponsored institution which included a "collegium" or secondary school (*Lyzeum*) and a teacher's college (*Lehrerinnenseminar*). She wrote and lectured on women's concerns. In 1933, eleven years after her conversion, she entered the Carmelite monastery at Cologne. The following year, she took the habit and her religious name, Sister Teresa Benedicta of the Cross, making her final profession in 1938. During this period she worked on her autobiography, *Life in a Jewish Family*, begun in 1933, continued off and on until 1935, then interrupted, resumed in Echt in 1939, but never finished. She completed a philosophical study, *Finite and Eternal Being* (1934–1936), and undertook in 1941 a study of the mysticism of St. John of the Cross, which was never completed.[42]

February 2000, personal correspondence.

[41]Published in 1917 at Halle by Buchdrucheri des Waisenhauses; reprinted 1980 in Munich by Kaffke. English translation: *On the Problem of Empathy*, trans. Waltraut Stein (The Hague: M. Nijhoff, 1964); 3rd rev. ed.: Collected Works of Edith Stein vol. 3 (Washington DC: Institute of Carmelite Studies, 1989).

[42]Edith Stein, *Life in a Jewish Family 1891–1916: An Autobiography*, trans. Josephine Koeppel, O.C.D., Collected Works of Edith Stein vol. 1, L. Gelber and Romaeus Leuven, O.C.D., series eds. (Washington DC: Institute of Carmelite Studies, 1986). One of the poignant details of this project was her fear of its discovery. Susanne Batzdorff suggests a reason in her 3 February 2000 annotation of my original draft: "Possibly she felt that this book, which emphasized the Jewish family background of a nun in this monastery could cause trouble for the community. Edith herself was already officially registered as a 'non-Aryan' and in a precarious situation." She buried the manuscript in the monastery garden for safe-

On 31 December 1938, she fled from Germany to the Netherlands where she took refuge in the Carmelite cloister of Echt, about 150 kilometers from Cologne. She records this flight in a letter of 3 January 1939, to Mother Petra Bruning, O.S.U., with whom she regularly corresponded:

> During the octave of Christmas, all documents necessary for departure arrived with almost miraculous speed . . . the good Sisters here had done everything possible to speed up the granting of an entrance permit [to the Netherlands], and received me with heartfelt love.[43]

Her blood sister Rosa left Germany for Belgium some time after April 1939,[44] but found that she had been swindled by the woman who had engaged her as a housekeeper for a new Carmelite foundation which she was organizing. With the help of her sister Edith, Rosa managed to escape from the clutches of this person after a couple of months and join Edith in Echt where she was taken in by the Carmelite monastery on 1 July 1939.[45]

The Nazi threat to Holland became more pressing after the 10 May 1940 invasion of Belgium and Holland.

> The Nazis subsequently applied the same anti-Semitic measures there that were already in place in the countries they ruled. Those who were defined by Nazi law as Jews had to register and, later on, wear the yellow emblem. In late 1941, all "German non-Aryans living in the Netherlands" were declared stateless and had to take steps to leave the country by 12-15-41. That's when Edith wrote to Dr. Borsinger asking for assistance for herself and Rosa to get to Switzerland.[46]

---

ty, later dug it up out of anxiety for its preservation, and gave it to one of her Carmelite Sisters to hide.

[43]Letter 290, to Mother Petra Bruning, O.S.U., Dorsten, in *Edith Stein, Self-Portrait in Letters 1916–1942*, 297-98.

[44]On a postcard from Echt dated 21 April 1939, to Karl and Katharina Lichtenberger, Edith Stein refers to the preparations her sister is making to move to Belgium. See letter 301, in *Edith Stein, Self-Portrait in Letters 1916–1942*, 310.

[45]See the details of Rosa Stein's conversion to Catholicism, attempt to leave Germany after *Kristallnacht* of 9-10 November 1938, her brief employment in Belgium which was really exploitation, and her eventual reunion with Edith Stein in Echt provided by Susanne Batzdorff, in *Aunt Edith: The Jewish Heritage of a Catholic Saint* (Springfield IL: Templegate, 1998) 161-63.

[46]Notation of 3 February 2000, kindly provided by Susanne Batzdorff to the

Edith requested refuge at the Carmel in Switzerland. In November 1941, she knew the Nazis were closing in. Writing to Mother Johanna van Weersth, O.C.D., she asks prayers for her family members. Her older sister Elfriede had been deported from Breslau to work with other women in an attic workroom in the country and her older brother Paul and his wife lived in fear of a similar action; efforts to bring them to the U.S. by their relatives who had already emigrated were proving unsuccessful.[47]

The delay dragged on for nine months after her registration in Maastricht, and a request for help with getting a Swiss visa, which was sent on New Year's Eve to Hilde Verene Borsinger, the Swiss lawyer and feminist scholar whom she had met in 1930.[48] There were various reasons given at different times during this period, with the most detail provided after the war in the memorial by Borsinger.[49]

Germany invaded the Netherlands. On 11 July 1942, the Dutch bishops and synod of the Reformed Church protested Nazi legislation denying Jewish children the right to public schooling, and denying citizens of Jewish descent the right to hold public office. Within a week, the Nazis retaliated against Christians of Jewish ancestry. On 2 August 1942, the SS knocked at the door of the Carmelite convent and took Sister Teresa Benedicta and her sister Rosa into custody. Edith and Rosa were interned at Auschwitz, where they died in the gas chambers, 8-9 August 1942.[50]

Conclusion

The paradoxes of Edith Stein's identity and her canonization present members of Catholic religious orders with a challenge to overcome the racial prejudices sustained by Catholic culture. It is the project of reexamining constitutions, addressing unspoken prejudices, and uncovering theologically masked forms of antisemitism within congregational life that still exist as part of an order's culture of spirituality.

---

original draft of this article.

[47]See letter 328, to Mother Johanna van Weersth, O.C.D., at Beek, from Echt on 18 November 1941, in *Edith Stein, Self-Portrait in Letters 1916–1942*, 339–40.

[48]Letter 331 to Hilde Verene Borsinger, Bern, Switzerland, from Echt, 31 December 1941, in *Edith Stein, Self-Portrait in Letters 1916–1942*, 341–43.

[49]See n. 12, above.

[50]See also esp. the overview of her life published on the occasion of her canonization: Steven Payne, "Edith Stein: A Fragmented Life," in *America* (10 October 1998) and online at <http://www.americapress.org/articles/payne.htm>.

The commitment of members of religious orders to work for justice involves not merely a decision to resist racism in "the world," but to acknowledge that antisemitism sustains a covert life "inside" the convent or monastery as well. Antisemitism so clearly identified in Jesuit congregational history suggests that the same dynamic is waiting to be acknowledged in historical studies of other congregations. Antisemitism does not afflict all individuals in a religious community equally. Some are more sensitized to its reality and summon their members to greater awareness, as demonstrated by Jan H. Nota, S.J.:

> For me the beatification of Edith Stein is not an end but the beginning of a dialogue between Christians and Jews. Our Jewish friends rightly say that Edith Stein's death is a challenge to the Christian churches to give up their anti-Jewish prejudices, which weakened their opposition to Nazi anti-Semitism. Edith Stein is not only the victim of brutal Nazis; her death was caused in part by Christians' excessive fear for their own lives while their Jewish brothers and sisters were murdered next door.[51]

Fr. Nota's insight coexists in a Jesuit congregation with less enlightened members James Reites, S.J., assistant novice director, and Peter Gumpel, S.J., postulator for the cause of Pius XII. The question is whether individual members can effectively offset a congregational culture which, left unattended by rigorous reform, will surely generate another generation of the less enlightened, reversing or neutralizing the commitment to reform endorsed by Jan Nota, S.J.

This essay has provided hints that further investigation will likely uncover the reality of antisemitic bias among members, both past and present, of archdiocesan offices and other religious communities. The uncritical Fr. Reites and Fr. Gumpel have political predecessors in the order, and suspicious brother Jesuits in the community recreation room who cast an auto-da-fé eye toward Zuckerman to assess whether his true reaction to news about Israel is "Jewish" or "Catholic." In addition there have been Dominicans who advised Edith Stein, but whom she had reason to believe would not want to be associated publicly with her scholarship; the superior at St. Francis Priory in Nice, latest in a succession of right-wing clerics who for more than forty years shielded Paul Touvier, the "Hangman of Lyon" and enthusiastic acolyte to the

---

[51]Jan H. Nota, "Edith Stein: Sign of Contradiction, Sign of Reconciliation," in *Never Forget*, 123. See also his essay "Edith Stein—Philosophin und Karmelitin," in *Edith Stein: Ein neues Lebensbild*, 156-70.

infamous "Butcher of Lyon," Klaus Barbie; Benedictines like the Nazi sympathizer Hermann Keller and his archabbott, Bauer; Swiss Carmelites who changed their minds about sheltering Edith and her sister Rosa. Another source of pro-Nazi, anti-Jewish sentiment is associated with the cast of clergy "behind the scenes" in Roman curial offices and their contacts at the International Red Cross, who intentionally aided Nazi emigration after the war to South America, as recorded in the report by Vincent La Vista in 1947.

Acknowledging and reforming an internal culture which fosters antisemitism is a continuing task facing all Catholic orders of men and women. This is because the ordained and the vowed live, by intention and practice, Catholic biblical and theological tradition as a matter of personal dedication. Members of Catholic orders, further, seek to embody the theological and spiritual tradition as an expression of their mission. It is inevitable, given the history of antisemitism's long life in Catholic theology, that members of Catholic orders would not be exempt from its distortions in deeply established patterns of thought and reaction.

The canonization in 1998 of Edith Stein is a signal to engage a new stage of communal repentance for Christianity's history of antisemitic racism, reinforced by unexamined theological structures of interpretation, and instinctive resistance to Jews reinforced by decades of preaching. Both individual members and religious congregations as a whole can follow the lead of Pope John Paul II, as in his speech delivered at the Yad Vashem Holocaust Memorial on his visit to Jerusalem in March 2000:

> As Bishop of Rome and successor of the Apostle Peter, I assure the Jewish people that the Catholic Church, motivated by the Gospel law of truth and love and by no political considerations, is deeply saddened by the hatred, acts of persecution and displays of anti-Semitism directed against the Jews by Christians at any time and in any place. The Church rejects racism in any form as a denial of the image of the Creator inherent in every human being. In this place of solemn remembrance, I fervently pray that our sorrow for the tragedy which the Jewish people suffered in the twentieth century will lead to a new relationship between Christians and Jews.[52]

---

[52]Quoted from the official Vatican text of Pope John Paul II's speech at the Yad Vashem Holocaust Memorial, as reported in the *New York Times*, 24 March 2000, A8.

Chapter 6

After Auschwitz:
Jews, Judaism,
and Christian Worship

Robert W. Bullock

So where is the truth to be found? Who are the elect blessedly
walking the true path to salvation . . . and who are the misguided others? Can we tell? Do we know? We think we know—of
course we think we know. We have our belief. But how do we
distinguish our truth from another's falsity, we of the true faith,
except by the story we cherish? Our story of God. But, my
friends, I ask you: Is God a story? Can we, each of us examining
our faith—I mean its pure center, not its comforts, not its habits,
not its ritual sacraments—can we believe anymore in the heart of
our faith that God is our story of Him? What, for instance, has
the industrialized carnage, the continentally engineered terrorist
slaughter of the Holocaust done to our story? Do we dare ask?
What mortification, what ritual, what practice would have been
a commensurate Christian response to the Holocaust? Something
as earthshaking in its way as Auschwitz and Dachau—a mass
exile, perhaps? A lifelong commitment of Christians wandering,
derelict, over the world? A clearing out of the lands and cities a
thousand miles in every direction from each and every death
camp? I don't know what it would be—but I know I'd recognize
it if I saw it. If we go on with our story, blindly, after something
like that is it not merely innocent but also foolish, and possibly
a defamation, a profound impiety? To presume to contain God
in this unknowing story of ours, to hold Him, circumscribe Him,
the author of everything we can conceive and everything we cannot conceive . . . in *our* story of *Him*? Of Her? Of whom? What
in the name of our faith—what in God's name—do we think we
are talking about?

—E. L. Doctorow, "Heist"

The first Russian patrol came in sight of the camp about midday on 27 January 1945. . . . They were four young soldiers on horseback, who advanced along the road that marked the limits of the camp cautiously holding their Sten guns. When they reached the barbed wire, they stopped to look, exchanging a few timid words, and throwing strangely embarrassed glances at the sprawling bodies, at the battered huts and at us few still alive. . . . They did not greet us, nor did they smile; they seemed oppressed not only by compassion but by a confused restraint, which sealed their lips and bound their eyes to the funereal scene. It was that shame we knew so well, the shame that drowned us after the selections and everytime we had to watch, or submit to, some outrage: the shame the Germans did not know, that the just man experiences at another man's crime; the feeling of guilt that such a crime should exist, that it should have been introduced irrevocably into the world of things that exist, and that his will for good should have proved too weak or null, and should not have availed in defense.

—Primo Levi, *The Reawakening*

After a trip to Europe with a group of staff members and teachers from "Facing History and Ourselves,"[1] I was a guest on a radio program. It was one of those early Sunday morning interreligious panels. Our group had been to Germany, Poland, and Czechoslovakia. We had visited Treblinka, Auschwitz, Theresienstadt, and Sachsenhausen. We had met with teachers, survivors, and government officials. During the radio program I often mentioned the Holocaust and antisemitism. One panelist, an Episcopal priest, sounding annoyed, said, "I am sick of the Holocaust and I am sick of antisemitism." The air went dead, eyes went down, papers were shuffled. I finally said something to the effect that I was sickened as well, but we have to study and learn. We are obliged. It is not an

---

[1]Facing History and Ourselves: The Holocaust and Human Behavior, based in Brookline, Massachusetts, is a national educational and professional development organization whose mission is to engage students of diverse backgrounds in an examination of racism, prejudice, and antisemitism in order to promote the development of a more humane and informed citizenry. By studying the historical development and lessons of the Holocaust and other examples of collective violence, students make the essential connection between history and the moral choices they confront in their own lives.

option to do so but a necessity. The rabbi on the panel agreed and expanded on that idea.

Later I wondered if the priest spoke for a large number of Christians. Is it a common view that we have heard enough, and as dreadful as this history is, it is now more than a half century since, and don't we all need to get on with our lives? There is evidence for this: a sense that students of this history need to justify their continued concern; the need to insist that Holocaust studies include other victims; it is seen in forms of denial. What the priest said is a form of denial, not of the fact but of the meaning. Holocaust deniers have been named and debunked.[2] They are haters and liars. "Holocaust denial in the crude sense is a thoroughly discredited affair of crackpot racists."[3] But what of those, like the priest, who deny the meaning of the Holocaust or refuse to remember? To talk as he did is sinful. It is a sin of silence and of indifference. When Pope John Paul II visited Auschwitz-Birkenau in 1979 there was a series of plaques in many languages between crematoriums II and III. The site has since been redesigned. When the pope came to the one in Hebrew he paused and said, "It is not permissible for anyone to pass by this inscription with indifference."[4] Johann Baptist Metz has written, "For me there is no truth that I could defend with my back turned to Auschwitz. There is no sense for me that I could save with my back turned to Auschwitz. For me, there is no God to whom I could pray with my back turned to Auschwitz."[5]

How, then, are we after Auschwitz? The name is not limited to the killing center or its time of operation. It embraces the whole Holocaust crime in all its parts and all the years since. Auschwitz "epitomizes the Holocaust."[6] It stands for the evil universe. Auschwitz is a history we are within. It is of Catholicism and all of Christianity. We are not living beyond. It has not ended. It is a new moral universe. Metz calls it our

---

[2]Deborah E. Lipstadt, *Denying the Holocaust* (New York: Free Press, 1993); Pierre Vidal-Nasquet, *Assassins of Memory* (New York: Columbia University Press, 1992).

[3]Robert Conquest, *Wall Street Journal*, 4 March 1999.

[4]Homily at Auschwitz, 7 June 1979, in Eugene Fisher and Leon Klenicki, eds., *Spiritual Pilgrimage* (New York: Crossroad, 1995).

[5]Johann-Baptist Metz and Jürgen Moltmann, *Faith and the Future*, (New York: Orbis Books, 1995) 41.

[6]Richard L. Rubenstein and John K. Roth, *Approaches to Auschwitz* (Atlanta: John Knox Press, 1987) 9.

situation.[7] Christopher Browning has written, "In retrospect we can see that the inauguration of the Final Solution in 1941 was a monumental event in history, when old notions of human nature and progress were shattered and mankind passed forever into the post-Auschwitz era."[8] The figure of a landscape is often used, one that has been radically altered and remains unsettled. "Nazi Germany defaced our century's moral landscape with a chasm so grotesque that it still won't close. Mangled at its bottom lie the remnants of millions of human beings, victims of the most fiercely focused genocide the world has ever known. And mangled there as well is the confidence the world once had in the possibility of human progress."[9]

Yet, in the midst of this dark landscape there is light and hope. New directions are being set. *Nostra Aetate*[10] was pivotal for Roman Catholics and for Christianity. Over the past twenty years, Pope John Paul II has referred to it scores of times, often noting as well subsequent Vatican documents that are more detailed.[11] For Americans, a great hope and substantial guidance can be seen in the work of the late Cardinal Joseph Bernadin of Chicago and his associates.[12] After many years of leadership in Christian-Jewish relations, the cardinal's final words were these: "If I could offer one piece of advice on where you go from here it would be this: Continue to build the relationship between the two communities on friendship, and then be sure to support it with structures of implementation and continuity. Then just keep going."[13]

Those relationships are building. Christian and Jewish leaders publish statements, join in common efforts, and create an agreeable public image. Local clergy and staffs meet together. They develop a common social agenda. When there are outbreaks of antisemitic acts—graffiti on walls, breaking of windows, or other hate crimes—responses are generally quick

---

[7]Metz and Moltmann, *Faith and the Future*, 8.

[8]Christopher R. Browning, *The Path to Genocide: Essays on Launching the Final Solution* (New York: Cambridge University Press, 1992) 143.

[9]Walter Reich, *New York Times Book Review* (31 January 1999): 8.

[10]Vatican Council II, *Declaration on the Relationship of the Church to Non-Christian Religions*, #4.

[11]*Guidelines and Suggestions for Implementing the Conciliar Declaration*, Nostra Aetate no. 4, 1 December 1974; *Notes on the Correct Way to Present Jews and Judaism in Preaching and Catechesis of the Roman Catholic Church*, 24 June 1985.

[12]See *A Blessing to Each Other, Cardinal Joseph Bernadin and Jewish Catholic Dialogue* (Chicago: Liturgy Training Publications, 1996).

[13]*A Blessing to Each Other*, 174.

and effective. Holocaust scholarship is extensive and widening. Thousands of American students are enrolled in educational programs like Facing History and Ourselves and Teaching Tolerance. Millions have visited the Holocaust Memorial Museum in Washington.

Nevertheless, for all the good words from our leaders and all the new directions being set, Jewish-Christian renewal is remote to the lives of most people. Cardinal Bernadin seemed to realize that we are still at the beginning, making first steps, when he urged structures for implementation. One of the measures has to be about local implementation. When Christians visit Jews, when they talk about Vatican II and the new directions, when they recount the words of the pope at Auschwitz-Birkenau or in the Roman Synagogue, the response invariably is, "Yes, but. . . . " People wonder about local implementation. They are concerned about their neighbors. Are attitudes changing and are Christians, in significant numbers, confronting the teachings of contempt?

The answer is surely "Yes." Progress over the past decades has been extraordinary. The history of Jewish-Christian relations, including the Holocaust, is being studied by an increasing number of Christians. They are often staggered by its content. Joshua Trachtenberg wrote: "The most vivid impression to be gained from a reading of medieval allusions to the Jews is of a hatred so vast and abysmal, so intense, that it leaves one gasping for comprehension."[14] For American Roman Catholics, the Secretariat for Catholic-Jewish Relations of the National Conference of Catholic Bishops provides significant leadership. Biblical scholarship is advanced on these issues. The Sacra Pagina New Testament series is most valuable, the Matthew and John volumes particularly.[15] There are twenty institutes for Jewish-Christian Relations in American colleges and universities. Religious catechetical texts have long been sensitive to the negative depiction of the "other." The problem is not in the classroom. It is in church.

Millions go to churches every Sunday. They enter a sacred environment of word, song, prayer, and art. How Jews and Judaism are depicted in this environment, in the lectionary, hymns, prayers, and art is highly

---

[14]Joshua Trachtenberg, *The Devil and the Jews: The Medieval Conception of the Jew and Its Relation to Modern Anti-Semitism* (reprint: Philadelphia: Jewish Publication Society of America, 1993, 1983; original: New Haven CT: Yale University Press; London: Oxford University Press, 1943) 12.

[15]Daniel J. Harrington, *The Gospel of Matthew*, Sacra Pagina 1 (Collegeville MN: Liturgical Press, 1991); Francis J. Moloney, *The Gospel of John*, Sacra Pagina 4 (Collegeville MN: Liturgical Press, 1998).

problematic. In the liturgical environment, supersessionism is endemic. It is found in liturgy's words and structures.

For American Roman Catholics, a new lectionary went into use on the first Sunday of Advent 1998.[16] The translation is better. The language tends toward inclusivity. But the lectionary does not regard the depiction of Jews and Judaism in the texts as a concern. In the introduction there is no indication that the lectionary is in any way influenced by *Nostra Aetate* or the subsequent Vatican documents of 1974 and 1985 urging its implementation. On 31 October 1997, in a speech to a symposium on the roots of anti-Judaism, Pope John Paul II warned about "erroneous and unjust interpretations of the New Testament regarding the Jewish people and their alleged culpability." His remarks are quoted in "We Remember: A Reflection on the Shoah" of March 1998. This warning is not reflected in the introduction to the lectionary. On a number of occasions the introduction supports supersessionist attitudes. At one point, Augustine's often-used quotation—that in the Old Testament the New is concealed, and in the New the Old is revealed—is repeated, adding, "Christ himself is the center and fullness of the whole of Scripture." After Auschwitz this truth needs to be qualified by the enduring Covenant between God and Judaism. In section 7, the lectionary introduction says that the church is aware of "being a new people in whom the covenant made in the past is perfected and fulfilled." In section 67: "The present Order of Readings selects Old Testament texts mainly because of their correlation with the New Testament texts read in the same Mass and particularly with the Gospel text." The enduring Covenant suggests the need to examine this principle as well. Section 76 is headed "Difficult Texts" and 77 is "The Omission of Certain Verses." No specific texts or verses are mentioned. Some could readily be suggested, for example, those sustaining anti-Judaism or presenting Jews as menacing. The readings from Acts on Easter Sunday and on the third Sunday of Easter repeat the deicide charge. (There will be more on these texts below). Would it be pastorally sensitive to omit "for fear of the Jews" as the reason the disciples are locked in the upper room? This is in the Johannine Gospel for Pentecost.

Reading the introduction to the lectionary cannot but lead to the conclusion that any awareness of the problem of how Jews and Judaism are presented in the texts, even to recommendations of careful interpretation or of homiletic sensitivity, is remote in the extreme. Clear papal leadership and Vatican documentation urging change have not been heeded.

---

[16]*Lectionary for Mass. For Use in the Dioceses of the United States of America* (Mahwah NJ: Catholic Book Publishing Co., 1998).

The Passion Narratives

In all four Passion narratives, the Jews are presented as guilty of the death of Jesus, and the guilt becomes more extended from the first Gospel to the last. For the Roman occupiers it goes in the opposite direction. There is a gradual exculpation of Roman responsibility and an inculpation of Jewish guilt. Pilate becomes a more sympathetic figure. History knows him as a killer, a cruel and dreadful human being, but in the Passion narratives he is weak, indecisive, and benign. This is particularly so in John where "the Jews" clamor for Jesus' death, intimidating Pilate in their efforts. In Matthew 27:25 the most damaging verse is found, a text of terror: "His blood be on us and on our children!" The text suggests that all the Jewish people cry this after Pilate gives in. Mark is a source for other vilifications, and its Passion scene is one of extreme suffering and abandonment. The religious leaders are the villains who manipulate the crowds against Jesus. In Luke, the Gospel of forgiveness, there is some mitigation. The women of Jerusalem weep for Jesus, he forgives his executioners, and after he dies, the crowd "saw what had taken place, [and] they returned home, beating their breasts" (23:48).

How these narratives are proclaimed in church should be a matter of grave concern. Sometimes passion plays are enacted. In one Florida parish on Good Friday, when the narrative is John's, the congregation goes outside when the reading begins. In an ample outer area, a volunteer parishioner is strapped to a cross and hangs before the people while the narrative is amplified for the large assembly. There is no commentary or homily. The hostility of "the Jews" clamoring for Jesus' death is not interpreted for the people. Afterward the congregation reassembles in the church while the volunteer is placed on a gurney, which is drawn up and down the aisles, accompanied by pallbearer-like ushers. The people all sing, "Were You There When They Crucified My Lord?"

In most churches there is a dramatic reading of the Passion narratives. The congregation with missalettes, like scripts, takes the part of the crowd. They become the Jews, calling for Jesus to be crucified. The congregation, the children included, cry out, "Crucify him!" When Matthew is used, everyone quotes 27:25 together, calling for his death and for his blood to be on them and their children. We hardly realize what a damaging thing we are doing. When we create environments where the sacred center of our faith is framed in such violence, accusation, and role-playing, it deforms the Paschal mystery and deepens anti-Judaism. People protest that it is not that way with them. The deicide charge is false because Jesus died for all our sins. But that spirituality has room for deicide. We all are responsible for the death of Jesus but the Jews are the guilty ones. The deicide charge has been abrogated, denied, and condemned by Vatican II and subsequent documents, by vigorous biblical scholarship, and by theological studies,[17] but it is supported and sustained in the ways we worship.

The damage done by these forms is aggravated by what we are coming to understand about the nature of prejudice, how it is learned, and how it grows within and among us. There has been considerable modern scholarship on prejudice, including recent work by Elizabeth Young-Bruehl.[18] Her central contributions are that prejudices are plural and that they are noncognitive.[19] If this is correct, the implications for the worshiping environment are most worrisome. We learn by hearing even when we are not listening. It is the reverse of the song, we do not need to be carefully taught but carefully untaught. This effort, however, is challenged by liturgical structures. A woman walked out of church one Sunday as soon as a reading from Ephesians began. It was 5:22ff., about wives being subject to their husbands. She left because her husband, a member of a small fundamentalist sect, used these verses to justify his abusive control. The pastor saw her leave and knew her reason. He later told her she should have stayed since the homilist gave a good interpretation. She answered, "You do not understand. After the homily you do not say 'The Word of the Lord.' "

The first rule for being in a hole is to stop digging. Churches can find ways not to make matters worse or to deepen anti-Judaism. One would be to stop dramatizing the Passion narratives. Another would be to avoid Passion plays in all forms and for all people, surely for children in religious education programs. Were passion plays ever the intent of the biblical authors? Such plays are most often unscriptural conflations of the four accounts into one. The Passion narratives are proclamations to be chanted or read. When read, it should be by a number of trained lectors with musical interludes and silences.

---

[17]Elizabeth A. Johnson, *She Who Is* (New York: Crossroads Publishing Co., 1993) 158.

[18]Elizabeth Young-Bruehl, *The Anatomy of Prejudices* (Cambridge: Harvard University Press, 1996).

[19]See *New York Times Book Review*, 19 March 1996.

"The Jews" in John and Acts

In the Gospel of John, the term "the Jews" is used 70 times. Modern New Testament scholars are sensitive to the problems about this term. To the congregation it sounds like all the people. The term is used in a variety of ways, but is most often menacing and hateful. Judas seems like the term personified. Pheme Perkins says that "None of the characterizations in the Fourth Gospel stirs as much dispute."[20] Raymond Brown indicates the term refers, most frequently but not exclusively, to the hostile religious leadership.[21] In lectures and conferences, Brown frequently said that it is imperative that on Good Friday homilists give a proper interpretation of the term. For Perkins the term is "emblematic of unbelief." She concludes her treatment by saying: "Since the evangelist has clearly shaped the characterization of 'the Jews' to the plot of his story of belief and unbelief, one cannot derive from his statements canonical warrant for anti-Semitism among Christians today."[22]

In the more recent Sacra Pagina commentary on John, Francis Moloney treats the problem early on and more extensively. For him the term must always "be placed in quotation marks because it does not represent the Jewish people." In the Gospel they are "those characters in the story who have made up their minds about Jesus." The Johannine community is on the other side of the debate. "The conflicts between Jesus and 'the Jews' are more the reflection of a Christological debate at the end of the first century than a record of encounters between Jesus and his fellow Israelites in the thirties of that century. *They do not accurately report the experiences of the historical Jesus.*"[23]

It is not the primary task of biblical scholars to help liturgists and worshipers. But we could hope for some. Whatever Pheme Perkins means by "canonical warrant for anti-Semitism among Christians today," it is anti-Judaism that is the concern in liturgy. There will be more on that issue below. And writing "the Jews" within quotes is no help to the lector or to the assembly of believers. Again, the problem is not what

---

[20]*The New Jerome Biblical Commentary* (Englewood Cliffs NJ: Prentice Hall, 1990) 948 at §61:15.

[21]Raymond E. Brown, *The Gospel according to John*, two vols., Anchor Bible 29, 29A (New York: Doubleday, 1966 and 1970; 2nd ed., 1979). "[T]he Fourth Gospel uses 'the Jews' as almost a technical title for *the religious authorities, particularly those in Jerusalem, who are hostile to Jesus*" (lxxi; italics in original).

[22]*The New Jerome Biblical Commentary*, 948 at §61:15.

[23]Moloney, *The Gospel of John*, 10; emphasis added.

their students and readers come to understand but what people *hear* in church, and how they hear it.

For Christians who follow the lectionary, during the Easter season there are no readings from the Hebrew Bible except the Psalms. The first readings are from the Acts of the Apostles and a number of these are problematic, particularly on Easter Day and the third Sunday of Easter. In both of these the deicide charge, Jewish guilt for the death of Jesus, is clearly made. On Easter it is in Acts 10. Peter is speaking to the people: "We are witnesses to all he did in the land of the Jews and in Jerusalem. They killed him, hanging him on a tree" (Acts 10:39). On the third Sunday, the Acts readings from all three lectionary cycles are deicide charges.[24] In cycle A, Peter says to the Jews, "You even used pagans to crucify and kill him" (Acts 2:23b). It is particularly disturbing on Easter Sunday for the charge to be made in such a formal and solemn setting. The churches are packed. The people hear these words from the ambo or pulpit, the altar of the book. The lector concludes with "The Word of the Lord." When the deicide content is pointed out, most will say it does not mean that or they did not hear it that way or they were not listening. But if prejudices are noncognitive, it is not necessary to be listening in order to learn. This is an anomaly of incomplete renewal, that the deicide charge, proscribed by the highest authority, is repeated Easter after Easter, after Auschwitz. How can we possibly imagine that this has no effect in sustaining anti-Judaism?

Anti-Judaism

The distinction between anti-Judaism and antisemitism is a work in progress. A stage in that progress is apparent in the Vatican document from the Commission for Religious Relations with the Jews, "We Remember: Reflections on the Shoah" of March 1998. In the text anti-Judaism is mentioned five times. It is not condemned. Antisemitism is mentioned three times and is strongly condemned, with a forceful citation from *Nostra Aetate*. Anti-Judaism is called a sentiment "in some Christian quarters." It was "essentially more sociological and political than religious." It is "long-standing sentiments of mistrust and hostility . . . of which, unfortunately, Christians also have been guilty." It is not the root of Nazi antisemitism. The response to the question of whether these anti-Jewish sentiments, "imbedded in some Christian minds and hearts," made the Nazi persecution easier, is the weakest part of the document.

---

[24]A. Acts 2:14, 22-28. B. Acts 3:13-15, 17-19. C. Acts 5:27b-32, 40b-41.

The question is, in effect, left unanswered. The moral reasoning is indefinite. It bystands the history.[25] There is no attention to the teaching of contempt for Jews, which for centuries was relentless and official. "We Remember" ends with a strong hope for the future, that "the spoiled seeds of anti-Judaism and anti-Semitism must never be allowed to take root in any human heart." This effort must entail attention to the worshiping environment and how Jews and Judaism are depicted in texts, art, prayer, and in the liturgical structure itself.

In the post-Vatican II period, the first comprehensive study of these matters for many Christians, surely for most Roman Catholics, was by Edward Flannery.[26] Father Flannery, who died in October 1998, made an enormous contribution to these studies. For his readers it was an awakening to a part of Christian history that had been ignored. There were no seminary courses about this part of Christian history. It was not part of higher education. Research had not been done. It was not part of religious education to any significant degree on any level. Flannery was widely praised but there was a major reservation. It was in the way he dealt with anti-Judaism. This was the concern of a number of Jewish scholars who reviewed his work in *Continuum*, a quarterly at the time. They were grateful for what he had accomplished. He was moving in the right direction. The problem, however, was in remarks by Flannery such as these:

> Did anti-Semitism exist in the Church during the first three centuries? Opinions differ. It is difficult, on our part, to categorize: first, hostile Christian writings or actions effectively provoked by Jews; second, theological or apologetical treatises or teachings which expounded an anti-Judaism that is essential to the Christological dogmas of the Church; third, the indignation of writers

---

[25]"We Remember: Reflections on the Shoah," IV. Nazi anti-Semitism and the Shoah: "Any response to this question must take into account that we are dealing with the history of people's attitudes and ways of thinking, subject to multiple influences. Moreover, many people were altogether unaware of the "final solution" that was being put into effect against a whole people; others were afraid for themselves and those near to them; some took advantage of the situation; and still others were moved by envy. A response would need to be given case by case. To do this, however, it is necessary to know what precisely motivated people in a particular situation."

[26]Edward H. Flannery, *The Anguish of the Jews: Twenty-Three Centuries of Anti-semitism* (New York: Macmillan, 1965).

gravely worried about the dangers Judaism posed for the often superficially Christianized populace.[27]

The critics were disturbed by accusing Jews of provoking hostile writers and by an anti-Judaism that is an essential apologetic. Flannery published a revised edition in 1985. The changes were not substantial, and the distinction between anti-Judaism and antisemitism was left to others. A more recent study criticizes Flannery's "fuzzy distinction" between anti-Judaism and antisemitism and his justifying anti-Judaism as a "rejection of Judaism as a way of salvation, not of the Jews as a people."[28] This "justification," or distinction, is not found in Flannery's revised edition.[29]

Flannery's concept of antisemitism's spreading over twenty-three centuries is challenged by Gavin Langmuir. In *History, Religion, and Antisemitism* and in *Toward a Definition of Antisemitism*, Langmuir has made a considerable effort to understand these prejudices. His research is essential to the work in progress of distinguishing anti-Judaism and antisemitism. It is imperative for Christians to do this work. The question so often asked, about antisemitism's being in the New Testament, is the wrong question. It avoids Christian responsibilities. The correct one is about anti-Judaism in the texts. Langmuir's distinction, while too sharp for many, is helpful and on the right track. Antisemitism, for him, is hatred of Jews based on chimerical fantasies—Jews as a racial threat, world conspirators, well poisoners, and ritual killers. "[B]y 'antisemitism' we mean not only its racist manifestations but instances in which people, because they are labeled Jews, are feared as symbols of subhumanity and hated for threatening characteristics they do not in fact possess."[30] The term, "anti-Semitism," was coined in the 1870s by a proto-Nazi, Wilhelm Marr, "to describe the policy toward Jews based on racism that he and others advocated."[31] For Marr and cohorts, and later for the Nazis, Jews were a disease, endangering everyone, like an infection, and it constituted the world's greatest threat. The name of the disease was Semitism. There is, of course, no such thing. Those who insist on the upper case and the hyphen give it reality, as though there was a "Semitism" you could be

---

[27]Ibid., 43.

[28]Gavin I. Langmuir, *History, Religion, and Antisemitism* (Berkeley: University of California Press, 1990) 34.

[29]Edward H. Flannery, *The Anguish of the Jews: Twenty-Three Centuries of Antisemitism*, rev. ed. (New York: Paulist Press, 1985).

[30]Gavin I. Langmuir, *Toward a Definition of Antisemitism* (Berkeley: University of California Press, 1990) 301-302.

[31]Ibid., 311.

"anti." Langmuir wrote: "If the meaning of antisemitism for its original proponents is clear, their use of the term is empirically meaningless for us because the Aryan myth on which it depended is now recognized as obviously false."[32] For Langmuir, antisemitism with its fantasy base of hatred began long before the Nazis. It was in 1150 with the first accusation of ritual killing.[33]

Anti-Judaism is hostility toward Jews for who they are, what they do, what they believe, and what they do not believe. It predated antisemitism and is its major source. Langmuir's distinction between hostilities, those based on fantasy and those on fact, while helpful, seems clinical. The space between what is fact and what is fantasy is murky. And to see Christian anti-Judaism as hostility toward real Jews, for beliefs and practices, for who Jews are, is to make them somehow complicitous. Steven Katz insists that

> Jewish conduct is not in the first instance the primary cause of Jew hatred. Christian Judeophobia preceded and, in actuality, creates the Jewish usurer, and modern racial antisemites oppose Jews whether they are bankers or farmers. Auschwitz and Treblinka are not created as a result of Jewish behavior but, rather, are the consequence of a specific metaphysical theory regarding Jewish behavior.[34]

Conclusions

Historians and theologians have described a "Theology of Supersessionism."[35] There is also a "Liturgy of Supersessionism." It is present in liturgical structures, in the choice and use of texts, in prayers, hymns, and in religious art. The "spoiled seeds" the pope deplored are rooted in the worship of vast numbers of Christians. To liberate worship from these elements is an enormous task. For such an effort to be engaged and to succeed, leadership must be clear about its importance. Roman Catholics, for example, need their bishops to help them, and their Offices of Worship to give explicit direction. National organizations like the Liturgi-

---

[32]Ibid.

[33]Ibid., 209.

[34]Steven T. Katz, *The Holocaust in Historical Context* (New York: Oxford University Press), 389.

[35]William Nichol, *Christian Antisemitism: A History of Hate* (Northvale NJ: Jason Aronson, 1993); Rosemary R. Ruether, *Faith and Fratricide: The Theological Roots of Anti-Semitism* (New York: Seabury Press, 1974).

cal Conference could apply their considerable energies and resources. Christians need to understand that this work is a priority for us; to be rid finally of anti-Judaism is demanded of us. It is a matter of conscience. What is happening in our worship is in grave need of reform. *Lex orandi, lex credendi,* the way we worship is the way we believe. If liturgy is laced with anti-Judaism, then Christians, despite all the progress otherwise, will tend toward sustaining the great hate that has been a nightmare for its victims and for its agents. And it is hate. Hatred need not be visceral and emotional. Ideas are enough—that Jews are replaced, their Covenant is ended, and the only purpose of Judaism was to prepare for Christ and Christianity. Saul Friedländer has written significantly on forms of religious anti-Judaism, that its impact is "a vast reservoir of almost automatic anti-Jewish reactions . . . as a result of early exposure to Christian religious education and liturgy, and to everyday expressions drawn from the pervasive and ongoing presence of the various denominations of the Christian creed."[36]

The Sunday lectionary is problem. It needs to be examined for anti-Judaism. The Hebrew Bible sections should be proclaimed for their own spiritual and biblical integrity, as they are for the most part in daily lectionaries. Catholics are instructed by the Constitution on Revelation of Vatican II that "the interpreter must investigate what meaning the sacred writer intended to express and actually expressed in particular circumstances as he used contemporary literary forms in accordance with the situation of his own time and culture."[37] This principle must be respected in liturgy as well as in Bible classes. The purpose of the Liturgy of the Word is the proclamation of the Lord Jesus Christ. But how can this be a true proclamation of the Lord when the text is misused and the structure is supersessionist?

The term "Good News" for Christians is holy. It is the proclamation for us of God's saving presence in the life, death, and resurrection of Jesus Christ. The Good News is his word, the word of love and peace, the word of justice and truth. The search after Auschwitz cannot be for it, for the word, but for how to undo what we have done. In *The Last of the Just,* the lovers, Ernie and Golda, who are about to be deported to Auschwitz, have this conversation:

---

[36]Saul Friedlander, *Nazi Germany and the Jews,* vol. 1, *The Years of Persecution, 1933–1939* (New York: HarperCollins, 1997) 83.

[37]Walter M. Abbott, ed., *The Documents of Vatican II: All Sixteen Official Texts Promulgated by the Ecumenical Council, 1963–1965* (New York: America Press; Association Press, 1966) 120.

"Oh, Ernie," Golda said, "you know them. Tell me, why, why do the Christians hate us the way they do? They seem so nice when I can look at them without my star."

Ernie put his arm around her shoulders solemnly. "It's very mysterious," he murmured in Yiddish. They don't know exactly why themselves. I've been in their churches and I've read their gospel. Do you know who the Christ was? A simple Jew like your father. A kind of Hasid."

Golda smiled gently. "You're kidding me."

"No, no, believe me, and I'll bet they'd have got along fine, the two of them, because he was really a good Jew, you know, sort of like the Baal Shem Tov—a merciful man, and gentle. The Christians say they love him, but I think they hate him without knowing it. So, they take the cross by the other end and make a sword out of it and strike us with it! You understand, Golda," he cried suddenly, strangely excited, "they take the cross and they turn it around, they turn it around, my God. . . ."[38]

Before he died, Pope John XXIII composed this prayer. He wanted it read in all churches. He called it, "Act of Reparation":

We are conscious today that many centuries of blindness have cloaked our eyes so that we can no longer see the beauty of Thy chosen people, nor recognize in their faces the features of our privileged brethren. We realize that the mark of Cain stands on our foreheads. Across the centuries our brother Abel has lain in blood which we drew or shed tears we caused forgetting Thy love. Forgive us for the curse we falsely attached to their name as Jews. Forgive us for crucifying Thee a second time in their flesh. For we knew not what we did.[39]

---

[38] André Schwarz-Bart, *The Last of the Just* (New York: Atheneum, 1960) 364-65.
[39] Quoted in Eliezer Berkovits, *Faith after the Holocaust* (New York: KTAV Publishing House, 1973) 26.

Chapter 7

Good News after Auschwitz: Binding the Brokenhearted

Jolene Chu and James N. Pellechia

In the minds of many, it would be stretching matters to say the road to Auschwitz originated in Eden. Yet the silhouette of fallen humanity already cast its shadow over the opening chapters of Genesis, as paradise disintegrated into a society rife with scapegoating, jealousy, fratricide, and vengeance. The intimacy between God and man had been ruptured by apostasy, the seeds of genocide had been sown, and humanity desperately needed good news.

The need has only grown. The scourge of Nazism stands as a terrible monument to humanity's spurning of its Maker and all that God stands for. Its scourge was an evil conspiracy that aimed with one crushing blow to destroy innocent lives and to shatter faith in a benevolent God. Out of the ashes of Auschwitz arise anguished cries for good news. And yet, after Auschwitz, what news could possibly be good enough?

An ancient herald of good news, the prophet Isaiah, foretold the coming of a messenger entrusted with good news of tremendous power. It could bind up the brokenhearted, liberate the captives, proclaim the year of goodwill and the day of vengeance, and comfort all who mourn (Isaiah 61:1-2).[1] Is there yet balsam in Gilead?[2] Can the good news indeed

---

[1] These verses in the *Tanakh* read: "The spirit of the Lord GOD is upon me, / Because the LORD has anointed me; / He has sent me as a herald of joy to the humble, / To bind up the wounded of heart, / To proclaim release to the captives, / Liberation to the imprisoned; / To proclaim a year of the LORD's favor / And a day of vindication by our God; / To comfort all who mourn."

The *New World Translation* renders Isaiah 61:1-2 as follows: "The spirit of the Sovereign Lord Jehovah is upon me, for the reason that Jehovah has anointed me to tell good news to the meek ones. He has sent me to bind up the brokenhearted, to proclaim liberty to those taken captive and the wide opening of the eyes even to the prisoners; to proclaim the year of good will on the part of Jehovah and the day of vengeance on the part of our God; to comfort all the mourning ones."

[2] The prophet Jeremiah alludes to the medicinal and healing properties of the resin ("balm") of the balsam plant from Gilead. See Jer. 8:22; 46:11-13; 51:8-10.

heal the wounds of the victimized? Is liberation possible from the shackles of bitter disillusionment, cynicism, and hopelessness? Will the good news comfort the contrite who mourn the collective failure and bloodguilt of human society? Will justice finally be done? Does the good news have the power to conquer the flames of the Shoah? Or, after Auschwitz, does the good news merely echo empty illusions of a mythical golden age?

Isaiah announced the tidings of restoration, exclaiming: "How comely upon the mountains are the feet of the one bringing good news, the one publishing peace, the one bringing good news of something better, the one publishing salvation, the one saying to Zion: 'Your God has become king!' " (Isaiah 52:7)[3]

The prophet identifies four vital facets of the good news: its message of peace; its promise of better things; its provision for salvation; and its jubilant affirmation of God's Kingship.[4] "Your God has become king!"— this proclamation to Zion epitomized the good news that reconciliation between God and humankind lay ahead. The Kingdom—a royal heavenly government—would express God's universal sovereignty by means of the messianic Prince of Peace.[5] The Kingdom was to be the key to the fulfillment of good news, the means by which would come a restoration of paradise lost, a new age of universal peace and justice, an end to humanity's lonely and terrible alienation from the Divine One. Thus, the good news of the Kingdom became the central theme of the message preached by Jesus and his disciples.[6] As H. G. Wells observed:

> Remarkable is the enormous prominence given by Jesus to the teaching of what he called the Kingdom of Heaven. . . . This doctrine of the Kingdom of Heaven, which was the main teaching of Jesus . . . is certainly one of the most revolutionary doctrines that ever stirred and changed human thought.[7]

---

[3]Scripture quotations are from the *New World Translation of the Holy Scriptures* unless otherwise noted.

[4]See Psalms 72:3; 93:1; 96:2; Isaiah 40:9-11.

[5]See Isaiah 9:6, 7.

[6]Implicit in both the Hebrew term *bawsar* and the Greek term *euaggelion,* variously translated as "good news," "gospel," and "glad tidings," is the action of announcement or declaration. See W. E. Vine, *Vine's Expository Dictionary of Old and New Testament Words* (Old Tappan NJ: Revell, 1981) 2:167; and Robert Young, *Analytical Concordance to the Bible* (Grand Rapids MI: Eerdmans, 1970) 987.

[7]H. G. Wells, *The Outline of History,* vol. 1 (New York: Garden City Books, 1920) 422. The passage in its entirety reads: "Remarkable is the enormous

The Christian gospel of the first century CE opened to all, Jew and non-Jew alike, the opportunity to reap the blessings of the Kingdom—this was good news indeed. But citizenship in the Kingdom brought with it responsibilities, requiring faithful obedience to God as Sovereign Ruler, along with an unbreakable commitment to God's law of neighbor love and to human brotherhood (James 2:8).

The purpose of this essay is to consider the relevance of the Christian gospel in a world that witnessed the Holocaust. The participation of professed Christians in Nazi genocide mocked the messianic expectations of faithful Jews throughout the ages, as millions of their descendants were savaged and murdered by individuals who claimed to follow the Messiah from Nazareth. To say that such followers had strayed from the path laid down by the Master seems a grotesque understatement. Where did the deviation occur? Was the deflection total? Is the damage irreparable? The following brief discussion of early Christianity and violence bears heavily on these issues and on the question of the relevance of the good news in the post-Auschwitz world.

The Christian's Role as Peacemaker

The life and teachings of Jesus illuminated humanity's pathway to peace with God and with all persons. Basic to the way of life that he taught was a commitment to nonviolence. Jesus never issued an explicit prohibition for his disciples against participation in war; nevertheless during Christianity's first three centuries Jesus' followers repudiated war and military service. They took their cue from his object lessons against violence, such as the dramatic incident involving the sword-wielding Peter in Gethsemane on the night of Jesus' arrest. "Return your sword to its place," directed the Master, "for all those who take the sword will perish by the sword" (Matthew 26:52). If violence could not be justified even in defense of the Son of Man, how could Christians take up weapons for lesser causes?

Furthermore, earlier that same evening, Jesus gave his apostles a new commandment that would be enjoined on all his followers: "Love one

---

prominence given by Jesus to the teaching of what he called the Kingdom of Heaven, and its comparative insignificance in the procedure and teaching of most of the Christian churches. This doctrine of the Kingdom of Heaven, which was the main teaching of Jesus, and which plays so small a part in the Christian creeds, is certainly one of the most revolutionary doctrines that ever stirred and changed human thought."

another." In itself this law was not new. It had its counterpart in the ancient mitzvah "Love your fellow as yourself" (Leviticus 19:18). What made it new was Jesus' proviso indicating the extent of Christian love: "This is my commandment, that you love one another *just as I have loved you.*" Defining the outermost boundaries of this love and alluding to his impending sacrificial death, he added, "No one has love greater than this, that someone should surrender his soul in behalf of his friends" (John 15:12-13).

Drawing on the principles embodied in these final exhortations, early Christians concluded that they could not obey the mandate to love their fellow believers and at the same time slaughter them in obedience to the command of a secular power. Moreover, the second of the greatest commandments of the Law required the same degree of love for one's neighbor as for oneself (Matthew 22:39). In case his followers should be tempted to adopt a narrow definition of "neighbor," Jesus further commanded them, "Love your enemies" (Matthew 5:44). The shedding of human blood would violate this basic Christian law of love. The professor of theology Ronald Sider notes the historical context of Jesus' injunction and concludes: "Jesus advocated love toward enemies as his specific political response to centuries of violence and to the contemporary Zealots' call for violent revolution."[8]

The majority of Christians up to the time of Constantine refused to take up weapons. "The pacifism of the early church," writes Roland Bainton, "was derived not from a New Testament legalism, but from an effort to apply what was taken to be the mind of Christ."[9] However, as

---

[8]Ronald J. Sider, *Christ and Violence* (Scottdale PA: Herald Press, 1979) as quoted in Dick Ringler, ed., *Dilemmas of War and Peace—A Sourcebook* (Madison WI: Board of Regents of the University of Wisconsin System and the Corporation for Public Broadcasting, 1993). Dietrich Bonhoeffer discusses the obligations connected with this text in *The Cost of Discipleship* (New York: Touchstone, 1995) 148-54. Bonhoeffer's developing views on Christian pacifism are discussed in the editors' introduction to *A Testament to Freedom: The Essential Writings of Dietrich Bonhoeffer*, ed. Geffrey B. Kelly and F. Burton Nelson (New York: HarperCollins, 1995) 9-12.

[9]Roland H. Bainton, *Christian Attitudes toward War and Peace: A Historical Survey and Critical Reevaluation* (Nashville: Abingdon Press, 1960) 53-54. Some would argue that the early Christians, although abstaining from war, were not purely pacifistic because they approved of wars waged by God. See Rev. 16:14; 17:14; 19:15, 16. See also, for instance, "Should Christians Be Pacifists?" *Awake!* 8 May 1997, 22-23. For further discussions of the term "Christian pacifism," see Theodore J. Koontz, "Christian Nonviolence: An Interpretation," in Terry Nardin,

fundamental as the law of love was to this early Christian position, additional principles governed the individual Christian's response to state-sponsored violence.

Like their Exemplar, the followers of Christ maintained political neutrality, having no part in the government-led conflicts and the bloodletting of the nations. But Christians' abstention from armed conflict by no means meant a monastic retreat from society. Jesus had pronounced the "peacemakers" blessed.[10] They were sent forth as emissaries of the Kingdom and bearers of the good news. As ambassadors of that Kingdom, they were to venture out into the world that God so loved, bearing the entreaty: "Become reconciled to God" (John 3:16; 2 Corinthians 5:20; see also John 17:16).

Indicative of the hostility Christian envoys would face is the apostle Paul's letter, written when he was in a Roman prison, where he was "acting as an ambassador in chains."[11] Paul evoked the imagery of battle as he mingled the language of conflict with the language of reconciliation: messengers of peace would henceforth wear "the complete suit of armor from God," their comely feet "shod with the equipment of the good news of peace" (Ephesians 6:13, 15).[12] Their obligations toward the good news

---

ed., *The Ethics of War and Peace—Religious and Secular Perspectives* (Princeton: Princeton University Press, 1996) 169-80; David R. Smock, *Perspectives on Pacifism* (Washington DC: United States Institute of Peace Press, 1995) 11-20.

[10]Matt. 5:9 AV/KJV: "peacemaker," *eirenopoios*, calling for the active pursuit of peace. Coins of the Roman emperors were struck with this same title. See Bainton, *Christian Attitudes toward War and Peace*, 64.

[11]Eph. 6:20. One commentary notes: "His being in chains is a demonstration of the hostile attitude of this world toward God, Christ, and the Messianic Kingdom government, for ambassadors have since time immemorial been considered inviolate." "Ambassador," *Insight on the Scriptures*, vol. 1 (Brooklyn NY: Watch Tower Bible and Tract Society, 1988) 89.

[12]"Equipment," literally meaning "in readiness; in preparedness." Interestingly, in this passage Paul presents the activity of spreading the good news as a protection, a defensive posture. He urges Christians to maintain a readiness to promote the good news as one means to protect their spiritual lives and stand firm against satanic attack, even while they waged an offensive to spread the good news as soldiers engaged in spiritual warfare. Of Greek Scripture writers, only Paul uses the term "soldier" in referring to Christians engaged in spiritual battle. (See Philippians 2:25 and 2 Timothy 2:4.) Bainton suggests that Roman readers related easily to the military metaphors in Paul's writings. See Bainton, *Christian Attitudes toward War and Peace*, 64.

were thus to preserve it, to preach it, to live by it, and, if called upon to do so, to die for it.

It might seem odd that bearing good news could bring fatal consequences. Yet first-century Christians[13] were to struggle with and suffer for their loyalty to the good news of the Kingdom. Jesus warned that the world would hate those who were not its own. His prescient words would echo in the ears of Christians facing wild beasts in the Roman arenas: "Whoever wants to save his soul will lose it; but whoever loses his soul for the sake of me *and the good news* will save it" (Mark 8:35). In the first-century Roman world, the official cult of emperor worship posed a challenge to Christian neutrals, who would not violate their prior loyalty to the Kingdom by acknowledging the divinity of Roman rulers. Catholic writer A. Hamann observed:

> It was impossible to take a step without encountering a divinity. The Christian's position brought him daily problems; he lived on the edge of society. . . . He faced recurring problems in the home, in the streets, at the market. . . . In the street, whether a Roman citizen or not, a Christian should bare his head when passing a temple or a statue. How could he refrain from doing so without arousing suspicion, yet how could he comply without committing an act of allegiance? If he was in business and needed to borrow money, he had to swear to the moneylender in the name of the gods. . . . If he accepted public office, he was expected to offer a sacrifice. If enlisted, how could he avoid taking the oath and participating in the rites of military service?[14]

The Deflection

As the centuries passed, however, boundaries became blurred and loyalties began to drift. In *The City of God*, Augustine wrote: "The church now on earth is both the kingdom of Christ and the kingdom of heaven."[15] With the Kingdom safely entrenched within the fortress of the church,

---

[13]Considering the lack of consensus on the term "Christian," we use the term here to mean one who professes belief in the teachings of Jesus. Gavin Langmuir discusses the problem of defining and using religious terms in historiography in *History, Religion, and Antisemitism* (Berkeley: University of California Press, 1990) 3-17.

[14]A. Hamman, *La vie quotidienne des premiers chrétiens (95-197)* (Paris: Librairie Hachette, 1971) 97-99.

[15]*Encyclopaedia Britannica*, vol. 8 (1970): 697.

Christians felt free to render their allegiance to more tangible entities. As Wells observed: "Men shifted the reference of their lives from the kingdom of God and the brotherhood of mankind to those apparently more living realities, France and England, Holy Russia, Spain, Prussia. . . . They were the real and living gods of Europe."[16]

Such a migration in loyalties resulted in both a lapse of vigilance for the Kingdom's good news and a disastrous marriage of religious fervor with political agendas. Defense of the Kingdom became synonymous with defense of Christendom's domain. Christians began to spill the blood of their own and of others, not for the sake of the Kingdom of heaven, but for the sake of their "living gods," the ones of flesh.

A long string of bloody religious conflicts involving populations claiming to follow the Prince of Peace climaxed in the twentieth century. World War I, the so-called Great War, involved primarily Christian nations in a mutual bloodbath. Repudiating the heavenly government and its good news, men once again declared Caesar to be their king and slaughtered one another in the name of God. What would prevent them from joining themselves to a new kingdom and a new messiah who promised a thousand-year Reich, a restored Holy Roman Empire, a positive Christianity, and a holy crusade against the Jews?

Not all, however, would be carried along by the seductive appeal of the Nazi messiah. A few urgent voices could be heard decrying the sinister agenda of this new counterfeit kingdom.[17] One small Christian group, the *Bibelforscher*, or Jehovah's Witnesses, struggled to retain their stewardship of the good news. As a group, they rejected the pseudo-messiah, his illusory millennium, his claim on human souls, his racism and inhumanity, and his trampling of the children of Israel.[18] As

---

[16]Wells, *The Outline of History*, 664.

[17]For example, Paul Schneider, Martin Niemöller, Dietrich Bonhoeffer, Bernhard Lichtenberg, Franz Jäggerstätter, and others like them, who took a stand, often without the backing of their hierarchy.

[18]*The Golden Age*, the Witnesses' international journal, stated in the article "The German Crisis": "Probably there is nothing so indicative of primitive consciousness in the entire Nazi program as the anti-Jewish sentiment it so passionately advocates. Racial prejudices and religious creeds for hundreds of centuries have formed the fulcrum on which was balanced the destiny of nations. Civilization has been extremely slow in realizing the incipience of such prejudices. The Occident, of course, has made the greatest progress in minimizing the importance of religious and racial differences. However, when such contemptible sentiment arises in a modern country like Germany, it serves as the very mockery of human progress" (*The Golden Age*, 4 January 1933, 209). In the German edition of *The*

emissaries of peace, they were bound to take a nonnegotiable stand on the side of God and God's Kingdom, to tell the good news, and to "obey God as ruler rather than men" (Acts 5:29).[19]

Choice and Consequences

"I am strongly convinced in my belief that I am acting correctly," Franz Reiter wrote from his Nazi death cell. "Being here, I could still change my mind, but with God this would be disloyalty." Reiter, a thirty-six-year-old Austrian Jehovah's Witness, took a stand of conscience, refusing to join the German army and support the Nazi wars. He was executed by guillotine on 7 January 1940.[20]

The Nazis brutally persecuted Jehovah's Witnesses precisely over the issue of loyalty to and good news about a rival Kingdom. In February 1936 the *Manchester Guardian* reported:

Golden Age, 15 October 1929, National Socialism is called "a movement that is acting, either by accident or design, directly in the service of man's enemy, the devil, and against Jehovah the exalted Creator of heaven and earth" (316).

[19]The 7 October 1934 protest letter from the German Witnesses to German government officials stated: "This is to advise you that at any cost we will obey God's commandments, will meet together for the study of His Word; and will worship and serve Him as He has commanded. . . . We have no interest in political affairs, but are wholly devoted to God's kingdom under Christ His King. We will do no injury or harm to anyone" (*Golden Age*, 24 October 1934, 50-51).

[20]Reiter's letter to his mother, written the night before his execution, read: "I am strongly convinced in my belief that I am acting correctly. Being here, I could still change my mind, but with God this would be disloyalty. All of us here [Reiter and five other Austrian Witnesses from his region who were all condemned to death] wish to be faithful to God, to his honor. . . . With what I knew, if I had taken the [military] oath, I would have committed a sin deserving death. That would be evil to me. I would have no resurrection. But I stick to that which Christ said: 'Whosoever will save his life will lose it; but whosoever will lose his life for my sake, the same will receive it.' And now, my dear Mother and all my brothers and sisters, today I was told my sentence, and don't be terrified, it is death, and I will be executed tomorrow morning. I have my strength from God, the same as it always was with all true Christians away back in the past. The apostles write, 'Whosoever is born from God cannot sin.' The same goes for me. This I proved to you, and you could recognize it. My dear ones, don't get heavy-hearted. It would be good for all of you to know the Holy Scriptures better still. If you will stand firm until death, we shall meet again in the resurrection. . . . Your Franz. Until we meet again." *1989 Yearbook of Jehovah's Witnesses* (Brooklyn NY: Watch Tower Bible and Tract Society of Pennsylvania, 1988) 121-122.

Amongst the victims of religious persecution in Germany are the so called 'Ernste Bibelforscher,' a society for the study and propagation of the Scriptures independently of the Churches. . . . They have something of the character of early Christians and there are some that recall the Anabaptists. . . .

There has been a tendency to laugh at them as 'cranks,' but since the establishment of the Nazi dictatorship they have earned a good deal of respect and have increased their following (which was always considerable) by their absolute refusal to compromise in religious matters. Some have been arrested or sent to concentration camps for their refusal to say 'Hail Hitler!' because they maintain that no temporal authority is entitled to this expression of reverence. . . .

They have nothing to do with politics. . . . Nor is any political charge brought against them; in fact, the indictment expressly states that, whereas they belonged to a forbidden society, "some of them went from house to house spreading the Word of God in accordance with the beliefs of the society, others discussed, exchanged, or circulated publications . . . and held meetings at which they expounded the Bible."[21]

During the early years of Nazi rule, many Witnesses lost their jobs and property. As Nazi terror advanced across Europe, Witnesses were arrested, beaten, interrogated, incarcerated, and tortured. A few were sterilized. Others were committed to mental institutions. The Nazi government took hundreds of Witness children into custody and sent them to Nazi homes and reeducation centers. Witnesses were sent to prisons and camps by the thousands; about 2,500 would die as a result.[22] Of these, some 350 were formally executed.[23]

---

[21]"Mass Trial of Bible Students—A German Religious Society Which Defies Persecution," by special correspondent, *Manchester Guardian*, 14 February 1936, 11. The article states that forty-seven Witnesses, eight of whom were over sixty and three of whom were over seventy, stood trial at Elberfeld, Germany.

[22]Estimate based on latest figures, as reported in *Spiritual Resistance and Its Costs for a Christian Minority—A Documentary Report of Jehovah's Witnesses under Nazism 1933–1945* (Brooklyn NY: Watch Tower Bible and Tract Society of Pennsylvania, 1999).

[23]Of this number, about 250 were sentenced to death by military courts for refusing military service. Others, men and women, were executed for a variety of reasons including refusal to perform war-related labor, doing underground printing and courier activity, harboring fugitives, and so forth. German Witnesses

About 10,000 Witnesses went to Nazi prisons and camps, the largest single Christian group to offer organized and individual nonviolent resistance to the evils of Nazism.[24] They regarded the purple triangles on their camp uniforms as evidence of their loyalty to God's Kingdom.[25] Clearly, the Nazis also saw loyalty as the key issue. They gave Witness prisoners the chance to offer a pinch of incense on the Nazi altar.[26] Freedom could be purchased with a signature pledging agreement to the following terms:

1. I have come to know that the International Bible Students Association is proclaiming erroneous teachings and under the cloak of religion follows hostile purposes against the State.

---

suffered the highest number of executions, approximately 260, followed by 54 for Austria. The Witnesses thus constitute the largest group of conscientious objectors executed during the Nazi period.

[24]That the Witnesses constituted the largest group of resisters on religious grounds is well attested by scholars. See, for instance, Detlef Garbe, "Gesellschaftliches Desinteresse, staatliche Desinformation, erneute Verfolgung und nun Instrumentalisierung der Geschichte?" in Hans Hesse, ed., *Am mutigsten waren immer wider die Zeugen Jehovas: Verfolgung und Widerstand der Zeugen Jehovas im Nationalsozialismus* (Bremen: Edition Temmen, 1998) 302; Christine King, *The Nazi State and the New Religions: Five Case Studies in Nonconformity* (New York: Edwin Mellen Press, 1982); and Gabriele Yonan, "Spiritual Resistance of Christian Conviction in Nazi Germany: The Case of the Jehovah's Witnesses," *Journal of Church and State* 41 (Spring 1999): 307-22.

[25]The SS assigned the purple triangle uniform insignia as designation specifically for the *Bibelforscher*, or Jehovah's Witnesses. Clergy of other religions usually wore the red triangle of the political prisoners. However, there are a few cases of members of other religions, such as Adventists, members of the Salvation Army, and others, having worn the purple triangle. (See, for instance, letter regarding Buchenwald camp from Björn Hallström, London editor of the *Svenska Morgonbladet*, to the International Bible Students Association, London Office, dated 18 May 1945.)

[26]Daniel P. Mannix writes: "Very few of the Christians recanted, although an altar with a fire burning on it was generally kept in the arena for their convenience. All a prisoner had to do was scatter a pinch of incense on the flame and he was given a Certificate of Sacrifice and turned free. It was also carefully explained to him that he was not worshiping the emperor; merely acknowledging the divine character of the emperor as head of the Roman state. Still, almost no Christians availed themselves of the chance to escape." *Those About to Die* (New York: Ballantine Books, 1958) 137.

2. I therefore left the organization entirely and made myself absolutely free from the teachings of this sect.
3. I herewith give assurance that I will never again take any part in the activity of the International Bible Students Association. Any persons approaching me with the teaching of the Bible Students, or who in any manner reveal their connections with them, I will denounce immediately. All literature from the Bible Students that should be sent to my address I will at once deliver to the nearest police station.
4. I will in the future esteem the laws of the State, especially in the event of war will I, with weapon in hand, defend the fatherland, and join in every way the community of the people.
5. I have been informed that I will at once be taken again into protective custody if I should act against the declaration given today.

Choice was a commodity virtually beyond the reach of most Nazi victims. For Jehovah's Witnesses, however, the option of freedom was almost always as close as the nearest pen. Their Nazi captors made sure that Witnesses had ready access to the declaration of renunciation. Sometimes the SS arranged a torture session or a public execution as an added incentive.[27] Most Witnesses refused to sign, viewing such an act as a renunciation of their God, their brothers, and their Christian principles.[28]

---

[27]See "Germans Execute Objector to War, First Conscientious Resister Was Member of Jehovah's Witnesses' Sect," in the *New York Times*, 17 September 1939, 26, for details about the shooting of August Dickmann in Sachsenhausen. Several hundred fellow Witness prisoners stood by during the execution and were threatened with a similar fate if they refused to sign the declaration of renunciation. Not one Witness signed. Eyewitnesses describe the shooting in the video documentary *Jehovah's Witnesses Stand Firm against Nazi Assault* (Brooklyn NY: Watch Tower Bible and Tract Society of Pennsylvania, 1996).

[28]Detlef Garbe, leading authority on the history of Jehovah's Witnesses during the Nazi period, estimates that no more than a few dozen German Witnesses signed the document and obtained release. The wording of earlier versions of the declaration varied. For instance, some Witnesses were offered and signed documents stating that they were aware that continued practice of their religion would result in a concentration camp sentence. See also Harald Abt, "Faith in God Sustained Me," *The Watchtower*, 15 April 1980, 8. In addition, see Jürgen Harder and Hans Hesse, "Die Zeuginnen Jehovas im Frauen-KZ Moringen: ein Beitrag zum Widerstand von Frauen im Nationalsozialismus," in *Am mutigsten warn immer wieder die Zeugen Jehovas*, 49-50. For a detailed discussion of Nazi terror tactics and the Witness response, see Detlef Garbe, *Zwischen Widerstand und Martyrium: Die Zeugen Jehovas im Dritten Reich* (Munich: Oldenbourg, 1994). Garbe's massive monograph on the Witnesses is one of the most authoritative and

Like the early Christians, they lived and were prepared to die for the sake of the good news. They were confident of their place in God's Kingdom. But they were not immune to the pains of the moment, nor were they oblivious to the agonies of their fellow victims. Having themselves been the objects of church-inspired persecution, the Witnesses abhorred and mourned the murder of European Jewry at the hands of those claiming to follow the Christ.

J. F. Rutherford, the second president of the Watch Tower Society, stated: "The Devil has put his representative Hitler in control. . . . He cruelly persecutes the Jews because they were once Jehovah's covenant people, and bore the name of Jehovah, and because Christ Jesus was a Jew."[29]

This statement, made in the autumn of 1938, one month prior to *Kristallnacht*, embodies the essence of the Witnesses' theological position toward the Jews. On the one hand, they readily and respectfully acknowledged the Jewish origins of Christianity and its founder.[30] On the other hand, according to their doctrine, the period of exclusive chosenness of the Jews based on the Torah, embodying as it does a lasting covenant between God and the sons of Israel, had concluded. With the coming of Jesus as the Messiah, the fulfillment of the promises God made to Abraham became available to all the families of the earth, in keeping with its original purpose.

Moreover, they saw the Shoah, not as the act of an angry God avenging the death of his Son[31] but as the failure of the church to lead its flocks

---

comprehensive works to date on the subject.

[29]The lecture, "Fascism or Freedom," was given on 2 October 1938, at Madison Square Garden, New York City. It was carried by sixty radio stations and reprinted in booklet form in millions of copies. The booklets were banned in Europe.

[30]Witness literature contained frequent references to the Hebrew Scriptures, the history of the Jews, and prophetic passages concerning Israel. Nazi officials cited this as one proof that the Witnesses were enemies of the state. See court opinion for Germany vs. Honemann et al., reprinted in *The Golden Age*, 27 February 1935, 323, which states that the Witnesses "are subject to foreign influences which cannot be gone into and examined and show Jewish tendencies." See Han Jonak Von Freyenwald, *Die Zeugen Jehovas: Pioniere für ein jüdisches Weltreich. Die politischen Ziele der Internationalen Vereinigung Ernster Bibelforscher* (Berlin: Buchverlag Germania Aktien-Gesellschaft, 1936) for a Nazi writer's extensive analysis of Watch Tower literature.

[31]The statement in *Consolation*, 4 May 1938, 7, is typical: "History never recorded a more systematic, efficient, devilish obliteration of Jews than at present in Germany."

in the ways of the Master[32] and as conclusive evidence of humanity's inability to rule itself without God. For if a civilized, educated, technologically advanced, and well-churched society could perpetrate such barbarity, what further proof of human incompetence was needed? It only remained for the Lord to bring the present order to an end and to usher in the Kingdom rule. But before the end would come, said Jesus, "this good news of the kingdom will be preached in all the inhabited earth for a witness to all the nations" (Matthew 24:14). The Witnesses saw it as their duty to do their part in announcing earthwide the coming of the real new world.

Binding the Brokenhearted

And what good news could they offer to the suffering masses of the Holocaust kingdom? The Yiddish-language daily *Der Tog* reported of Jehovah's Witnesses in Danzig:

> They quote various Bible texts and want to show the Jews that things will get better. In a time of moral depression and total loss of rights, of despair and disillusionment, when one does not know what the morrow will bring, the active work of the widespread religious society of the "International Earnest Bible Students" and "Jehovah's Witnesses" is evidence that we still have a very great number of friends among the German common people who actually weep over the great destruction which has befallen the German people.[33]

---

[32]"The pope declared 1933 a 'holy year.' . . . That very so-called 'holy year' saw the Nazi dictator assume the misrule of Germany. . . . all for the purpose of robbing Jews and wrongfully acquiring territory. . . . In all of these things religion and state acted together. Religionists now laud and praise the dictators and the leaders in war, who in violation of God's everlasting covenant have shed much innocent human blood." From the lecture "Government and Peace," by J. F. Rutherford at Madison Square Garden, New York City, on 25 June 1939, and reprinted in the booklet *Government and Peace* (Brooklyn NY: Watchtower Bible and Tract Society, Inc., 1939) 14-15.

[33]See Yitzhak Kirschbaum, "How the Sect 'Jehovah's Witnesses' Is Clandestinely Working to Undermine Hitler's Regime," *Der Tog*, 2 July 1939, 5. The article also reported: "There were numerous cases in Danzig where members of the same religious sect have defended Jews against attacks by Nazis, or when these sincere women of the common people intentionally patronized Jewish stores just when Hitlerites picketed those Jewish shops. Only a half a year ago, when like a plague all kinds of food stores began to post the well-known signs *Juden unerwünscht*

A Jewish woman who encountered the Witnesses in Lichtenburg camp said of them: "They prayed for us as if we belonged to their family, and begged us to hold out."[34] To them, the good news and only the good news could offer genuine comfort to their fellows in suffering, who needed more than ever to hear the simple message penned by the Hebrew prophet: the promise of peace on earth, the prospect of a better future, the hope of salvation, and the herald of paradise restored. As a true test of their belief that all humans have the opportunity to become reconciled to God, surviving Witnesses even ventured back into the camps after the war to preach the good news to the new captives, their former persecutors.[35]

If these Christians who passed through the crucible of Auschwitz were to answer the question: "What is the good news today?" they would surely respond that the good news is the same—but its realization is nearer than ever. They would urge people never to cease praying for God's Kingdom to come, so that God's will can be done on this earth as it is done in heaven. They would tell of the time when God will open the graves and "actually swallow up death forever, and [when] the Sovereign Lord Jehovah will certainly wipe the tears from all faces" (Isaiah 25:8). They would affirm the healing power of the good news to "bind up the brokenhearted," so that "the former things will not be called to mind, neither will they come up into the heart" (Isaiah 61:1; 65:17).

To believe that the good news can actually extinguish the fires of Auschwitz from tormented minds and hearts is in itself an immense act of faith. For good reason, Jesus himself issues the appeal: "Have faith in the good news" (Mark 1:15).[36]

[Jews not wanted], the same German women regarded it as a sacred duty to provide their Jewish neighbors or mere acquaintances with food or milk without asking anything in return."

[34]*Consolation*, 26 July 1939, 4.

[35]*1946 Yearbook of Jehovah's Witnesses* (Brooklyn NY: Watch Tower Bible and Tract Society, 1945) 169; *1947 Yearbook of Jehovah's Witnesses* (Brooklyn NY: Watch Tower Bible and Tract Society, 1946) 115-17. Shortly before he committed suicide, Heinrich Himmler encountered a *Bibelforscher* at masseur Felix Kersten's estate Harzwalde and was given "a thorough witness" (*1974 Yearbook of Jehovah's Witnesses* [Brooklyn NY: Watch Tower Bible and Tract Society, 1974] 211).

[36]"Have faith," from the Greek *pisteuo* meaning "to think to be true; to be persuaded of; to credit, place confidence in." Joseph Henry Thayer, *The New Thayer's Greek-English Lexicon* (Lafayette IN: Christian Copyrights, Inc., 1979) 511.

Chapter 8

The Holy Ground
of Hospitality: Goods News
for a Shoah-Tempered World

Henry F. Knight

Whatever else we may say about the period of history we call the Shoah, it was a time of radical inhospitality. Jews, the quintessential "other" in Christendom, were radically unwelcome not simply to share place but also life and breath in the Nazi universe of the Third Reich. Simple hospitality toward Jews took on increased significance, for it involved life-and-death affairs for those who were its recipients as well as those who were its hosts. In this essay I hope to show how hospitality, when understood as making room for the other in one's life and in one's worlds of relation and significance, holds an important key for rethinking Christian expressions of good news after Auschwitz. Radical hospitality becomes the countertestimony to the radical inhospitality of the Shoah, but no longer in the triumphant voice of exclusivism and supersessionism. Indeed, I will maintain that the good news of Christianity is also chastened news, for the witness of hospitality is sparse and often encountered in spite of the articulated theologies and beliefs of faithful Christians, especially during this dark period of world history. Moreover, such hospitality is not necessarily dependent upon any affiliation with the church or its witness. Still, the witness of Christian faith is grounded on the affirmation that in Jesus the rule and realm of God has[1] come near, breaking forth in human life. It will be my contention that the radical hospitality Jesus embodied is the still-encounterable gestalt that Jesus identified as the rule and realm of heaven and the threshold on which we must stand if we are to have good news to offer our Shoah-tempered world.

---

[1] I have intentionally chosen to use a singular form of the verb with this compound subject because the rule and realm of God is an attempt to render the singular reality identified in Greek as *basileia* and most often in English as *Kingdom*. I am guided by the Hebraic use of the singular understanding of the plural word for God (*Elohim*) to identify the Eternal One of Israel.

The Absence of Hospitality

At the center of the Shoah was the inability of the Nazi mind-set to view the Jewish people as worthy of life. The Nazi worldview defined certain classes of otherness as outside the framework of its universe of care. In its particularity, the Nazi *Weltanschauung* showed its inability to accept not only the identity but also the very presence of its Jewish other. Integrating the antisemitism of Christendom, along with the antireligious sentiments of its pagan history, Nazi Germany responded to the economic, political, social, and religious temper of the time with an intensely focused loathing for anyone and anything Jewish. Fear was linked to prejudice, and both were carefully cultivated in a climate of caricature and hatred. There was no room for the other, particularly the Jewish other, in this world.

Christian identity, when conceived in either an imperialistic mode or in supersessionary readings of its relationship with the Jewish people (that is, most of Christian theology up to the current era), also provides no room for the presence of the other, as other, to have independent standing. The other, so conceived, must be transformed into the likeness of the Christian identity. Still, and to some extent in spite of this, there were Christians during the Shoah and throughout history who demonstrated that they valued the stranger as bearing the image of God shared by all humanity. During the Shoah, the actions of rescuers demonstrated that even in such radically inhospitable times there were persons, some of them Christian, who welcomed the other into their homes, even at the risk of death. However, as Samuel and Pearl Oliner have pointed out in their research on the motivating factors of rescue,[2] Christian identity was not necessarily the deciding factor in this regard. In some cases, hospitality was practiced in spite of supersessionary dismissal of Jews as the people of God. They were neighbors who needed help.

What the Oliners uncovered in their research was that rescuers simply practiced hospitality to the other in an "extensive" and including manner. They opened their lives and their homes to others and gave them sanctuary. We call these acts rescue. Their recipients knew them to be lifesaving. In hindsight, the rescuers typically saw what they did as simply extending the inclusive character of how they were raised.[3]

---

[2]Samuel P. Oliner and Pearl M. Oliner, *The Altruistic Personality. Rescuers of Jews in Nazi Europe* (New York: The Free Press, 1988) 171-222.

[3]Ibid.

Strangers were welcome in their homes. It did not matter if they were Jews; they were neighbors and were to be extended hospitality. In the aftermath of what happened, we see these acts as extraordinary, even if the rescuers themselves did not. And because these acts happened, we know that hospitality to the other was possible, even in this universe of destruction we call the Shoah. And because such hospitality took place, we can hold our world even more accountable for hospitality's not happening more than it did.

The Witness of Hospitality

In significant ways, the behavior of rescuers, whether specifically Christian or not, gives Christians a way to rethink their identity as they stand before God and every other. For Christians, like me, who have taken the work of Irving Greenberg and Johann Baptist Metz[4] to heart and have begun to rethink even their most precious theological assertions, these actions are not simply instructive. They are essential to our hope for the future of Christianity. For without them, we must ask, what good news is left for us to proclaim after Auschwitz? Imperialistic notions of truth and supersessionary visions of ourselves as the people of God can no longer be tolerated. After the Shoah, no one can stand at the threshold of heaven's door as its gatekeeper. With such a far-reaching confessional adjustment as this, what shall we, as Christians, declare as our good news for a post-Shoah world? And how may we declare it knowing what we know about ourselves and the world around us?

Seeking Hospitality. We may begin where the first disciples began, venturing into an inhospitable world and looking for people and places of hospitality. According to Matthew 10, Jesus sent his disciples to the "lost sheep of the house of Israel" (Matthew 10:6) to proclaim the good news that God's rule and realm had drawn near. As he sent them, he instructed his disciples to look for hospitality. When hospitality was found, the house that offered it was deemed "worthy" (Greek *axios*) or

---

[4]Here I have in mind Irving Greenberg's oft-quoted criterion, "No statement, theological or otherwise, should be made that would not be credible in the presence of the burning children," and Johann Baptist Metz's admonition that no theological assertion should be trusted if it is unaffected by what happened at Auschwitz. See Greenberg's article "Cloud of Smoke, Pillar of Fire: Judaism, Christianity, and Modernity after the Holocaust," in Eva Fleischner, ed., *Auschwitz: Beginning of a New Era?* (New York: KTAV, 1977) 23; and Metz, *The Emergent Church: The Future of Christianity in a Postbourgeois World* (New York: Crossroad, 1987) 17-32, esp. 28.

deserving.[5] In return, the disciples were to bless that household with their peace and to share their message of the nearness of God's reign among them. And where needed, they were to bring healing. On the other hand, if they were not welcomed, they were to move on, shaking the dust from their feet. In other words, the connection between the good news of the dawning rule and realm of heaven and hospitality is essential. The disciples, in the presence of hospitality, were to identify its significance, blessing those households where it was practiced with the good news of what they beheld: the rule and realm of heaven/God was breaking forth in their midst.

A warning accompanied their mission: "Be wise as serpents and gentle as doves."[6] They were being sent "like sheep into the midst of wolves."[7] But here, too, we must be careful. In Matthew's text, there is animosity awaiting the disciples—in the synagogues as well as with "governors and kings."[8] Biblical scholarship alerts us that Matthew's wording reflects a situation sometime after Jesus, one in which there was competitive hostility between synagogue leaders and the sect constituted by Jesus' followers. Embedded in this story is a record of the relationship between Jews and Christians sometime near the end of the first century of the common era, as well as the message Jesus' followers were to proclaim to their Jewish siblings. In our post-Shoah context, we must read Matthew with critical eyes and resist the supersessionist temptation while remaining attentive to the heart of the matter: the wise and cautious practice of hospitality, even in the face of resistance and violence.[9]

Our task, like theirs, is to go out into our own world seeking hospitality at the same time we embody it. When we find it, we are to announce its presence and proclaim its significance, recognizing that in hospitality the rule and realm of God breaks forth in the world. In the gestalt of hospitality we meet the promise of creation breaking forth in respectful encounter with the other. Because it happened before, it can

---

[5]The meaning here is not based on merit. Rather, it seeks to express the reciprocal relationship between the good news the disciples were sent to proclaim and the life of hospitality that expressed the very reality they sought to proclaim. Hence, when they encountered those who practiced hospitality, they were blessed with the same reality they were sent to practice and spread.

[6]Matthew 10:16.

[7]Ibid.

[8]Matthew 10:18.

[9]See my *Confessing Christ in a Post-Holocaust World: A Midrashic Experiment* (Westport CT: Greenwood Press, 2000) esp. chap. 2.

happen again. Because it happened even in the Shoah, it can happen anywhere, anytime.[10] This is, indeed, good news.

Practicing Hospitality. If we are to seek hospitality in the spirit of Jesus, we must not overlook that Jesus sent his disciples to heal when he sent them in search of hospitality's welcome embrace (Matthew 10:1, 8). While we, with our modern temperament, may be uncomfortable with this linkage, it was not accidental for Jesus. After Auschwitz, knowing what we know about the importance of hospitality, that linkage and its essential bonds with hospitality may be even clearer.

From our vantage point we know that hospitality heals. Its practice serves life and restores life to a greater—though still wounded—wholeness. Whenever and wherever it is truly (and radically) practiced, the intention for creation is fulfilled. Or to use the language of Matthew's Jesus, the rule and realm of heaven has drawn near.

With this in mind, we may read Matthew 10 with new insight. The disciples were sent to heal (that is, to practice hospitality) and proclaim the good news of God's rule and realm—when, and only when, they were welcomed by hospitality. They were to announce the very gift that they encountered being offered to them, even as they were to offer it to those they met, deepening and extending its embrace as they announced it to be the good news that it was and is. They were to practice what they sought—hospitality—and to proclaim its significance as the rule and realm of heaven configured in their midst.

---

[10]Emil Fackenheim makes the point with poignant clarity in his analysis of the ontological and moral imperative that, if there was to be any continuing claim for Jews to seek the mending of the world in the present, there must have been a single act of Jewish *Tikkun* (mending of the life) that occurred during the rupture of reality that the Shoah embodied. As Fackenheim made equally clear, this same logic applies to Christian self-understanding as well: "*Has the Good Friday, then, overwhelmed the Easter? Is the Good News of the Overcoming itself overcome?*" (italics in the original). Because there were acts, such as the public prayers of Bernhard Lichtenberg on behalf of Jews, Fackenheim could say, "It is rather that in a world in which *nothing* is well, *all* was happening, a terrible Good Friday was every day overwhelming the old Easter, *Lichtenberg's prayer was actual, and therefore, possible.* The Good News is in the prayer itself, and in the Holy Spirit that dwells in it. This *Tikkun* is the *Boden* on which Christian theology can undertake the 'destructive recovery' of the Christian Scriptures, of the Christian tradition, of the Christian faith. It is the rock on which Christian faith can rebuild the broken church." Emil L. Fackenheim, *To Mend the World: Foundations of Future Jewish Thought* (New York: Schocken, 1982) 286, 292-93.

In other words, the practice of hospitality in an inhospitable world offers healing to those who provide it as well as to those who receive it. This is good news; but still, healing is not automatic. It does not occur simply if hospitality is practiced. Likewise, healing is not an act of magic, even though the two are often confused. Rather, healing is the restoration of health and wholeness to unhealthy and broken lives. Healing reestablishes fractured ties between others and within communities. Healing binds our wounds in often unexpected, but nonetheless needed, ways. Often mediated by human touch, healing reconnects isolated individuals and communities with the resources from which they draw meaning and support. However, in a time like ours where human touch can express unwelcome intrusion and violence, we must be alert to the boundaries of otherness that true healing respects.

Hospitality heals when it restores alienated and marginalized others to community. It bestows respect when the regard of one recognizes the infinite value and work of another. Hospitality opens up closed worlds when boundaries of community and care are extended to include others who stand at or just beyond their thresholds. Hospitality mends broken relationships and shattered communities when wounded souls meet in the acknowledgment of fragile ties that bind them together, even in their pain.

Hospitality heals both guest and host when it binds them in a larger gestalt of care and wholeness. It connects guest and host at the thresholds of their worlds, asking each to be open to the other and to grow in turn. In a broken world, hospitality heals when it is practiced by vulnerable hosts and extended to wounded guests. It even brings healing to wounded hosts when they risk opening their lives and exposing their wounds to and for the sake of others.

In this way we see the healing promise of hospitality at work in the lives of its hosts as well as its guests. Those who extend hospitality break open their closed lives as they welcome others into their domain and care. Those who are embraced as guests are reconnected to life and others similarly embraced. When either of them participates in hospitality with those others who stand at the margins of their worlds of meaning and care, their shared worlds are made larger as their boundaries extend outward, like an expanding ellipse, from the hospitality provided by its participating host(s) and guest(s). As the spirit of hospitality grows in our lives, our worlds expand. This is the dynamic of creation itself, taken into our living with others. When hospitality takes place, the cup of life overflows. And this is good news.

At the same time, the inward movement of hospitality leads to the enlargement of one's inner resources. As otherness is taken in, embraced, and integrated into one's heart and soul, we grow in our capacities to meet and regard others with respect and care. That is, genuine outward expressions of hospitality to others are tied to an inner hospitality of soul. True intercession for the world requires making room in one's inner life for the other—and for God as the Other—in a progressive and steadfast manner. When prayer is viewed as the hospitality of the soul, it can be seen as the disciplined opening of one's inmost landscape to the Other who is the Host of creation. In an age of spiritual suspicion, this is good news for the wounded soul.

Confessing Hospitality. To be sure, we have good news to share; but it is deeply chastened news as well. It is good because if hospitality happened in the Shoah, there is no time when it cannot happen. If it happened in the camps, even if only once, its occurrence there declares that there is no place where the promise of creation cannot be honored.[11] However, this news is chastened because more often than not, hospitality did not take place during the Holocaust. Furthermore, the news is deeply wounded news because the countertestimony of the Shoah declares that even faithful people will not make room for the other in their lives. Some will radically deny the other a place in the world. And some will even actively oppose the other's very right to life. Consequently, confessing this good news in the shadows of betrayal and terror requires facing up to our complicity and the radical absence of hospitality our complicity supports and fosters. In other words, the integrity of our good news depends upon the honesty we bring to facing up to this dark night of our history.[12]

Facing the shame of our inhospitality also requires our facing up to the hostility in our received identities, narrated in the stories we tell about ourselves in scripture and tradition. We must recognize that there is contempt in our narrated identity directed toward otherness *per se* and

---

[11]Fackenheim's argument is essential here. When we look at the camps, we are faced with the walking dead, the *Muselmänner*. Only if there were those who did not succumb to the world they symbolized can we speak of healing (*tikkun*). Moreover, that healing, if it bespeaks the restoration of Jewish-Christian trust, must have been initiated from the Gentile side. See Fackenheim, *To Mend the World*, 306-307.

[12]See my article, "From Shame to Responsibility and Christian Identity: The Dynamics of Shame and Christian Confession Regarding the Shoah," *Journal of Ecumenical Studies* (Winter 1998): 41-62.

the otherness of our significant others, Jews. That is, in our narrated identity there is no room provided for Jews to be affirmed as Jews. They are discounted as Jews and even called upon to renounce their identity as Jews so that they may accept the good news of being free of its halachic obligations.

In this context, the good news of hospitality is announced when and where appropriate as a confessional witness to the significance of the occurring hospitality. Importantly, its proclamation is double-edged. It is rightly *confessed* as a declaration of the promise of hospitality for life as well as a penitential acknowledgment of our failure to be hospitable people. It is an invitation to participate in the grace of hospitality at the same time it is a summons to change. Likewise, it is a confession of need at the same time it is a declaration of will to resist the exclusion and violence among us and around us.

Furthermore, such a confession grounds Christian identity outside itself in the larger, including reality it identifies as the rule and realm of God, the purpose of creation which we as Christians have encountered in Christ—and in every one who welcomes the other as other. It also calls forth a companion moral imperative rooted in the knowledge of what is truly at stake in our relations to others. And it does so in a chastened, even ironic voice. In other words, it may no longer be appropriate to make this announcement in the same key as before. The triumphant proclamations of G major may need to be revoiced in the sober chords of E minor. The fanfare of trumpets may need to be muted by sensitive hands in recognition of other instruments otherwise drowned out.

This does not mean that there cannot be bold celebrations of life in the full and extraordinary scope of humankind's repertoire of symphony and song. But it does mean that the context and pairing of theme and purpose will require a more delicate and nuanced composition than we have exercised before, at least in the realm of human relations to the sacred and each other. How we bear our witness will make all the difference in whether or not our professions of faith are truly confessional acts of hospitality.

Facing the Sacred—Facing the Other. In recognizing the significance of hospitality, we must draw another distinction. Hospitality to others is not necessarily identical to hospitality to the Other. Nonetheless, the two are intimately related. As John Koenig indicates in his study of New Testament hospitality, hospitality to others is "a catalyst to the partner-

ship of the gospel."[13] By partnership of the gospel, he means the covenantal partnership of life in which God and all others are welcomed in
right relationship with each other. When one makes room for the other
in his or her life, or when a community makes room for others in its
world of relationships, the rule and realm of God are near. This gestalt
of hospitality places us before the One who is Other and embraces all life
in hospitality. And the One who chooses otherness in the ongoing work
of creation is set apart by our being other to this One.

Lest we misread the import of these relationships, we might ponder
the essential connection between otherness, the other/Other, and the
meaning of our term *holy*. In Hebrew, the word we render as *holy* is
qadosh. The word itself designates the quality of being set apart, hallowed,
wholly Other, majestic, and pure. In other words, otherness partakes of
the very nature of the holy. In fact, in Hebrew the word to designate
holiness or sacredness also means apartness.[14] The connections between
hospitality and the holy are significant, perhaps essential. Consequently,
we remind ourselves that the One who elects otherness in the decision
and act of creation is the One before whom we stand in our otherness,
addressed by One who always remains Other to us. In the radical
hospitality of creation, every other is called into presence before this life-
giving Other.

It is no accident that the primary Christian prayer of thanksgiving,
the great thanksgiving of the Eucharist, includes a sung or recited "Holy,
Holy, Holy Lord. . . . " The song is derived from the sixth chapter of
Isaiah, which reports the call of Isaiah and recounts Isaiah's visionary
moment before the throne of God as he overhears the heavenly chorus of
qadosh, qadosh, qadosh—Holy, Holy, Holy. In the presence of God, Isaiah
confronts the majestic otherness of the creator and ruler of life. At the
same time, he realizes he is summoned by precisely this same One who
is Other to him and before whom he is wholly other as well. Furthermore, he recognizes that this selfsame One who has welcomed him as his
host has also chosen him to speak on this One's behalf to others. In the
face of otherness, therefore, we are invited to glimpse the One who
welcomes us, and like those Isaiah heard, we dare to declare: *Holy, Holy,*

---

[13]John Koenig, *New Testament Hospitality: Partnership with Strangers as Promise
and Mission* (Philadelphia: Fortress Press, 1985) 10. He goes on to explain that,
throughout the Gospel of Luke, hospitality constitutes the contours of the
inbreaking rule and realm of God that Jesus seeks, serves, and embodies.

[14]For a detailed analysis, see *The New Brown-Driver-Briggs-Gesenius Hebrew-
English Lexicon* (Peabody MA: Hendrickson Publishers, 1979) 871.

Holy. But in addition to encountering the awe-evoking otherness of God, we are invited to hear the more silent voice of the Other whose otherness also hospitably declares: "Here I am and I have made room for you." That is, the voices of Abraham Joshua Heschel and Rudolf Otto can meet in hospitality; and after the Shoah, even in the *Tremendum* of their violation[15] as well as in the grace of their confirmation.

The Life of Hospitality

Hospitality begins in the recognition of the other and in making room for the other's presence. Consequently, the linkage between otherness and the sacred is the threshold of standing before the Other who grants us room to be. This is not a broad, open-door policy to relativism; boundaries still matter. But inclusion within them is given to the other in whose presence hospitality is practiced. Whether or not the other accepts the invitation to dwell with his or her inviting other depends upon the invited one. Hospitality is not complete until the guest dwells with the host as guest and accepts the responsibilities that accompany the proffered place in their host's world. Furthermore, hospitality is not fully embodied unless those who have been guests extend to others the hospitality they have known. The good news of hospitality includes a summoning dialectic regarding the other in one's life, which is an essential facet of the life of hospitality. Whether one is welcomed as guest or welcoming another as his or her host, hospitality unfolds as one makes room for the other in one's life. The dynamics are similar to those grasped by John Calvin and, in different and more problematic ways, by Martin Luther as the dialectic of Law and Gospel. However, the privatized restriction of that dialectic's activity and its pejorative linkages with supersessionist logic bled into their theological insights and still renders suspect the framing of this dialectic as one of Law and Gospel. Nonetheless, the essential linkages they sought to express—between the good news of God's choice to embrace the other in hospitality and the summons to practice hospitality ourselves—are right. That is, it is not the good news of Christianity and the Law of Israel, but the good news of God's love and the obligation to others such love calls forth. As Calvin

---

[15]I have in mind the work of Arthur Cohen, *The Tremendum: A Theological Interpretation of the Holocaust* (New York: Continuum, 1993) and in "In Our Terrible Age: The *Tremendum* of the Jews," in Elisabeth Schüssler Fiorenza and David Tracy, eds., *The Holocaust as Interruption* (Edinburgh: T.&T. Clark, 1984) 11-16.

saw and expressed in this relationship in his "third use of the Law,"[16] the problem lies in sundering the dialectical bond that exists between the good news of hospitality and its summons to live out its obligations. In other words, Christianity may rightfully speak of its good news only when it also speaks of its accountability to live hospitably with others. After Auschwitz, however, we must be more forthright: as post-Shoah Christians, we must learn to speak of our good news while recognizing that Jews may speak of theirs in similar fashion. That is, the good news that we claim to know confessionally by grace is not ours to grant or possess. Rather, it is ours to accept and to embody—confessionally—and to recognize in others as they dwell in it and, in turn, offer it to others.

Not surprisingly, this dialectic expresses itself in a number of ways. Hospitality's confirming embrace of inclusion and care calls forth reciprocal expressions of care for others in an expansive spirit of engagement with the world. Similarly, hospitality holds a taste of life which, as it overflows with respect and mutual regard, participates in a reality that is yet to be sustained or shared beyond the extraordinary moments in which it occurs. As such, these moments are manifestations of the promise borne by creation. That is, they are foretastes, threshold moments, of a reality yet to come. If the emphasis is temporal, the dialectic focuses on the quality of a day not yet come but glimpsed in the threshold moments of its dawning. If the emphasis is spatial, the dialectic focuses on places in which life manifests itself in the momentary fulfillment of its promise at the same time it identifies places where that promise is absent—even if, and when, they are the same place. Note, too, that as we focus on the temporal, our expression unfolds spatially. This is also the case for spatial emphases. They are expressed in a temporal dialectic as well. Each requires the other.

With the lens of hospitality, we add another dimension that we are able to express in the relationship of host and guest, demonstrating the dynamics of self and other which unfold in essential ways *in* their dynamics. Hospitality requires a host as well as a guest, each recognizing the other as one who knows how to be a guest of another's hospitality. Thus, each participates in the life of hospitality that unfolds *around* them. As we learn to appreciate these dynamics, we recognize the interdependency of hospitality's aspects. A good guest recognizes not simply the offer of hospitality, but also his or her responsibility to dwell in hospitality as a host as well as a guest within the larger gestalt that is

---

[16]John Calvin, *The Institutes of the Christian Religion*, trans. Henry Beveridge (Grand Rapids MI: Eerdmans: 1972) 1:309-10, 319-22.

mediated by the practice of hospitality—what we have learned to call the rule and realm of heaven. Furthermore, as we recognize that this summoning dialectic is rooted in the very dynamics of creation, we discover that any notion of a Christian mission must participate in creation's larger, more inclusive mission.[17]

Empowered by this dialectic, our task is to recognize the sacred and threshold character of hospitality[18] as we seek it in our relationships with others. And we offer the gift of its including embrace by making room for those we meet as well as making clear our responsibility for extending it to others. When and as hospitality takes place, we identify its significance as *we honor it for what it is*. That is, we are always participants in this gestalt as guests—even as we act as hosts and extend our hospitality to others. Any loss of this perspective alters the gestalt; such loss undoes the hospitality we seek to offer. Our good news must be confessed as guests even when, as hosts, we are welcoming others.[19]

After Auschwitz, the good news is that this possibility remains. Indeed, it remains as an urgent summons to change and to enjoy new life as well. Not simply individuals, but peoples throughout the world must face the problem of the other and otherness, face the other and the issue of otherness in themselves, and thereby help their world become a new place. This is the summons to life that hospitality mediates. In Jesus, Christians face that summons anew, especially as they come to terms with the recognition that this one who embraces and includes them is a *bar mitzvah* (son of [the] Law) even as he is the *ben adam* (son of man). Furthermore, they discover, in the deeds of hospitality risked during the Shoah as well as in those moments of hospitality in their own dealings

---

[17]Douglas John Hall's *The Stewardship of Life in the Kingdom of Death* (New York: Friendship Press, 1985) is instructive in this regard. See also his later volume, *Confessing the Faith: Christian Theology in a North American Context* (Minneapolis: Fortress Press, 1996) 143-97.

[18]R. Kendall Soulen does a superb job of uncovering the structural dimensions of supersessionism in Christocentric theology in his *The God of Israel and Christian Theology* (Minneapolis: Fortress Press, 1996). As an alternative, he offers a theology of creation which sees in the presence of the other the unfolding promise of creation. Hospitality marks its threshold. He writes, "Each member of the human family finds himself or herself 'always already' a Jew or a Gentile and in this way confronted in one way or another by the offer and invitation of the blessing of an other" (40).

[19]As Koenig points out in his study of hospitality, conversion to God's way with creation is, therefore, not to Christianity but to God's way with life. *New Testament Hospitality*, 85-120, esp. 103-106.

with others, the dawning presence of God's intention for all life, the *rule and realm of heaven*. In the gestalt of hospitality, the rule and realm of heaven is tangibly present in our midst.

The good news, chastened by our own inhospitality to others, is that even in a post-Holocaust world, hospitality is possible, for at times hospitality happened during the Holocaust. It happened even there. Even then. Because it happened, even if only once, hospitality is a real possibility for life. It is not simply a pipe dream. More important, hospitality is the gift of life for persons trapped in an inhospitable world. In some cases, it was lifesaving then, and it still is. That is, hospitality is good news in troubled times, and lifesaving in radically inhospitable ones. And the call for hospitality becomes an urgent summons for redemptive action in the face of evil.

After Auschwitz, hospitality to the other takes on increased significance. Simple actions take on added meaning when we remember that creation is at stake in every interaction with the other—literally as well as figuratively. Minor moments of disdain point to the evil that lurks in the shadows ahead. Every other reminds us of our place in life. The good news of hospitality places our interactions with others in different light. Even in the aftermath of the Shoah, hospitality bears the promise of healing to a world torn asunder by our inhospitality to others. In this way, hospitality bears the redemptive promise of a renewed creation, one set back on course through a divine commitment to the abundant unfolding of life in the richness of its otherness. In other words, when hospitality happens, creation is fulfilled, at least in the momentary part we are blessed to see.

The Promise and Risk of Hospitality

We cannot forget that hospitality is a vulnerable reality. To be sure, it has always been so. However, in the aftermath of the Shoah, we must acknowledge, with significant trepidation, the risk of radical hospitality, for in embracing the other who rejects the other, one may risk death, even participate in annihilation. Including all others indiscriminately can lead to a diminishment of hospitality, especially when large numbers of those so included, exclude and give exclusion increased power and presence. This was fearfully clear in the case of Nazi Germany. Consequently, we are driven back to Jesus' admonition to his disciples when he sent them forth to look for hospitality. They were commissioned to look for places where they would be welcome as guests.[20] As guests, they were then charged to proclaim their good news, the significance of their host's action and the inbreaking of God's ways in their midst. Embracing the rejecting other was reserved for other times and other places. In the case of a rejecting, imperial power, the rejection risked in that situation was a one-time, life or death affair, no matter how much the dynamic of radical inclusion informed the overall movement toward that occasion.

After Auschwitz, we must be careful not to confuse the radical hospitality of Jesus with the indiscriminate embrace of any other. This recognition places us, as it were, between the admonition of Jesus to search for hospitality with caution (Matthew 10 and parallels) while honoring the apostle Paul's proclamation that we must embrace the risk of hospitality, as Jesus did, if we are truly going to follow him. On the other side of innocence, we must live in and work with this tension. After the Shoah, those who follow this path must do so with caution, fully aware of what is at stake at the same time that they recognize this tension to be part of the very shape of God's way with creation.

Surely the way of the cross can mean nothing less than embodying the life of hospitality in inhospitable times and places while facing inhospitable others. For those sheltered during stormy times, such action remains good news indeed. Still, the risk of hospitality is complicated as well as intensified by the Shoah. Too easily, hospitality can be used in the service of violent ends, in spite of noble goals. The Shoah has demonstrated that, too, in forceful fashion. Hospitality, even radical hospitality that embraces the rejecting other, must be carefully, if not cautiously, expressed. It must always, and at times, be cautiously guided by the intentionality of creation, the goal of life unfolding in abundance, which is the end toward which the risk of the cross is oriented. Concisely stated, any responsible, post-Holocaust theology of the cross is self-consciously and self-critically located within the more encompassing intentionality of creation, oriented by the providential movement of its hospitality to life.

This recognition is of no small moment. As R. Kendall Soulen makes convincingly clear, Christocentric faithfulness, even when supporting positive commitments to Jewish identity, participates in a structural form of supersessionism that fails to take Jewish otherness seriously, not to

---

[20]Drawing on insights from process theology, Clark Williamson develops this theme in his explication of a Christian theology for post-Shoah times. For his interpretation of how the church's life is rooted in the life of Israel, see Williamson, *A Guest in the House of Israel: Post-Holocaust Church Theology* (Louisville: Westminster/John Knox Press, 1993) 40-47.

mention the identities of others outside the covenantal framework of Israel and its fidelity to God.[21] For this reason, Christologies rooted in theological confessions like this one develop representative understandings[22] of the reality brought to expression in and through the life of Jesus. That is, the hospitality manifest in his life and ministry is the hospitality expressed by God from the very beginning and the promise borne by creation as its abiding possibility. Jesus re-presents this divine wager in his life and ministry, even in the face of abandonment, rejection, and death. He is the representative one, host and guest, in whom and through whom we find ourselves included in the hospitality that is God's way with the world.

The Providence of Hospitality

If hospitality is the way of God with the world, the manner of God's engagement with creation is neither control nor indifference, nor even interference, but that of making room for life to unfold in its manifold otherness. The good news is that the evil of the Shoah is not blessed with or by divine intention, for it is the very denial of hospitality to the other. Nonetheless, it is given place in the very embrace of otherness that is the divine choice for life. That is, in hospitality to every other and form of otherness, life can and may deny itself—at the human and any other level. And yet, in order that life may bear good fruit, the denial of hospitality must be resisted by any who dares enter into partnership with this divine choice for life. In this way, the providence of hospitality places the matter of human freedom in a larger, yet distinctly oriented framework. Such a framework, however, does not provide an explanation for evil, even though it does recognize that the full embrace of otherness must extend even to the other who, or that,[23] rejects otherness in any and every form. In other words, from the beginning creation has been a radical risk embraced by God in the pursuit of life, with God making room for its unfolding otherness. To participate in that hospitality is to participate in the life of God's choosing. To participate in that hospitality is to know the grace and, with it, the risk of creation. To participate in that hospitality is to share the risk of making room for others in one's

---

[21]See Soulen, *The God of Israel and Christian Theology*, esp. 1-21 and 81-106.

[22]See my treatment of this point in *Confessing Christ in a Post-Holocaust World*.

[23]At the cellular level, cancer gives expression to the same dynamic—likewise, other forms of bacterial and viral life forms. Surely, whatever we posit as the providential dynamic guiding all creation should be true at all levels of life.

own life. To participate in that hospitality is to know both the promise and urgency of that task, knowing that in every act of hospitality creation and its promise of life are at stake. To participate in that hospitality is to taste the fruit of creation's promise and to know its good news.

Hospitality, so understood, is not a means to something else, although it is a threshold invitation to something more. In hospitality we encounter the blessing and the promise of creation, radically open and vulnerable to its own rejection. In this way, hospitality is its own end, which in being proclaimed can be embraced for what it is: the holy ground on which we stand as guests in the presence of a welcoming other/Other. When hospitality is truly practiced, we make room for the presence of the other/Other in our own lives and identities as well as in our encounters in the world around us. In this fashion, there is room for the creator and every creature to be present, each to the other on this sacred terrain.

A fundamental paradox stares us in the face, daring those who confront it to embrace it boldly, albeit with deep and abiding humility: *the rejection and absence of hospitality is possible only in the presence of radical hospitality.* The good news of hospitality is the good news that has been the promise of creation from the beginning. But it is borne with great risk and in radical vulnerability. Even so, the good news of hospitality is not an explanation of the vexing question of why innocent people must suffer at the hands of unloving/inhospitable others. Even in the freedom of hospitality, we are left with that unyielding mystery. Nonetheless, it is a joining of the question with a larger framework that deepens the anguish by placing it within the lament of God. No matter how deep our grief over the violence that stalks our lives, the One who remains the faithful host of life knows a grief we cannot fathom.

The providence of hospitality does not answer the question of evil, nor diminish our anguish as we face it and face up to our complicities in it. We remain vulnerable. However, as a prism for understanding the providence of God, hospitality does provide a distinctive context for viewing the freedom that we as human beings have to do good and evil. Moreover, the providence of hospitality neither removes nor diminishes the anguish we feel in the presence of evil or of freedom turned against life; instead, our anguish is joined by divine anguish. As a result, our anguish is relativized, like Job's, in the face of the creator's, who has borne the loss and anguish of all creation, not simply the part we know. Still, such a view of divine providence does not frame an answer to the question of evil. Nor, in particular, does it offer an explanation for the Shoah. Rather, it provides a paradoxical affirmation of divine fidelity to life, lived with the confident hope that death has not and will not have the final word.

Furthermore, the lens of hospitality provides a way to conceive of God that, while it retains the agency and ongoing activity of God, also insists on the responsible partnership of human beings in the unfolding of providential care. In this perspective, God is the Hospitable One in whom we dwell in freedom to choose our place in the unfolding dynamic of creation. God remains active, as host, making room for our presence and setting the table of life for our delight. As well, God dwells in our midst, as guest, as we make room for God's presence to share and delight in what we provide. In this way, the creating, sustaining, and redeeming qualities of divinity are manifest in hospitality as we take our place in the covenantal partnerships that serve creation. Their interpenetrating qualities, of course, suggest insights associated with traditional understandings of the Trinity. But in the context of hospitality they do not require doctrinal elaboration. We need only affirm that these essential relational qualities also participate in the paradoxical character and summoning dialectics of hospitality. In other words, the creating, sustaining, and redeeming activity of God that finds its fulfillment in the partnership each offers the other/Other in the life of hospitality is the ongoing and unfinished work of creation.[24]

An Unfinished Wager—The Venture of Creation

The good news that hospitality happened in spite of its widespread absence during the Holocaust carries with it an abiding summons to remain hospitable and to increase its presence and practice in all the domains in which we reside. That is, hospitality is not simply the good news of and for post-Shoah faithfulness; it is also the prophetic summons to repent and change, at the level of behavior as well as in the ways we understand ourselves vis-à-vis the significant others in our lives. The good news of hospitality is accompanied by an ethical summons that is fundamental to life[25] and dialectically essential to the identities we bear,

---

[24]Conceptually this is also good news. Such a perspective offers persons of faith a way of conceiving of divine engagement with history that is able to move beyond notions of divine intervention and rescue that are made problematic, if not untenable, by the Shoah.

[25]Emmanuel Levinas argues that the fundamental character of this revelation is captured in the summoning presence of the other mediated by the human face; indeed, he contends that this reality is the foundation of ethics. See Emmanuel Levinas, *The Levinas Reader*, ed. Sean Hand (Oxford: Basil Blackwell, 1989) 72-86.

even when those identities betray that very same demand. Moreover, as this good news reflects the divine mission of creation itself, it calls forth a life lived in fidelity to the other/Other. The task of faithful discipleship is to join in extending the mission of creation as followers of one who represented that mission. In this way, Christians may honor their calling as disciples of Jesus without having to disregard the identity of the others whom they embrace in hospitality. Instead, they can reach out to the other, as other, in an unfettered expression of hospitality. Moreover, they can join in partnership with others in hosting an even larger circle of otherness, extending the reach of hospitality further. After Auschwitz, this possibility is good—though chastened—news at the same time that it brings an urgent summons to choose life in the unfinished wager and venture of creation.

Chapter 9

What Can a Christian Say about Forgiveness after Auschwitz?

Carol Rittner

No statement, theological or otherwise, should be made that would not be credible in the presence of burning children.
—Rabbi Irving Greenberg[1]

The Holocaust and the Christian. There is something obscenely incongruous about the juxtaposition of these two phrases. How can they exist together? When I say "Christian," I think of goodness, love, understanding, acceptance, respect, graciousness, friendship, forgiveness, generosity unto death—everything that for me exemplifies that *extraordinary* Jewishman Jesus whom I accept as the Christ of God. But when I say "Holocaust," I think of evil, terror, horror, absurdity, absolute obedience, absence of self doubt, godlessness—everything that for me exemplifies a descent into a terrifying human and spiritual abyss that contradicts entirely my understanding of "Christian." And yet, I have to face the fact that the Holocaust—Nazi Germany's planned total destruction of the Jewish people and the murder of nearly six million of them in the heart of "Christian" Europe—was carried out by human beings like myself, almost all of whom were baptized Christians. This is no small matter for me, a believing, professing Christian who has struggled for nearly twenty-five years with this obscenely incongruous juxtaposition and with the profound challenge it poses to my Christian faith.

Knowing what I know about Christians during the Holocaust—that most were not "victims" of the Nazis—at least not in the same way Jews were, hunted to their death all over occupied Europe; that during the Holocaust most Christians failed to live out Jesus' "Great Command-

---

[1]Irving Greenberg, "Cloud of Smoke, Pillar of Fire: Judaism, Christianity, and Modernity after the Holocaust," in *Auschwitz: Beginning of a New Era?*, ed. Eva Fleischner (New York: KTAV, 1977) 23.

ment" of "love of God and love of neighbor"; and that during the Holocaust the overall record of Christians was anything but stellar when it came to helping Jews, I hesitate to raise the issue of forgiveness after Auschwitz, and yet, I must. Why? Because whenever Christians and Jews confront the reality of the Holocaust, they find themselves on the boundaries of forgiveness; because forgiveness occupies a pivotal place in both our traditions and is central to Christian identity; and because I am confounded by something Elie Wiesel said in January 1995 at a ceremony commemorating the fiftieth anniversary of the liberation of Auschwitz-Birkenau.

Many Christians exhibit a remarkable resistance to reflecting on and even learning about the Holocaust. I have, for example, heard Christians say such things as, "What's the matter with those Jews? Why do they keep harping on the Holocaust? Don't they know that other people also suffered under the Nazis? Why can't Jews move on? Why do they keep talking about what Christians did, and didn't do, during the Holocaust? Why can't they just forgive and get on with it?" Such questions put the onus on the victims—Jews—and make it easy for the perpetrators—Christians—to avoid acknowledging that the ideological parents of Nazi antisemitism were Christian anti-Judaism and Western philosophy, both of which marginalized and even demonized Jews and Judaism for nearly two thousand years. Such questions also impact on discussion about the Holocaust and often come to the fore when Jews and Christians discuss Simon Wiesenthal's book, *The Sunflower*, which deals with the question of whether one person can forgive another for what was done to someone else.[2]

The Sunflower is the story of a Jew named Simon, probably Wiesenthal himself, forced to listen to the "confession" of a dying SS man named Karl, baptized at birth as a Roman Catholic Christian. Karl is consumed by guilt and longs "to beg forgiveness" from a Jew—*any Jew*—before he dies. ("I do not know who you are, I only know that you are a Jew and that is enough."[3]) Karl wants to tell all, "to come clean" about atrocities he committed while serving with his SS unit on the Russian front. Simon is horrified by what the dying man tells him, but he recognizes that Karl is remorseful. ("In his confession there was true repentance, even though he did not admit it in so many words. Nor was it necessary, for the way

---

[2]Simon Wiesenthal, *The Sunflower: On the Possibilities and Limits of Forgiveness*, 2nd ed. (New York: Schocken, 1997).

[3]Ibid., 54.

he spoke and the fact that he spoke to *me* was a proof of his repentance."[4]) What Karl wants before he dies is "forgiveness." ("I know that what I have told you is terrible. In the long nights while I have been waiting for death, time and again I have longed to talk about it to a Jew and beg forgiveness from him."[5]) But Simon cannot bring himself to say anything, neither a word of condemnation nor a word of consolation, much less a word of forgiveness. ("At last I made up my mind and without a word I left the room."[6])

The burden of the encounter with Karl haunts Simon. Perhaps he should have said *something* to the dying man. At first, Simon says nothing, then he talks about it endlessly, for days and weeks, even up to two years after the incident happened. He asks some of his friends—prisoners like himself—what they would have done had they had been in his place. Predictably, they are divided. Josek, for example, a Jew, tells Simon, "You had no right to forgive him, you could not have forgiven him."[7] Bolek, a Polish Catholic seminarian arrested in Warsaw by the Nazis, tells him that the SS man "deserved the mercy of forgiveness."[8] This is an example of what I mean when I say that Christians and Jews find themselves on the boundaries of forgiveness whenever they confront the reality of the Holocaust. One man is willing to forgive Karl, the murderer of Jewish men, women, and children, while the other is unwilling to forgive him.

The two positions represented by Josek ("You had no right to forgive him") and Bolek (he "deserved the mercy of forgiveness") reinforce for many Christians a prevailing negative stereotype about Jews and Judaism that stems from a misreading of both the Jewish and Christian scriptures ("Old" Testament and "New" Testament). That stereotype can be summed up as follows: Jews worship a "God of wrath" who insists on "an eye for an eye, and a tooth for a tooth" (Exodus 21:24), while Christians worship a "God of love" who forgives and insists on unending forgiveness (Matthew 18:22).

Christians need to learn more about Jews and Judaism, just as Jews need to learn more about Christians and Christianity. As David Blumenthal writes, "The spiritual task of interfaith dialogue requires each party to understand what the other teaches, and what the other does not

---

[4]Ibid., 53.
[5]Ibid., 54.
[6]Ibid., 55.
[7]Ibid., 75.
[8]Ibid., 82.

teach."[9] Making the effort to do so could help clear up theological logjams and expose distortions each has about the other. Likewise, it could help Christians and Jews to realize that the boundary of forgiveness they find themselves on when they confront the reality of the Holocaust is not a boundary that separates a "God of wrath" from a "God of love"—that is a false boundary in any case—but a boundary that delineates Jewish and Christian understanding about *what* can be forgiven and *by whom*. To some extent, this is exemplified by the discussion Simon and Bolek have in Mauthausen:

> We talked for a long time, but came to no conclusion. On the contrary, Bolek began to falter in his original opinion that I ought to have forgiven the dying man, and for my part I became less and less certain as to whether I had acted rightly.
>
> Nevertheless the talk was rewarding for both of us. He, a candidate for the Catholic priesthood, and I, a Jew, had exposed our arguments to each other, and each had a better understanding of the other's views.[10]

If Simon Wiesenthal raised the "earthly" question of who can forgive whom for what in *The Sunflower*, Elie Wiesel raised the question about what can be forgiven and by whom to a "heavenly" level when he spoke at a ceremony in Poland on 26 January 1995 commemorating the fiftieth anniversary of the liberation of Auschwitz-Birkenau.

From the beginning, the event was problematic—who had the right to remember the victims of Auschwitz, the overwhelming majority of whom were Jews, and how should they be remembered? Newspapers reported that the ceremonies, organized by President Lech Walesa's Polish government, were plagued by an ugly dispute between Jewish groups and Polish officials over how to appropriately honor the dead. Jean Kahn, president of the European Jewish Congress, said that ninety percent of those who died in Auschwitz were Jews and the ceremonies should reflect that fact. Polish officials said the ceremonies should be ecumenical, reflecting the fact that in addition to Jews, Poles (meaning Polish Catholics), Gypsies, Russian POWs, Jehovah's Witnesses, homosexuals, and others also died at Auschwitz, but Jewish groups protested that the government-sponsored ceremonies did not accurately reflect Jewish deaths in the camp. The World Jewish Congress accused the Polish

---

[9]David R. Blumenthal, "Repentance and Forgiveness," *Cross Currents* (Spring 1998): 75.

[10]Wiesenthal, *The Sunflower*, 83.

government of insensitivity and bungling in planning the two-day com-memoration.[11] It got so heated that Elie Wiesel threatened not to participate unless changes were made in the program. He accused Polish officials of trying "to de-Judaize the tragedy of Auschwitz,"[12] but in the end Wiesel did participate:

> It may seem paradoxical, but if in the end I decided to accept President Walesa's invitation it was precisely because of the con-troversy surrounding this fiftieth anniversary. I convinced myself that I did not have a right to evade the issues. Perhaps in my dual role of Nobel laureate and representative of the American president, and with a little luck, I might succeed in building some kind of consensus.[13]

No such luck! The controversy was so acrimonious that two cere-monies were held, an *official* one, organized by the Polish government, at which Wiesel spoke as the representative of President Bill Clinton, and an *unofficial* one, "entirely Jewish,"[14] organized by the European Jewish Congress,[15] at which Wiesel also spoke. The *unofficial* ceremony, held at Auschwitz-Birkenau during a lunch break of the Polish government's official schedule of events, was where Wiesel told the crowd that the Nazis must not be forgiven and that the genocide symbolized by Auschwitz must never be forgotten. His remarks included a prayer, which he said, "will offend some Christians"[16]:

> Although we know that God is merciful, please God, do not have mercy on those who created this place. God of forgiveness, do not forgive the murderers of Jewish children here. Do not forgive the murderers and their accomplices. . . . God, merciful God, do not have mercy on those who had no mercy on Jewish children.[17]

---

[11]See further the *Washington Post*, 27 January 1995, A1, 21; the *New York Times*, 27 January 1995, A3; and *Christian Century* (22 February 1995): 201-202.

[12]Elie Wiesel, *And the Sea Is Never Full: Memoirs, 1969–* (New York: Alfred A. Knopf, 1999) 195.

[13]Ibid., 196.

[14]Ibid.

[15]*Christian Century* (22 February 1995): 202.

[16]Wiesel, *And The Sea is Never Full*, 194.

[17]Although Wiesel includes a version of this prayer in his memoir, *And the Sea Is Never Full*, 194, I have taken the version I am using from the *New York Times*, 27 January 1995. This version is corroborated by what was reported in the *Washington Post*, 27 January 1995, and also by the excerpt of his speech reprinted

These are very tough words coming from anyone, but from Elie Wiesel, they are tough indeed, even harsh, though perhaps justifiably so. Still, they seem out-of-character for a man who has been described "as a messenger to mankind" who came "from the abyss of the death camps . . . not with a message of hate and revenge but with one of brotherhood and atonement."[18] Wiesel's words at Auschwitz-Birkenau are anything but a message of "brotherhood and atonement." They are angry words, words prayed in the tradition of the imprecatory Psalms. To my Christian ears, they are confounding and challenging at the same time. Confounding, because this man whom I so admire and respect, this "Messenger to All Humanity," as Robert McAfee Brown called him, pleads with God, who is merciful and forgiving, *not to be merciful* and *not to be forgiving*. Challenging, because what Wiesel said sounds to my Christian ears too much like a "message of hate and revenge," and yet, I do not think that is the message he intended to communicate. What, then, is the message Elie Wiesel wanted us—Christians and Jews alike—to hear and to heed?

I think Wiesel wanted us to hear the message that human beings are responsible for their deeds, for what they have done and for what they have failed to do, and that they will be held accountable, if not in this life, then in eternity. This is a message that surely is compatible with Christian belief and understanding about the dignity of the human person. Human beings, for better or worse, are responsible for the deeds they do. They also are responsible for the consequences of their actions. To deny this responsibility is to diminish the significance of all human actions. The passage of time does not rescue a person from the consequences of wrongdoing. If it did, time would, in turn, rob human beings of the credit for the good they have done.[19]

What I hear in Wiesel's words at Auschwitz-Birkenau is a plea to God *not* to allow time to rescue Nazi murderers from the consequences of their actions. He wants God to hold them accountable for eternity. That is how I understand Wiesel's plea to God *not* to forgive murderers of Jewish children and their accomplices, and *not* to "have mercy on

---

in *McLean's* (22 February 1995). The version in Wiesel's memoir appears to be slightly edited from what appeared in the news media almost immediately following his presentation.

[18]Egil Aarvik, "The Nobel Presentation Speech," in *The Nobel Peace Prize 1986, Elie Wiesel* (New York: Summit Books and Boston University Press, 1989) 4-5.

[19]Mary Jo Leddy, NDS, Carol Rittner, RSM, and Eva Fleischner, "The Appearance of Forgiveness, the Reality of Justice" in Mary Jo Leddy, *Say to the Darkness, We Beg to Differ* (Toronto: Lester & Orphen Dennys, 1990) 221-22.

those who had no mercy." While it is a plea that lumps everyone together, whether repentant or not, and while it is a plea that shakes my understanding of what it means to affirm that God is merciful and forgiving—for if God who is merciful will not forgive those who committed such acts, but who may have repented, what hope has the sinner?—it is a plea for God to take us and what we do with our lives seriously, as seriously as we are asked to take God. For many Christians, however, myself included, I think the question Wiesel's prayer raises is whether it is possible to reconcile Wiesel's plea—"please, God . . . do not forgive the murderers of Jewish children"—with Walter Wink's understanding of God as merciful and forgiving:

> We expect evildoers to repent and seek forgiveness. Jesus, however, reversed all that. He declared to an incredulous world that could not finally accept it, that God already forgives us, whether we ask for it or not, whether we like it or not. We can repent, in fact, precisely *because* God has already forgiven us. The gospel declares to us, You are forgiven! Now you can repent! "The kingdom of God has come near; repent, and believe in the good news" (Mark 1:15). It is because God already loves us that we can dare to approach God. God accepts us as we are; the prodigal son's father runs to greet him, and receives him back as son. God, moreover, makes no exceptions; whether we are able to forgive or not, God does, and this applies even to Hitler, Stalin, and Pol Pot.[20]

Wiesel's and Wink's positions draw attention to another of those boundaries of forgiveness on which Christians and Jews find themselves when they confront the reality of the Holocaust. Which comes first? Repentance, or forgiveness? Wink says, "forgiveness," but not Wiesel, who is adamant that those who were not merciful then should not be shown mercy or granted forgiveness—ever.

I confess to straddling this issue: agreeing with Wink one day, and with Wiesel another. When I'm in Wiesel's circle, Wink's position seems triumphalistic, fatuously superficial and glib, all fluff. Yet, when I think about it, pray about it, I remember that God—the God of Abraham, Isaac, Jacob, *and* Jesus—is *always* on the side of human beings, always with *all* God's creation. How did Abraham Joshua Heschel put it? "Man is not

---

[20]Walter Wink, *When the Powers Fall: Reconciliation in the Healing of Nations* (Minneapolis: Fortress Press, 1997) 18. Wink, a Christian, is professor of Biblical Interpretation at Auburn Theological Seminary in New York City.

alone."[21] We are not abandoned; we are not orphaned, even by God's disgust! And, then, through the "fluff" I see the rugged truth of God's faithfulness, and I am pulled toward Wink's position. When I am in the Wink circle, I find Wiesel's position too judgmental to accept, too final, despairing even. To my Christian ears, Wiesel's plea carries echoes of unmendable rips and tears in the fabric of creation—rips and tears, grotesquely horrid though they may be, that I believe God can mend, even if we human beings cannot. The tears and rips in the fabric of creation are grotesquely horrid, and, even if mended, will leave ugly, vivid scars. That's when I sense in Wiesel's plea the simple truth of eternal accountability and the demand that those who perpetrated such evil must not be allowed to evade it—in this life or in the next—and I am drawn back to Wiesel's side. Because all of this was so difficult and confounding for me, I asked Elie Wiesel if I could interview him. In October 1996, more than a year and a half after his January 1995 prayer at Auschwitz-Birkenau, I talked with him.

Rittner: In the Jewish tradition, is there a concept of an unforgivable sin?

Wiesel: The unforgivable sins are those committed between human beings. If I commit a sin against God, God can forgive me, but if I commit a sin against you, it is up to you to forgive me, and I have not heard yet that the six million Jews have issued a pardon. Who can speak on their behalf?

Rittner: Doesn't it constrain God, even "frustrate" God in God's very nature to ask a merciful God *not* to forgive, *not* to have mercy on some people?

Wiesel: I would say to God, please, have mercy on the children, not on their killers. There was no mercy for them then, so why should God have mercy on the killers? Of course, God can and will do what God wants. God is God and, with some trepidation, I would abide by His judgment. But, if I have anything to say for myself, I don't want these murderers to be forgiven.

Rittner: What does it mean to you, as an observant Jew, as a believer, and what does it mean in the Jewish tradition, to speak of God as merciful, as forgiving?

Wiesel: I speak with pain. I want God to be forgiving. I want Him to be a merciful God. There was a Hasidic rebbe, the rebbe of Kotzk, who said that we must address God as "God, our Father" in

---

[21]Abraham Joshua Heschel, *Man is Not Alone: A Philosophy of Religion* (New York: Farrar, Straus and Giroux, 1951).

order to make Him become our Father. In the same way, I hope we go on saying, "God be merciful" so that He will become merciful, but first of all God must be merciful toward the victims. That's the main issue. And if I have my problems with God, if I protest against God, it is because during the Holocaust so many victims were not objects of mercy, neither human mercy nor divine mercy.

Rittner: Robert McAfee Brown, a friend and admirer of yours, writes that "the Holocaust raises the possibility that forgiveness is a weak virtue that encourages the repetition of wrongdoing rather than the amendment of life." Consequently, he argues, Christians need to struggle with the second part of the exhortation, "Never forget—Never forgive!" Help me, a Christian, to understand the exhortation, "Never forgive!"

Wiesel: As always, I agree with Bob Brown. We are so close that we think alike, and we feel alike. We simply feel that either we decide that the Holocaust was a unique crime, or we declare that it was a crime like many others, and, therefore, there was nothing unique about it. I believe it was a unique event, a unique crime, a unique murder. Therefore, all the principles that governed religious compassion *before* the Holocaust do not apply when it comes to the murderers of children *during* the Holocaust. That's what he meant. That's what I mean. In this case, all the compassion which I am for—and I am always for it—should not apply to the murderers.

Rittner: In his book, *Elie Wiesel: Messenger to All Humanity*, Brown wrote, "And yet, if there is not a resource of forgiveness, of mercy, of grace—human or divine, human and divine—we are caught in a web of guilt that finally destroys us all." Isn't it dangerous to ask God *not* to forgive?

Wiesel: I am asking God not to forgive the murderers. I pray God not to forgive them. And I hope He hasn't done so. Remember one thing: I believe the question is really the wrong question, because forgiveness, even if it is permitted in certain cases, presupposes an admission of guilt, contrition, and remorse. I have not seen the killers express remorse or contrition, much less guilt, so why is this question even being raised?

Rittner: What message did you want to convey at Auschwitz-Birkenau in January 1995?

<u>Wiesel</u>: My message was one of compassion for the victims. My message was to say that I believe the victims deserve a special compassion, just as the murderers deserve a special punishment.[22]

Is despair, then, the last word? No, I do not think so. I believe God's last word about human history will not be a word of condemnation or anger but a word of mercy and liberation. This is what provides the basis for lasting hope.[23] I even think Wiesel might agree with me on that, but, to be honest, I don't know. What I do know is that I want to make sense of his prayer at Auschwitz-Birkenau in January 1995, and I want to do so in a way that is faithful to my own religious tradition, but that challenges me to think again about what I believe. Likewise, I want to do so in a way that does not allow me to evade the difficult questions, for if there is anything I have learned from Elie Wiesel, it is that questions are more important than answers. Questions are fundamental, and "questions—especially religious ones . . . deserve lasting priority because they invite continuing inquiry, further dialogue . . . and openness."[24] Religious questions are important questions. Questions about forgiveness and mercy fall into the category "religious," and because they are "important" we have to face the possibility that there may not be any satisfactory answers, only more questions. Indeed, the questions may well remain questions,[25] articulated but, ultimately, unanswerable.

Why did Elie Wiesel use the language of prayer to convey what he wanted to say about mercy and forgiveness? I think he did so because he was profoundly angry, perhaps more angry than he had ever allowed himself to be, and I think he wanted to communicate his profound pain and anger to God, as well as to human beings. (Miroslav Volf says that

---

[22]I interviewed Elie Wiesel in New York City in early October 1996. I faxed him a copy of my transcription on 16 October 1996. Unlike other interviews I have done with him, Wiesel did not respond with any clarifications or comments. The excerpts from that interview are as I transcribed and edited them from the taped interview, which is still in my possession. Subsequently, after finishing this essay and as a courtesy, I faxed Wiesel a copy of my essay. On 6 July 2000, he faxed two pages back to me with a few "corrections," which I have incorporated into the text of my interview with him.

[23]Edward Schillebeeckx, *God Is New Each Moment* (New York: Seabury Press, 1983) 51.

[24]John K. Roth, *Private Needs, Public Selves: Talk about Religion in America* (Urbana: University of Illinois Press, 1997) 206.

[25]Elie Wiesel, "Telling the Tale," in *Against Silence: The Voice and Vision of Elie Wiesel*, 3 vols., ed. Irving Abrahamson (New York: Holocaust Library, 1985) 1:234.

"Deep within the heart of every victim, anger swells up against the perpetrator, rage inflamed by unredeemed suffering."[26]) I think Wiesel wanted to make clear to everyone who heard—or read—his words, God and human beings alike, that "an admission of guilt, contrition, and remorse" is the prerequisite for forgiveness, human or divine, human and divine. And, finally, I think Wiesel also wanted to counter the human propensity for *certainty*—*certainty* about what can be forgiven and by whom, what can be forgiven and when.

In the shadow of the chimneys of Auschwitz-Birkenau, and in the twilight of a century of genocide, I think Elie Wiesel wanted to provoke us to ask ourselves some fundamental questions: What is mercy? What is forgiveness? Did mercy and forgiveness die in Auschwitz? (Wiesel told Philippe de Saint-Cheron, "Everything died in Auschwitz in every way."[27]) The Prophet Ezekiel, common to both our religious traditions, reminds us that God can and does give life to even our dead, dry bones (Ezek. 37:1-14). Should we not ask, therefore, Is there no overriding mercy to which guilt-tormented souls can entrust themselves? Will human beings have to learn to live with eternal guilt? What is the purpose of religion? (Is it to escape the just consequences of our actions?)

Again and again, alone and together, we Christians and Jews must explore these questions, and we must try to expose "our arguments to each other" so that we can gain "a better understanding of [each] other's views." This is a daunting challenge, but one we must embrace and engage—for the sake of our common future together as human beings in our fragile world.

In her book *Proclaim Jubilee! A Spirituality for the Twenty-first Century*,[28] Maria Harris, a Christian scholar, has a chapter entitled "Forgiveness as a Way of Being in the World."[29] In it, she asks, "Forgive what?" and responds, "Forgive everything we can," but that is easier said than done. Suppose the one(s) I/we must forgive stubbornly refuses "an admission of guilt, contrition, and remorse"? What then? Harris writes that forgiveness—and the acknowledgment of wrong—can take a long, long time. As human beings, we are called "to forgive everything that it is in our

---

[26]Miroslav Volf, *Exclusion & Embrace: A Theological Exploration of Identity, Otherness, and Reconciliation* (Nashville TN: Abingdon Press, 1996) 120.

[27]Philippe de Saint-Cheron and Elie Wiesel, *Evil and Exile* (Notre Dame IN: University of Notre Dame Press, 1990) 54.

[28]See further Maria Harris, *Proclaim Jubilee! A Spirituality for the Twenty-first Century* (Louisville KY: Westminster/John Knox Press, 1996).

[29]See further 36-55 in *Proclaim Jubilee! A Spirituality for the Twenty-first Century*.

power to forgive," which suggests that there are some things that *are not* in our power as human beings to forgive. Hannah Arendt "names as the exception those things we are unable to punish, saying, 'It is quite significant, a structural element in the realm of human affairs, that human beings are unable to forgive what we cannot punish and unable to punish what has turned out to be unforgivable.' "[30] But, Harris and Arendt are talking about human forgiveness. What about divine forgiveness? Are there sins so heinous as to be beyond forgiveness? I do not want to believe that. I want to believe that God's mercy and forgiveness will endure forever, that God's memory will endure forever, which means, therefore, so also will accountability endure. I want to believe that God's creative, restorative power is eternal and that God's ability to mend all wounds is unsurpassed by the destructive ability of God's creatures. And yet, I know that many faithful Jews murdered in Auschwitz also wanted to believe in God's faithfulness, wanted to believe that God's mercy and forgiveness would endure forever.

Does my belief about God make sense in the presence of burning children? This is the dilemma I face whenever I think about what Elie Wiesel said at Auschwitz-Birkenau in January 1995. I can only hope that God will hold in eternal memory all we human beings have done, all we have become. I can only hope that God's eternal faithfulness—even in the face of radical evil—God's refusal to abandon us—even in the face of "disgust"—will draw forth, in this world and in the world to come, a greater, finer potential—a healing, mending potential for all creation.

---

[30]Ibid., 42.

Part Three

Proclamations

To proclaim something involves declaring it plainly and publicly. Wherever it can honestly be found, good news deserves to be the subject of proclamations. Chastened, challenged, and changed by the Holocaust, Christianity has more than words that a wounded world needs to hear. At its best, post-Holocaust Christianity offers a way of life that can join with the best in Judaism and other major religious traditions to mend the world. Post-Holocaust Christianity will not appeal to everyone, but it is an option that can make a positive difference. Expressing that hope, Victoria Barnett, Douglas Huneke, David Gushee, and John Roth attempt to state key elements in that kind of Christianity.

Deeply influenced by the example of the German theologian Dietrich Bonhoeffer, Barnett develops her approach to post-Holocaust Christianity by emphasizing that "we Christians are called to discipleship—to follow the example and teachings of Jesus of Nazareth." In his essay, "A Post-Shoah Interventionist Christianity," Huneke calls attention to Herman Graebe and other Christians who resisted Nazism and rescued Jews. Their example gives him hope that post-Holocaust Christians can be "a mutually supportive community of conspirators for good." David Gushee urges post-Holocaust Christians to do their homework, which places a premium on a close reading of the New Testament. Not only does such reading provide "no grounds . . . for a hatred of the Jewish people in any form," but also Christianity's "good news" cannot be divorced from the fact that Jesus "intensifies and radicalizes the Hebrew Bible's moral demands." Identifying what he takes to be the heart of traditional Christianity—the claim stated in John 1:14 that "the Word became flesh, and dwelt among us, full of grace and truth"—Roth contends that this teaching can and should be a central element in the "good news" that post-Holocaust Christianity has to offer.

In no way do these authors think that their proclamations explain the Holocaust. Nor do their proclamations minimize Christian failure during those dark times. But these writers do testify that the Holocaust's darkness does not ultimately triumph, and it is their post-Holocaust Christianity that compels them to say so.

Chapter 10

The Message and the Means: Some Historical Reflections on the "Good News"

Victoria J. Barnett

Whatever our theological or denominational tradition, for most Christians the "good news" is part of our faith. We believe the essence of the Christian message is joyful and that we do indeed have some "good news" to share. A central part of our belief is that we Christians have to witness to this, in some form, in the world. Thus, this "good news" is significant both theologically—in *what* we believe—and ethically—in *how* we express and act upon that belief. Ideally, these two aspects are combined in the kind of lived discipleship that for me constitutes the heart of the Christian life.

But the actual history of Christian witness and its consequences, especially for those of other faiths, raises serious questions about the nature of this witness. This is particularly true when we look at the history of Christianity's relationship to Judaism. Much of that history has been marked by pogroms, the burning of Torah scrolls and desecration of synagogues, the Inquisition, ghettos, and numerous other forms of discrimination and persecution. Some of this was at the direct instigation of Christian churches, bishops and clergy; some of it was not. But these centuries of persecution are part of the Holocaust's historical foundation. The Holocaust therefore raises crucial questions for Christians.

For, although the National Socialist regime was based upon an ideology that in many ways was explicitly anti-Christian,[1] it never would

---

[1]Many Nazi leaders and ideologists viewed religion as an outdated myth that would die out as it was replaced by National Socialism. Such views were stressed by party ideologist Alfred Rosenberg in his polemics, especially against the Catholic Church. "My religion is my Führer Adolf Hitler, my people and my Fatherland," said one party stalwart in 1934. Quoted in Victoria Barnett, *For the Soul of the People: Protestant Protest against Hitler* (New York: Oxford University Press, 1992) 32.

have achieved its hold on German society without the complicity and support of many in the Christian community. Antisemitism was not a Nazi invention, nor did it prove to be a significant stumbling block for many Germans. The preaching in many churches helped to legitimate it, as did the churches' institutional passivity toward many of the Nazi regime's measures. In Auschwitz and the other camps, in the ghettos and forests of eastern Europe, millions of innocent men, women, and children were murdered only because they were Jewish. People who considered themselves Christian were among the perpetrators. Christians were among the bystanders who looked away from the genocide or pretended they knew nothing about it. For the most part, their church leaders were silent; in some cases, church leaders were complicitous. All too seldom, Christians attempted to help the victims through rescue or resistance.

We Christians cannot practice our faith as if all this had never happened. Our "good news" poses two central questions: *What* do we witness? *How* are we called to witness? Although these two questions, the theological and the ethical, have existed since the beginning of Christianity, they take on entirely new significance for us in the wake of the Holocaust.

The question of "how" to witness is more straightforward, although that doesn't make it any easier to practice. Essentially, we Christians are called to discipleship—to follow the example and teachings of Jesus of Nazareth. I once heard Raul Hilberg tell an unforgettable story that still moves me deeply. Bernhard Lichtenberg, dean of St. Hedwig's Catholic Cathedral in Berlin, was one of the few members of the clergy to pray and preach publicly on behalf of the Jewish victims of Nazism. The Gestapo arrested Lichtenberg in the fall of 1941; he was imprisoned for several years before dying en route to Dachau in 1943.

When he first heard the story of Bernhard Lichtenberg, Hilberg said, he went home and picked up a copy of the New Testament that someone had once handed him in Times Square. He then read it, from the beginning to the end, in one sitting. And when he had finished reading it, Hilberg said that he had the sense that this was a man—I think these were his exact words—"who simply followed in the footsteps of his Lord."

Hilberg recognized something that emerges in the accounts of Christian rescuers or heroes like Lichtenberg, Paul Schneider, and André Trocmé. Paul Schneider was a Protestant pastor in a small village in Germany. He excommunicated two leading Nazis in his congregation and condemned the Nazi regime so publicly and vociferously that he was imprisoned and tortured mercilessly until his death in 1939.[2] André Trocmé was the pastor of the French village of Le Chambon in France, which hid and rescued more than 2,000 Jewish children.[3] These people stand out, not only because there were so few of them during the Holocaust, but also because, with remarkable simplicity and directness, they tried their best to follow the teachings of Jesus Christ.

Most of the Christians of that era were a far more complicated group. The history of the church between 1933 and 1945 is a turbulent one, and its behavior was influenced by a number of factors, not just attitudes toward the Jews. While a detailed look at this history is beyond the scope of this essay, a brief list of some key developments illustrates some of the other factors that paralyzed the churches, inside and outside of Nazi Germany.

A Historical Overview[4]

At the beginning of the Nazi era, the Protestant church in Germany was strongly nationalist. On the whole, its leaders welcomed the new Nazi regime and expressed optimism about Hitler's promises to restore German pride and to end the chaos of the Weimar years. Protestants quickly became divided, however, by a bitter fight (the so-called "church struggle") between the *Deutsche Christen* (the "German Christians"), who wanted the churches to embrace Nazi ideology, and the Confessing Christians, who wanted to keep the churches free of ideology and state control. Some Confessing Christians eventually went even further, opposing the

---

[2]See Rudolf Wentorf, *Paul Schneider: The Witness of Buchenwald* (Tucson AZ: American Eagle Publishers, 1993).

[3]See Philip Hallie, *Lest Innocent Blood Be Shed: The Story of the Village of Le Chambon and How Goodness Happened There* (New York: Harper & Row Publishers, 1979).

[4]A number of books examine the history of the churches during the Holocaust. In addition to the other books mentioned in these notes are Doris Bergen, *Twisted Cross: The German Christian Movement in the Third Reich* (Chapel Hill: University of North Carolina Press, 1996); Ernst Christian Helmreich, *The German Churches under Hitler. Background, Struggle, and Epilogue* (Detroit: Wayne State University Press, 1979); Robert Ericksen and Susannah Heschel, eds., *Betrayal: German Churches and the Holocaust* (Minneapolis: Fortress Press, 1999); and Wolfgang Gerlach, *And the Witnesses Were Silent* (Lincoln: University of Nebraska Press, 2000). Also see "The Churches and the Holocaust: A Reconsideration," a special edition of *Dimensions: A Journal of Holocaust Studies* 12/2.

Nazi regime itself, and a few tried to help the Jews or joined the resistance against Nazism.

The majority of Protestant leaders fell somewhere in between; they were primarily concerned with preventing a church schism and preserving the viability of the institutional church. Their reactions to Nazi measures were cautious and conciliatory. At several church synods, for example, these church leaders actually prevented statements on behalf of the Jews from being passed, arguing that such public opposition would put the church itself at risk.[5]

The Catholic church in Germany, while not divided by ideological factions, viewed Nazism as a threat similar to that of Communism. Like their Protestant colleagues, Catholic leaders were more concerned with creating arrangements that would preserve their institutional independence within the Nazi state; the 1933 concordat signed by representatives of the Vatican and the Nazi regime was a striking example.

Outside Germany, the responses of Protestant and Catholic leaders were strongly influenced by the messages they received from their colleagues in Germany. The predominant tone of these messages, at least those that came from German church leaders, was that their foreign colleagues should support their efforts to preserve the church and refrain from open criticism of the Nazi regime. Particularly in the early years, some of these messages defended the Nazi regime, including its anti-Jewish measures.[6]

Still, some of the messages sent abroad by German church members had a different tone. The more radical members of the Confessing church—a small minority, it should be noted—did call for international protests against the Nazi racial laws and other measures.

Beginning in 1933, international church leaders in Europe and the United States issued several protest statements against the Nazi persecution of the Jews. One such statement from the Federal Council of Churches in this country condemned the November 1938 pogrom; in late 1942 and early 1943, U.S. and European church leaders condemned what they termed the "massacre" of European Jews.[7]

The principle focus of churches abroad was on the plight of the refugees fleeing Nazism. Especially during the 1930s, many of those refugees were Christians who were now categorized as Jews by the Nazi

---

[5]See the chapter on the Steglitz synod in Gerlach, *And the Witnesses Were Silent.*
[6]See, e.g., ibid., 13-16, 108-109.
[7]See my article, "The Role of the Churches: Compliance and Confrontation," in *Dimensions: A Journal of Holocaust Studies* 12/2.

racial laws. The churches felt a particular responsibility toward these people, but even those church relief agencies founded to serve Christian refugees suffered from a lack of support, financial or otherwise, from church members.[8] Christian advocacy and aid committees received far more financial support from international Jewish organizations than from their own Christian churches.

Antisemitism and theological anti-Judaism were often, but not always, factors in these various developments. Some of the European church leaders most active in trying to help Jewish refugees viewed their work in a way that was theologically supersessionist. They believed the Nazi persecution of the Jews was part of God's plan to eventually bring the people of Israel to the Christian faith.[9] With very few exceptions (the American theologian Reinhold Niebuhr is one) theologians and church leaders did not begin to challenge and condemn such supersessionism until long after 1945. At the same time, however, European and United States ecumenical leaders issued clear condemnations of antisemitism that were explicitly based more upon the churches' commitment to the political principles of democracy and civil liberties.

For the most part, the straightforward course of rescue and resistance was one taken only by individuals.[10] Much of the literature on rescue shows that religious faith was a factor among only a minority of rescuers; the literature on resistance suggests the same. Human decency and a commitment to humane and democratic values often existed independently of religious belief. One of the many aspects of this history that should shame the churches, particularly in Germany, is that there was so little support for such courageous individuals. Far from supporting church members or clergy who did speak out in protest or attempt to

---

[8]See Haim Genizi, *American Apathy: The Plight of Christian Refugees From Nazism* (Ramat-Gan, Israel: Bar-Ilan University Press, 1983).

[9]I discussed some of these church leaders on a panel on "Religion and the Holocaust" at the Lessons and Legacies conference, Notre Dame, Indiana, November 1996. The proceedings were subsequently published by Northwestern University Press. See also Stephen R. Haynes, *Reluctant Witnesses: Jews and the Christian Imagination* (Louisville: Westminster/John Knox Press, 1995).

[10]See David Gushee, *The Righteous Gentiles of the Holocaust: A Christian Interpretation* (Minneapolis: Fortress Press, 1994); John J. Michalcyzk, ed., *Resisters, Rescuers, and Refugees: Historical and Ethical Issues* (Kansas City MO: Sheed and Ward, 1997); Samuel and Pearl Oliner, *The Altruistic Personality* (New York: The Free Press, 1988).

help Jews, the church leadership retreated as far as possible from identifying with them.[11]

Some Conclusions

Even this brief overview highlights several important points. The churches were not simply divided between hardcore supporters and steadfast opponents of Nazism; the vast majority of Christians fell somewhere in between. Some of them attempted to do the right thing. There were certainly Christians, including leaders, who recognized what was going on and believed that the churches were called to respond to it. Some of them did the wrong things—refusing to speak out about Nazi terror, making compromises with Nazi authorities—for what appeared to them to be valid and responsible reasons. Moreover, although antisemitism and certain theological teachings about Judaism certainly played a role in the churches' behavior, so did other factors.

Thus, some scholarly caution is called for when we look for the lessons this history holds for Christians and their churches. To view the Holocaust as primarily an act of Christians against Jews or as a "holy war," as some scholars have argued, is untenable historically. As I have tried to show above, the actual historical record—both of the churches and of the emergence of Nazism in Germany—is more complex.

What role did theology play here? In Germany, the Protestant church was preoccupied primarily with what kind of church it should be. Many of its greatest minds wrestled with the theological questions of "what" to witness—that is, with the question of the "good news." They took their theology seriously. They were convinced that they had to clearly define *what* they believed before the right course of action could become evident. The theological faculties in Germany and their endless *Denkschriften* and *Gutachten*, the voluminous writings of Karl Barth, the protocols of church synods in Germany and ecumenical meetings in Europe and this country—all show how seriously Christians during that period were pondering what they should proclaim.

Seen from our perspective today, some of what they produced is absolutely awful. A few documents show the first cautious signs of a rethinking of Christian teachings about Judaism and a critique of church nationalism and acquiescence to state authority. But none of it was the same thing as following the path of discipleship. Discipleship between 1933 and 1945 was not the act of endless theologizing or devising strate-

---

[11]See, again, Gerlach, *And the Witnesses Were Silent,* esp. 169-73.

gies to keep the institutional church intact, but speaking out on behalf of the Jews, excommunicating Nazis, and hiding children. None of us can know for certain whether we would have had such clarity and strength of faith. But we recognize that people such as Bernhard Lichtenberg, Paul Schneider, and André Trocmé witnessed to the "good news" through their actions in a way that their scholarly contemporaries failed to do.

So we remain torn between this question of *how* to witness and *what* to witness. On the surface, the question of the "good news after Auschwitz" concerns *what* our theology is: Who is Jesus? Is it possible to detach our Christian belief in his messiahship and message of salvation from the more problematic teaching that we should proclaim this to people of other faiths? How do we interpret those scriptures that have been used to condemn the Judaic faith? In the aftermath of the Holocaust, the church is called to rethink its teachings not only about Judaism, but about Christian doctrine itself. What is it we are being called to witness to, and how are we to witness? What does God want the Christian church to be in this world?

I do not wish to minimize the importance of such theological questions; it is very necessary that we wrestle with them. Yet the historical evidence shows that the churches' failures were not merely based upon bad theology or even upon prejudice against Jews. It also proves that theological clarity isn't necessarily the same thing as clarity of purpose and a commitment to human rights and democratic values. As the literature on rescue suggests, those values can be more important in bringing people to do the right thing than can religious faith.

Thus our task is not merely theological, and even ethically it concerns more than individual ethics. We must understand and change those patterns of institutional behavior that paralyzed the churches and put them on the side of the Nazi persecutors, not the victims. We must become more alert to the use of theology to rationalize injustice and evil. The statements and sermons of the German churches between 1933 and 1945 were full of such rationalizations: that the Nazi measures against the Jews were only "temporary," that they were "understandable" and "justified," that the church was being called to "patience" and "caution." Wherever the church finds itself using such language when people are being persecuted and murdered, it is time to look at the underpinnings of such complicity. If those underpinnings are theological, then it is time to examine our theology critically.

Two concrete tasks face us as Christians in the wake of the Holocaust. The first is to understand and acknowledge the various threads of Christian complicity: the ways in which our tradition, our teachings, and the practices of our religion laid the foundation for what was perpetrated against the Jews, not just between 1933 and 1945 but long before. The second is to acknowledge our failure to act when we should have acted. Only within that context can we explore the connection between theology and lived faith.

We are taught and believe certain doctrines and interpretations of scripture, and we experience life as people of faith. That *experience* is what can move us beyond what we think we are capable of, that can shake us out of old prejudices and make us act, think, and worship differently. The experience of the evil they confronted in the Holocaust moved some Christians, at the time and later, to witness to their faith in new ways. In Germany, it led the Catholic priest Bernhard Lichtenberg and the Protestant pastor Paul Schneider to condemn their government's treatment of the Jews, despite the silence of their church superiors. In Le Chambon, it led Pastor André Trocmé to move a congregation that he had described as "dead" in 1934 to a living church capable of rescuing hundreds of children. In this country, it led the theologian Reinhold Niebuhr to condemn the evangelization of Jews in 1941, and to try in his own theology "to strengthen the Hebraic prophetic content of the Christian tradition."[12] In 1994, it led the Evangelical Lutheran Church of America to condemn the anti-Jewish polemics of Martin Luther. In the past decade, it has led numerous theologians and seminaries to examine and teach the Hebrew Bible and the Christian Scriptures in a new way that not only acknowledges the Judaic roots of Jesus' teachings, but respects the integrity and validity of the Judaic faith.

This kind of process is really what the old conversion experience was about. Conversion, as many accounts show, is not always a move from nonbelief to belief, but a movement from the world of intellectually accepted dogma to a deep, living faith that can alter people and their actions in a fundamental way.

Finally—perhaps most importantly—we must accept that the questions with which the Holocaust confronts us have to be part of our "good news" from now on. The Holocaust was certainly an event in which the church's history and passivity played a role, theologically and institutionally. This means that we as Christians must rethink our interpretations of scripture. We must rethink our Christology. We must rethink our ethics. And we must engage in other acts of faith—such as genuine repentance and remorse at our weakness and complicity in acts of real

---

[12]Quoted in Abraham Joshua Heschel, *Moral Grandeur and Spiritual Audacity* (New York: Farrar, Straus and Giroux, 1996) 301.

evil—that acknowledge that the Holocaust was an event that occurred within *Christian* history, not just *world* history.

Only in this way can we lay the theological foundation that enables us to conceive of a "good news after Auschwitz." Ultimately, theology only makes sense when it has integrity as a form of witness—in the context of lived discipleship. That, for me, is the starting point for any "good news" after Auschwitz.

Chapter 11

A Post-Shoah Interventionist Christianity: Expanding the Ranks of the Faithful Remnant in the Third Millennium

Douglas K. Huneke

How do we explain them and what might they teach a post-Shoah church, those whose behavior placed them at the zenith of human dignity? The others, whose actions reached the depths of evil and depravity are well known, and, at some level, the behavioral sciences have learned from them. There were those who chose to act with compassion and courage, and those who chose murder, indifference, or complicity. The former offer the example of their lives as a model for the modern church in a world where genocide, indifference, war, and all manner of human pestilence endlessly threaten. The latter minimally teach the church the danger of grasping onto a self-indulgent piety and going into the world unprepared for the inevitable confrontations with violence and evil.

The victims and survivors of the Nazis, those who rescued the endangered from the enemy, and those who resisted the rise of National Socialism, demand to know. The present victims of systemic global evil and those threatened by its myriad forms demand to know. Addressing individual Christians and the institutional church, this cadre of victims and potential victims demand to know who or what Christendom will be, what Christians will do, and what lessons they have learned from the suffering. Today, the choice between good and evil, action and indifference, seems obvious on first impression. Upon reflection, however, the choices faced in war were complicated by the times and history, by personal loyalties and political allegiance, by systemic and personal fear externally crafted and imposed, and by the will to conform or the resolve to deny or ignore. The people in the following accounts made their choices. Compassion and complicity stood in stark contrast to any of the variables.

A Polish public health nurse, forced to serve the Reich regional government as it established a Jewish ghetto in her city, discovered the nature of evil. She was required to identify the sick and assured that they would be treated in regional hospitals and reunited with their families or communities. One day she was summoned to a wooded site where a "mobile killing unit" (as the SS *Einsatzgruppe*[1] execution units were sometimes called) had slaughtered or fatally wounded hundreds of Jews from the surrounding areas. She recognized from among the dead several people she had identified in reports the prior week.

She suddenly knew the truth about the Nazis. A devout, practicing Roman Catholic, apolitical, and dedicated to healing, she had to make a choice. She chose to rescue small Jewish children, removing them from the ghetto and placing them in the homes of a few trusted members of her extended family and with numerous friends. She sought the assistance of her priest, asking that he give her signed, incomplete baptismal forms in order to better protect the children. He refused, citing the scripture that, according to his narrow interpretation, forbade Christians to violate secular laws. The priest did not betray her, but she continued her operation without the support of her church.

She practiced with a chosen child for days, walking with the child hidden between her legs under the hooping in her dress uniform. Once she was certain that a child could follow her movements without verbal commands they set out for the two heavily guarded posts. At one guard post she was required to leave a daily report and at the second she signed out of the ghetto.

Twelve Jewish children found hospice because of this woman. The last child she sought to rescue was very sick. As they neared the first

---

[1][Editors' note.] *Einsatzgruppe* is variously translated "Special Force," "Action Group," "Task Force," and *Einsatzgruppe* troops sometimes were called "mobile killing units." (*Einsatzkommando* and *Einsatztrupp* were subunits.) The *Einsatzgruppen* were specially trained mobile units under control of the *Reichsführer-SS* (Heinrich Himmler). They followed the German armies into Poland in 1939 and into the USSR in 1941. *Einsatzgruppen* were indeed "mobile killing units," charged with eliminating captured communist military officers and political leaders, and then all Jews, the handicapped, psychiatric patients, Gypsies, and others considered "undesirable" by the Nazi state. Their victims routinely were executed by mass shootings (later, by gassing to save ammunition) and buried in unmarked mass graves. Later, many bodies were dug up and burned to conceal the evidence. It is estimated the *Einsatzgruppen* were responsible for the wholesale slaughter—euphemistically, "Jewish Action"—of at least 1.5 million Jews.

guard post the child began coughing; she could not mask his cough with her own. A Ukrainian militia man knocked the woman to the ground with the butt of his rifle, exposing the child. Other guards held the boy upside down and one shot him to death, then turned his rifle and summarily executed the nurse. The Nazi officer ordered that the bodies remain in place for three days as a warning to anyone else who might consider helping the Jews.

I asked the brother of this compassionate and courageous nurse why she took such dangerous actions on behalf of strangers. He responded that it was the nature of her religious values that gave her the vision and courage to care—even to the point of the ultimate personal sacrifice. Her family felt that she acted as a true and compassionate healer solely because of the teachings in scripture that required Christians to care for others.

Franz Stangl, a nominal and occasionally observant Roman Catholic, moved through the minor ranks of the police and eventually entered the service of the Third Reich as the commandant of the Treblinka death camp. Turning his back on his religious values, spiritual practices, and ignoring his charge as a law enforcement officer to protect human life, Stangl supervised an extermination program using carbon monoxide gas from a submarine engine pumped into truck trailers crammed full of Jewish women, children, and men. This hideous means of death was compromised by mechanical breakdowns that generated disapproval from Berlin because quotas were not met. Stangl co-opted learned professionals in his unfaithful and immoral endeavor, bringing to his death camp engineers and physicians to make the system more reliable and effective. The engineers offered their counsel and the system became efficient. In violation of their sacred oaths, the medical doctors offered their opinions, and the system became even more effective. There is no evidence that Stangl's faith or religious practices gave him pause in his murderous calling.[2]

We must know. What skills, traits, characteristics, family upbringing, and religious values distinguish a devout Roman Catholic public health nurse who rescued Jewish children awaiting certain death, from another Roman Catholic, a police officer, who used his knowledge and skills to become an energetic and potent mass murderer? What lessons do each

---

[2]The story of Franz Stangl's life is related in Gitta Sereny's book, *Into That Darkness: An Examination of Conscience*, Picador Edition (London: Pan Books Ltd., 1974).

of these persons offer post-Shoah Christians and the religious institutions that choose to be post-Shoah churches?

Herman "Fritz" Graebe was an active layperson in the Lutheran tradition.[3] His mother, Louise, instilled strong spiritual values in both of her sons. She taught them, by the example of her life, to be respectful of other traditions and people, and encouraged Fritz to be empathic and compassionate. Louise Graebe was the articulately moral parental role model for her son and the source and primary teacher of his faith, biblical knowledge, spirituality, and prophetic actions.

During the early years of the war, Graebe was assigned by his government to work with the Reich Railroad Administration in the Ukraine. One day, to his utter astonishment, he discovered a "mobile killing unit" (from an *SS Einsatzgruppe*, and supported by Ukrainian militia) at work adjacent to one of his job sites. As a mass grave filled with bodies shot by German marksmen, Graebe made the choice to oppose the government of his nation and set about establishing a rescue network that would eventually save or extend the lives of thousands of Jews seeking refuge from the Hitlerian madness.

Throughout the course of the war Graebe requisitioned ever-increasing numbers of Jews to work on his construction crews and, eventually, to perform nonexistent work that Graebe fabricated in order to distance them geographically from the hands of the killers. Graebe watched helplessly as militia men ripped infants from their parents' arms and smashed their heads against pillars. He observed a German soldier in one unit throw a screaming baby into the air and catch her with his bayonet. At one mass grave, Graebe watched as women were ordered to hold their children in front of them so that two victims could be killed with one bullet, a perverse economy of death when replenishment munitions were slow to arrive.

Graebe's voluntary testimony—an act as courageous as his rescues—opened the crimes against humanity portion of the Nuremberg Trials. He testified about the very real horrors that he witnessed and that caused him to resist the German command. William Shirer wrote of the moment when the British prosecutor, Sir Hartly Shawcross, read Graebe's testimony: "An eyewitness report by a German of how a comparatively minor

---

[3]Herman Graebe's story is recounted in Douglas K. Huneke's *The Moses of Rovno: The Stirring Story of Fritz Graebe, a German Christian Who Risked His Life to Lead Hundreds of Jews to Safety during the Holocaust* (New York: Dodd, Mead, 1985).

mass execution was carried out in the Ukraine brought a hush of horror over the Nuremberg courtroom when it was read."[4]

Graebe's simple, practical faith and his prayerful spirituality played a central role in his decision to become a rescuer of Jews. It also sustained him in that effort for nearly five years, through a heart attack, and the very real risks of betrayal that he routinely sidestepped. Indeed, Graebe's faith enabled him to find the calm inner core of his humanity as he endured these horrific experiences and nearly fifty years of phantasmagoric nightmares.

We must learn about the experiences and values that compelled a German engineer to design and implement a wildly dangerous and successful rescue operation while countless of his peers used their knowledge to design and implement death camps. Why were so many of these technologically proficient professionals unable to see the immorality and inhumanity in the deeds to which they dedicated their knowledge and training? Why, against all odds and the power of acculturation, was Graebe "pro active," "pro social," and faithful to his religious beliefs?

Another, more troubling contrast places the focus directly on pastoral calling and theological training. Ernst Biberstein was a student of theology with advanced degrees, for eleven years a parish minister, and the commanding officer (an *SS-Obersturmbannführer* or lieutenant colonel) of *Einsatzkommando* 6, a component of *Einsatzgruppe* C, a fierce and proficient military force that carried out deeds similar to those witnessed by Graebe in the Ukraine. Biberstein betrayed his calling from God; turned against the worlds of theological dialogue, pastoral care, and spiritual disciplines; and denied the biblical demands to be just and compassionate.

At some level, one may discern but not explain or justify how countless clergy acquiesced to the social ideology and self-serving propaganda of the Reich. In the face of the Reich one may comprehend the primal fear of the clergy inspired by the oath demanded in the thirty-point agenda for the National Reich Church whose motto was "One People, One Reich, One Faith." It is one thing to willingly or under duress ascribe to a political creed directing that "On the altars there must be nothing but *Mein Kampf* [to the German nation and therefore to God the most sacred book], and to the left of this a sword." It is altogether a different matter to lead and act in complicity with the Nazi death machine as Biberstein did.

---

[4]William L. Shirer, *The Rise and Fall of the Third Reich: A History of Nazi Germany* (New York: Simon & Schuster, 1960) 961.

There is no evidence to indicate that Biberstein struggled with his conscience in the periods before, during, or after his pastorate and his alliance with the executioners. His dispatches or notes, such as they were, do not reflect on the moral and spiritual implications of the Shoah nor do they offer any hint of resistance to Hitler or the Reich. What might his diary entry have been after he and his unit emptied a village, in a week's time, of its 5,000 Jewish inhabitants and left them in mass graves?

If Biberstein allied himself with the forces of death, pastor and theologian Dietrich Bonhoeffer did the opposite, choosing the Deuteronomic alternative of life and blessing rather than death and curse. The record of Bonhoeffer's soul searching, his prayerful process of discernment, his movement from pure pacifism to participation in the "Generals' Plot" to assassinate Hitler, and his role in the rescue effort known as "Operation 7," are well established by coconspirators, in his writings from Nazi prisons, and in his biography.[5]

After *Kristallnacht* ("The Night of Broken Glass," 9 November 1938), Bonhoeffer's strong commitment to pacifism, patience, and nonviolence drew a strong response:

> His seminarians recalled his remark . . . that, "if the synagogues are set afire today, tomorrow the churches will burn." . . . [T]hese words from Psalm 74:8 are marked with the date, November 9, 1938: "They say to themselves: Let us plunder them! They burn all the houses of God in the land. . . . "[6]

After traveling to the United States to teach in a seminary, Bonhoeffer was forced to wrestle with his role, conscience, and commitment to pacifism. This escape from Germany and the Reich left the theologian deeply conflicted. How could he remain in the relative security of New York City and still expect to have a role in the postwar reconstruction of a moral and civilized German nation if he did not return and ally himself with those who actively sought to overthrow the Reich?

As a witness to faith and human dignity, Bonhoeffer found inner serenity with his decision to return to Germany where he worked with the *Abwehr* in the conspiracy to bring down Hitler. Klaus von Stauffenberg failed in the attempt to assassinate Hitler. Bonhoeffer's role was

---

[5]The collection of Bonhoeffer letters, diaries, and notes is entitled *Letters and Papers from Prison*. The biography was written by Eberhard Bethge, *Dietrich Bonhoeffer: Man of Vision, Man of Courage*.

[6]Geffrey B. Kelly and F. Burton Nelson, eds., *A Testament to Freedom: The Essential Writings of Dietrich Bonhoeffer* (San Francisco: HarperCollins, 1990) 33.

uncovered. He was arrested and two years later executed at Flossenburg Prison on 9 April 1945. Contrast Biberstein's reports with Bonhoeffer's diary entry from one of his prison cells, where he wrote of his commitment to universal brotherhood and sisterhood in favor of national interests, and of his faith-based passion:

> There remains for us only the very narrow way, often extremely difficult to find, of living every day as if it were our last, and yet living in faith and responsibility as though there were to be a great future. . . . There are people who regard it as frivolous, and some Christians think it impious for anyone to hope and prepare for a better earthly future. They think that the meaning of present events is chaos, disorder, and catastrophe; and in resignation or pious escapism they surrender all responsibility for reconstruction and for future generations. It may be that the day of judgment will dawn tomorrow; and in that case, though not before, we shall gladly stop working for a better future.[7]

The underlying quest of this book is for the Christian proclamation or its expression of the "Good News" after the Shoah. Lest post-Shoah Christianity rush past the horrors of the Shoah to embrace the goodness of the rescuers or the heady acts of those who resisted, let us be firmly reminded that out of the tens of millions of people in Central and Eastern Europe who could have rescued, only a handful consciously assumed the risks of hiding or saving Jews. Their acts ranged from great personal inconvenience to extreme danger, from betrayal to the ultimate self-sacrifice. The rescuers compose a faithful remnant of biblical proportion. As always, it is from the faithful remnant that the community of believers is rebuilt after tragedy, unfaithfulness, assimilation, or outright violation of the highest scriptural standards of morality.

Before turning to the goodness of rescuers and the nature of faithful remnants, the post-Shoah church must come to terms with Lawrence L. Langer's admonition not to "co-opt mass murder for noble ends."[8] Langer speaks for the victims, survivors, and the rescuers when he warns against

> Using—and perhaps abusing—[the Shoah's] grim details to fortify a prior commitment to ideals of moral reality, community

---

[7]Dietrich Bonhoeffer, *Letters and Papers from Prison* (New York: Macmillan, 1972) 15-16.

[8]Lawrence L. Langer, "Preempting the Holocaust," *The Atlantic Monthly* (November 1998): 106.

responsibility, or religious belief that leave us with space to retain faith in their pristine value in a post-Holocaust world. . . . The Holocaust experience challenged the redemptive value of all moral, community, and religious systems of belief. A life more shrouded by darkness than radiant with light—one inevitable bequest of the mass murder of European Jewry—is not necessarily a hopeless one, but only the least sensitive among us could celebrate a return to normalcy after such chaos. . . . I am convinced that all efforts to enter the dismal universe of the Holocaust must start with an unbuffered collision with its starkest crimes.[9]

A post-Shoah church or theology cannot claim to be "post-Shoah" absent a barrier-free confrontation with the horrors of the Nazis, their co-conspirators, the indifference, and the complicity suffered by the victims and survivors, and witnessed or suffered by the rescuers. The fact that only a small remnant of post-Shoah era theologians, clergy, seminaries, and churches have undertaken the arduous soul searching required of an intentional, unbuffered confrontation with the evil and horror of the Shoah seriously tempers the possibility of a Christian "Good News" proclamation of faith and justice, love and hope, courage and compassion. For its lack of an open-souled engagement with the Shoah, Christianity is forever locked in the conscience-stupefying tension of being the religion of the murderers and the faith of those who rescued or resisted the Reich. This tension is complicated by the fact there were so many Christians numbered among the killers, the complicit, and the indifferent, and so dramatically few among the courageous and compassionate.

That Christianity provided the fertile ground for crusades, pogroms, and mass murder cannot be denied or diminished. Its contribution to the ideology of human destructiveness, to the policies of racial purity and genocide, and its arrogantly tenacious and unrepentant triumphalism clearly nurtured the antecedents of the Shoah. Curiously, these specific contributions to Nazism were turned around and employed against the very churches and individuals who promulgated them against the Jews. Having stated what has been clearly established in the history of the Shoah, it should be but is not equally apparent that the faith, spiritual practices, and religiously based moral values of Christian rescuers and resisters were central to their lives and transparently integrated into their altruistic actions. That a small but faithful remnant acted on behalf of

---

[9]Ibid., 105.

desperately endangered Jews is an expression of hope for the emergence of a post-Shoah church.

The fact that Christian teachings and the churches neither successfully kept most Christians from participation in or indifference to genocide, nor prepared Christians and their parishes to resist Hitler or rescue Jews, indicates a devastating system failure. Perhaps worse, the absence of a systemic Christian confrontation with and response to the Shoah indicts contemporary Christianity. The church is indicted as well for its general unwillingness to learn from and celebrate its coreligionists who saved the doomed. To address the lessons of courage and compassion taught by the rescuers is to be forced into Langer's "unbuffered collision with [the Shoah's] starkest crimes." After all, there is no need for compassion, courage, and rescue, unless there is great hostility, murderous cowardice, and real danger. To celebrate rescue demands candid acknowledgment of the need for it.

With sadness born of the contemporary indifference they experience, and with the uncertainty that what they did had meaning beyond that dark time, many of the rescuers ponder the fact that Christianity does not publicly acknowledge their efforts or appear to have learned from their actions. These same rescuers are embarrassed and suspicious when they are used by the church to point to the imagined grandeur of its teachings and heritage. One rescuer went so far as to say:

> The pastor in my community refused to help me. He rebuked me for endangering my family and friends. Another one, in a different town where I worked, refused to hide a Jew in one of the church buildings and I was afraid he would betray me to the authorities so I sent the Jew away. It does not surprise me when these men who denied my requests for help have counterparts today who ignore what I did. Love! Respect! I found that among Jews but not in my church.

To the shame of the modern American ecclesia, indifference to the rescuers is yet another insidious form of Shoah denial.

Christians who have confronted and attempted to respond to the reality, the implications, and the lessons of Auschwitz seek a reformation of the church and its manner of teaching and modeling Christianity, and a return to the prophetic justice, messianic inclusion, and humane values of the biblical tradition. A form of that reformation and return has had a halting and arguably lasting emergence, but not because of a genuine encounter with the Shoah. Quite the opposite, it is rooted in a modest response to modern racial injustices spotlighted by the civil rights movement of the 1960s and antiwar activity during the United States engagement in Vietnam.

Seminary education in mainline Protestant Christianity helps us understand the problem of attaining the reformation and return. Seminaries are saddled with denominational pressures to prepare clergy for parish ministry, which is all too often synonymous with the management of decline and irrelevance. Seminaries, once the hotbed of engagement with the world and all its harshness, injustice, and inhumanity, for the most part have slipped to the middle of the road, seeking consensus while mastering the art of political correctness. Where Bonhoeffer is taught, more attention is paid to his general theological thought than to his work in the *Abwehr* or his efforts in Operation 7, rescuing a group of Jews.

One must wonder how German theologians in 1937 and contemporary American theologians reconcile Bonhoeffer's introduction to his book, *The Cost of Discipleship*, and his role in saving Jews and resisting Hitler. And, one must question the dichotomy between those who were complicit or indifferent in that era and those today who proclaim Bonhoeffer's martyrdom without acknowledging his rescue and resistance efforts. Bonhoeffer wrote:

> When the Bible speaks of following Jesus, it is proclaiming a discipleship which will liberate mankind[10] from all manmade dogmas, from every burden and oppression, from every anxiety and torture which afflicts the conscience. If they follow Jesus, men escape from the hard yoke of their own laws, and submit to the kindly yoke of Jesus Christ. . . . We can only achieve perfect liberty and enjoy fellowship with Jesus when his command, his call to absolute discipleship, is appreciated in its entirety. Only the man who follows the command of Jesus singlemindedly, and unresistingly lets his yoke rest upon him, finds his burden easy, and under its gentle pressure receives the power to persevere in the right way. . . . Jesus asks nothing of us without giving us the strength to perform it. His commandment never seeks to destroy life, but to foster, strengthen and heal it.[11]

---

[10]Bonhoeffer wrote before theologians understood the need for gender-inclusive language and the importance of avoiding exclusively masculine references. One would hope that had he survived the Reich, Bonhoeffer would have used an inclusive vocabulary.

[11]Dietrich Bonhoeffer, *The Cost of Discipleship* (New York: Macmillan, 1974) 40.

While conducting my research, I read that paragraph to a Dutch rescuer and, later, to the German rescuer, Herman Graebe. The Dutch woman immediately identified the relief of her vulnerability and fear with the next-to-last sentence: "I truly believe today that what this man wrote explains my peace of mind in the midst of all the dangers I faced: 'Jesus asks nothing of us without giving us the strength to perform it.' " Graebe, on the other hand, enraged at the absence of church and clergy support for his efforts, loudly demanded to know "Why do these men of the cloth not obey such simple truths from the Bible? Either you help people or you hurt them, there was no other way for me!"

In a private conversation, a theologian commented that the Shoah is now a function of "historical memory." It did not find a place in theology, he observed, except in a few quarters, therefore, "It cannot be a paradigm for reformation of the church. Besides which, one can argue that the Holocaust was a particular crime against a particular people and not a universal experience." He was in no way dismissive of the tragedy, the crimes, or the possibility of repetition, somewhere else, to some other people. To his way of thinking, the Shoah was simply "not on the Christian radar—we did not commit those crimes and we cannot be judged for what other Christians did to the Jews of Europe."

This exchange illustrates Langer's point that Christians continue to seek to "retain faith in their [religious beliefs'] pristine value in a post-Holocaust world." There seems to be a correlation between this theologian's justification for ignoring the Shoah and Bonhoeffer's distinction between cheap and costly grace:

> Cheap grace is the deadly enemy of our church. We are fighting today for costly grace. . . . The sacraments, the forgiveness of sin, and the consolations of religion are thrown away at cut prices. Grace is represented as the church's inexhaustible treasury, from which she showers blessings with generous hands, without asking questions or fixing limits. . . .
>
> Cheap grace is the preaching of forgiveness without requiring repentance. . . .
>
> Such grace is costly because it calls us to follow, and it is grace because it calls us to follow Jesus Christ. It is costly because it costs a man his life, and it is grace because it gives a man the only true life.[12]

---

[12]Ibid., 45–46.

There can be no reformation and return absent the unbuffered confrontation and the difficult work of costly grace.

Given the terrible role of the institutional church in the Shoah and its duty to prepare and send into their workaday worlds people of faith who will resist evil and intervene on behalf of those endangered by it, post-Shoah Christians are faced with difficult challenges. The first challenge is an authentic engagement with the horrors of the Shoah and the theologies and political policies that enabled genocide. The second challenge is to genuinely listen, first to the victims and survivors and then to the faithful remnant of rescuers. Finally, post-Shoah Christianity must embrace a reformation of believing and being that constantly enlarges the faithful remnant until it can no longer be called a remnant.

The Christian proclamation, whatever we might dare to name "Good News" after the Nazi era, is the faithful remnant who held fast to the teachings of scripture and the revelations that inspired and empowered them to be compassionate, just, and engaged, and the inclusive values modeled for them from the wisdom teachings of the Bible. The majority of people seemed to "whore after other gods." They became assimilated into the dominant culture and indifferent to the disciplines of Christianity, or they sated their appetite for prejudice on the blood of European Jewry. But the faithful remnant persisted against all odds. In holding to their beliefs and commitments, the rescuers saved the tradition from utter moral bankruptcy. Their actions in no way restore the "pristine values" or allow the church to return to pre-Shoah normalcy. On the contrary, they are the impetus and foundation for the post-Shoah reformation.

By their very existence, the remnant demands of the church, its theologians, and its clergy full repentance—not confession, but repentance—of centuries of antisemitism and anti-Judaism expressed in the most vile transgressions of all that is holy. They demand that Christendom experience a profound metamorphosis, a new and different life born of love rather than hatred, of inclusion not exclusion, of resistance to rather than complicity in evil, of courage instead of complacency and conformity.

A post-Shoah church can be built on the foundation of the shared skills, values, role models, characteristics, and traits that enabled a Roman Catholic Polish public health nurse, a Lutheran German engineer, a German theologian, or an entire Huguenot parish to save the lives of the desperately endangered. Those who died at the hands of Nazi genocide cannot be restored, but the faithful remnant from the Shoah can be enlarged to ensure that future acts of genocidal madness, violations of human rights, and economic injustice are met with resistance, compassion, and courage by the churches.

Jews died when Christians were so saturated with antisemitic and anti-Jewish hatred that the Christians could look away from the horrors without feeling or conscience. The post-Shoah church is one that will value the faith experiences of those in other traditions. It will challenge the cultural forces that dehumanize and divide one group of people from another.

Jews died when Christians failed to create an institutional ethic that called for the sanctification of life and the protection of being. The Huguenots of Le Chambon or the priests of Assisi developed institutional values that defined membership or participation in their communities to include protecting all who were persecuted and hunted for execution.

Jews died when Christians were unable or unwilling to conform to the Gospel mandate to love others, because they busied themselves conforming to the world. During our interview, a Dutch rescuer did not answer any of the seven oblique questions about her motivation. Finally, I asked her directly, "Why did you rescue Jews?" She was quiet for a time and then responded pensively, "I've never thought to ask such a question. I must say that I did it because of what St. Paul said in Romans 12:2: 'Be not conformed to this world, but be transformed by a complete renewal of mind, so as to know for yourself the good and acceptable and complete will of God.' " Tears that filled her eyes began to cascade as she spoke, "If I had failed to open my door and my heart to the Jews who knocked, I would have conformed to the evils of the Nazis, but to bring them into my home, to hide them in my closet or under my bed, to share my food with them, that was to know and do the will of my God."

Rescuers benefitted from articulately moral parental role models whose spoken values were predicated on biblical teachings that stressed responsibility for others, care for strangers, the sharing of one's substance and person with those in need and alone. Frequently, the articulately moral parental role models acted on their spoken values in the presence of their children who went on to become rescuers. The biblical and humanitarian values were clearly linked and consistent, and their practice was expected.

Rescuers routinely described themselves as what I have titled, "religiously inspired nonconformists." The Dutch rescuer in the previous story is a perfect illustration of a person who elected to be a cultural and political nonconformist and a biblical conformist in the face of murderous deportations and the news of genocidal acts. Religiously inspired nonconformity is not as passive as the title suggests. A significant number of rescuers made an intentional choice to act contrary to the dominant flow of society and religion.

Many of the rescuers had empathic imaginations. That is to say, they had the skill to exchange roles with those threatened by the Nazis and to imagine what they experienced and what they would want someone to do for them in that instance. Employment of the empathic imagination produced a strong commitment to intervene and set the rescuer's mind to creating alternative means by which they could have a positive effect on the lives of the victims.

As he watched helplessly at a "Jewish Action," Herman Graebe observed "an old man and his twelve-year-old son" standing naked in the crowd, waiting to be called to the ledge to be shot by officers of the "mobile killing unit." The boy was in tears when the "old man" bent down, whispered something in his ear and pointed to the heavens. In an instant they were called to the ledge. I asked Graebe how he knew the man was old and the boy was twelve. He responded, "The man was my age; he just looked old because he was sick and malnourished. . . . I didn't know [the age of the boy] but he looked to be the age of my son who was visiting with my wife and staying in Sdolbonov." Then the rescuer said, "I know precisely what I would say to my son in that moment. I would point to heaven, comfort him, and say, 'Do not be afraid because where we are going, there are no SS or mass graves.' " That is empathic imagination. Then Graebe added, "In that moment . . . I heard my mother's voice say to me, 'Fritz, what will you do?' It was then that I knew I had no choice—I had to save the Jewish workers." Here we witness the powerful blending of the empathic imagination with the memory of the articulately moral parental role model.

Without reducing rescue to a single explanation or category, one may conclude that the skills and characteristics of the rescuers were fundamentally hospitable. Nazi era Christians who rescued Jews practiced a form of Christian hospitality and welcome described by the late Roman Catholic theologian Henri Nouwen:

> In a world full of strangers, estranged from their own past, culture, and country, from their neighbors, friends, and family, from their deepest self and their God, we witness a painful search for a hospitable place where life can be lived without fear. . . . That is our vocation, to convert the *hostis* into a *hospes*, the enemy into

a guest and to create the free and fearless space where brotherhood and sisterhood can be formed and fully expressed.[13]

The hospitality of the faithful remnant included the welcoming, caring for, and safeguarding of strangers and sojourners. There are two biblical passages rescuers most often used to explain the motivation behind their hospitality. The first was the parable of the "Good Samaritan," in which the most unlikely person helps a man (who is culturally and religiously an enemy of his helper) who is the victim of robbers, and concludes with Jesus' admonition, "Go and do likewise." The second most frequently cited passage was Jesus' parable in Matthew 25 in which Jesus is identified as having been treated with welcome and hospitality while imprisoned, without clothing, sick, hungry, thirsty, and a stranger. The parable concludes with the summons to the faithful to be hospitable and welcoming: "Whenever you did these things to one of the least of these . . . you did it to me."

Most rescues were single, serial interventions. Few communities of faith were organized to intervene. In those places where communal rescue occurred, the clergy and church leaders created a unifying ethic that supported interventions on behalf of victims and resistance to evil. These remnant communities of faith shared in common a clearly articulated interpretation of biblical mandates for compassion and inclusion, humanitarian values, and an ethic of moral responsibility and engagement with the "powers and principalities" of the world. Most importantly for their mission in the war, they formed a mutually supportive community of conspirators for good.

A reformation of post-Shoah Christendom on the basis of these practical lessons drawn from the lives of Christian rescuers will greatly enlarge the faithful remnant and ensure that in the face of the world's ongoing history of human destructiveness, intolerance, indifference, and exclusionary behavior there will be a voice of protest, acts of resistance, and an ever-expanding cadre of church people who may be counted on to intervene. Many of the rescuers quietly confide their concern that their deeds made no difference beyond those who directly benefitted from their courageous and compassionate labors. These rescuers want to know if lessons will be learned from their actions and applied to the crises of contemporary times. Theirs is not a wistful quest for validation—a surprising fact given the absence of notice by the churches—but an insistent,

---

[13]Henri J. M. Nouwen, *Reaching Out: Three Movements of the Spiritual Life* (New York: Doubleday, 1975) 46-47.

genuine concern for the world they are leaving behind that can only be addressed by a Christendom that is truly "post-Shoah."

Among the remnant of modern post-Shoah Christians there is dismay over the general absence of engagement with the Shoah by Christian theologians and clergy. There is deep concern that the church has not made progress in the post-Shoah reformation nor found eager audiences for the lessons of resistance and rescue. At one level, this is not surprising given the pervasive and often subtle antisemitism and anti-Judaism among the purveyors of Christianity. On the other hand, professional church people seem unable to confront the stark crimes of the Shoah or to envision trying to transform the monolith that is the church in response to the Shoah. Such a reality, if it continues to dominate, portends a dark future for the church in the world and a dramatically foreboding future for all of creation. The alternative for the current remnant of post-Shoah Christians is captured in Elie Wiesel's portrait of the prophet Jeremiah. Wiesel's words point to what may well be one of the only remaining viable routes to choosing life and blessing rather than death and curse. Wiesel wrote of Jeremiah and for many of us:

> [His] purpose is to teach his contemporaries and their descendants a lesson: there comes a time when one must look away from death and turn away from the dead; one must cling to life, which is made of minutes, not necessarily of years, and surely not centuries; one must fight so as not to be overwhelmed by history but to act on it concretely, simply, humanly.[14]

---

[14]Elie Wiesel, *Five Biblical Portraits* (Notre Dame IN: University of Notre Dame Press, 1981) 120-21.

Chapter 12

The Good News after Auschwitz: A Biblical Reflection

David P. Gushee

A major theme of this book is a question: Is it appropriate for Christians to speak of "Good News" after Auschwitz? It is a most provocative and important question—and one that is, in my context, almost completely incomprehensible. Let me explain.

Good News after Auschwitz? On the Comprehensibility of the Question

The context—or, better, set of contexts—in which I am situated includes a teaching post at a Tennessee Baptist Convention-sponsored undergraduate university (Union University); a role in pastoral leadership at a small "seeker-oriented" West Tennessee Southern Baptist congregation; a twenty-year affiliation with the denomination called the Southern Baptist Convention; and a ten-year identification with the broader evangelical family. In each of these contexts, the question under consideration would be viewed, with rare exceptions, as incomprehensible, for the following set of interrelated reasons.

- The theological and moral content of the Christian faith is understood to be established by the Bible.
- The Bible is viewed as the inspired, trustworthy, and authoritative Word of God.
- The basic Christian *kerygma*, or Gospel message, is seen as a particularly well-established part of Christian doctrine that is therefore particularly impervious to change or alteration.
- Historical events, in any case, are not understood as having any authority to alter the shape of Christian doctrine.
- The Holocaust, though viewed as a horrible event in human history, is not treated as an item of significant concern for Christians *qua* Christians.

I understand my own calling to be service as an "organic intellectual" (philosopher Antonio Gramsci's term) in relation to the faith-community from which I emerge and for which I do my scholarly work. I have no interest in walking away from that faith-community or in deriding its most cherished convictions. Loyalty to this particular branch of the Christian family is a fundamental part of my own personal identity and professional vocation. I happily remain engaged in these various contexts of service because of this sense of identity and vocation. Yet this does not mean an uncritical embrace of prevailing assumptions, beliefs, or practices. My vocation instead is to offer critical, sometimes prophetic, leadership from within the family, as it were, in an attempt to help lead the people I serve to follow Jesus in the most faithful way possible. This approach involves working within the parameters of cherished convictions about the inspiration, authority, and truthfulness of the Bible, but at times needing to demonstrate that precisely within such parameters a previously unseen demand exists for the change or transformation of prevailing behaviors and beliefs.

This, for example, is the process that Southern Baptist and evangelical leaders have followed in recent years on the issue of racism. If the Bible is the authoritative Word of God, and if the content of the Christian faith is established by the Bible, *and if it can be shown that racism is clearly ruled out for the Christian believer when Scripture is rightly understood,* then there can be no place for racism in the Christian life. That is precisely the process and the outcome of the best Southern Baptist and evangelical thought about race. Progress, where it has occurred, has not required the abandonment of core understandings of the sources and norms for Christian convictions, but instead a fresh reading of Scripture has provided potent evidence for acknowledging prior heresy (doctrine) and sin (practice). In my context, then, the revision of Christian practices and beliefs always involves a contest over the meaning and interpretation of Scripture.

I am well aware that some other branches of the Christian family construe the process of theological/ethical reflection and revision very differently. Some are far more open to radical revision of Christian convictions based on, for example, a very different understanding of the nature and authority of Scripture. Some place much greater emphasis on the role of tradition, or the illuminating intervention of the Holy Spirit, or the findings of contemporary science, or the authority of church leaders. If by conviction I belonged in one or another of those other branches and were serving there, my approach would surely be different. But I do not, and so my treatment of the issue under consideration must be understood to be shaped by the perspective and context I have just outlined.

With that in mind, let us revisit the five reasons articulated above as to why the "Can there be Good News after Auschwitz?" question would be generally incomprehensible in my context, and consider from within an evangelical/Baptist perspective which of these reasons are valid and which are not.

First, I share the two key convictions named there—that the Bible is the inspired and authoritative Word of God, and that the theological and moral content of the Christian faith is established by the Bible. Yet it is the case that no Christian, or Christian group, can claim an infallible interpretation of Scripture. We "see through a glass darkly." Our reason is corrupted by sin. Our self-interest, experience, and social location blind our perception. All interpretation of Scripture must in principle be seen as ever open to correction and revision. Jesus emphasized our need to work on clearing up our spiritual perception, both our "eyesight" (Matthew 7:1-5) and our "hearing" (Mark 4:9),[1] which are constantly prone to misunderstanding and misperception.

Further, the vast treasury of works that constitute the Bible contains a variety of strands and voices. The history of Christian thought, both in ethics and in theology, demonstrates a perhaps inevitable tendency in the diverse Christian family to develop various hermeneutical grids, to find distinct patterns in Scripture, to trace out certain key themes and push them to their logical conclusion while downplaying the significance of others. One might speak of the Bible as a brilliant collection of threads, but threads that do require some form of organization, which the church in its many expressions has spent 2,000 years doing—weaving Scripture together in varying designs and patterns. It is not inappropriate, then, to reconsider—especially in view of important new information emerging from church or culture or history—aspects of the way that "threading" has occurred.

Here is where I must part company with the latter three assumptions listed above. It is a mistake, I believe, when my coreligionists assume that historical events have nothing to teach the church. It is particularly erroneous, for reasons I will review below, to assume that the Holocaust is not a significant event for Christians precisely as Christians. That is a grievous error. Finally—and this will be the most controversial claim I will make, in the context of my faith-community—I believe it is even mistaken to assume that the basic Gospel message—*as we understand it*—is by definition impervious to change or alteration.

---

[1] Unless otherwise noted, scripture references are to the New Revised Standard Version (NRSV).

As we understand it—that's the key. We must be willing to acknowledge the revisability of Christian convictions, sometimes under the impact of historical events and sometimes simply due to fresh revisiting of the sources of Christian thought, both because of a sober awareness of our sinfulness and fallibility and because of our radical commitment to the Word of God rather than to any particular interpretation of that Word.

In this essay, I will argue that there can be Good News after Auschwitz. That Good News remains a biblical message centered around the person and work of Jesus Christ. But the content of that Good News, or Gospel, must be understood in light of a truthful encounter with the Holocaust and especially with Christian failure during that horrible event. The Holocaust is not the only historical occurrence that is worthy of sustained Christian attention with an eye to a reconsideration of scriptural interpretations. But it is one critical event in need of such reflection, and one that Christians in my context have rarely considered seriously. Only after embarking upon that painful journey of encounter are we prepared to return to the Scriptures to consider afresh the content of the Christian message and the shape of the Christian way of life.

Elements of Christian Failure during the Holocaust

Jesus said that "you will know them by their fruits" (Matthew 7:20). He also said that "Not everyone who says to me, 'Lord, Lord,' will enter the kingdom of heaven, but only the one who does the will of my Father in heaven" (Matthew 7:21). The founder of the Christian faith taught that doing the will of God and being morally "fruitful" are to be the central marks of his followers. On this basis, therefore, it is fully appropriate to assess actual lived Christian behavior against the standards established by the Christ whose name we claim.

There is no responsible Christian thinker today who would argue that the overall behavior of those who, during the Holocaust, claimed Christian identity was anything other than a failure. Surely there were scattered exceptions, such as those who risked their lives to rescue Jews, an inspiring group about whom I and many others have written. But in general the Holocaust constituted a devastating failure of "Christianity" and "the church," especially as they had come to exist by the mid-twentieth century in their Western, first-world incarnation, and most especially in Germany. It is a failure that forces Christians everywhere back to a fresh encounter with Christian faith at its very roots.

It is easier to make the relatively common claim of Christianity's failure during the Nazi era than to articulate exactly why it is a truthful claim. It is truthful not because the Nazi regime was led by numerous devout, pious Christian people, because instead it was headed by thoroughly amoral, paganized, racist ideologues. Nor is it the case that the mass murder of the Jews was incited, organized, sponsored, and/or led by the church, as in the Crusades, the Inquisition, or the Salem witch trials, because instead it was administered by a modern state through its bureaucracy and governmental apparatus. We must guard against a guilt-driven conceptual sloppiness on these critical points.

Christian responsibility for—and failure during—the Holocaust was more subtle. It begins with the role of historic Christian anti-Judaism, that cluster of Christian theological beliefs about Jews and Judaism (such as the deicide charge, collective bloodguilt, and displacement theology) which through the centuries had led to profoundly antisemitic behavior at both the individual and the social levels. Eighteen centuries of this Christian anti-Judaism laid the groundwork for the nationalist/racist antisemitism that emerged in the nineteenth century—though there was real discontinuity between these two forms of anti-Jewish sentiment as well. What is less frequently noted is that the older, religiously based anti-Judaism was also visible in Europe during the Holocaust, especially at the grassroots level in eastern Europe. Jews looking for succor under persecution frequently found themselves the objects of religiously incited scorn, rejection, assault, and murder.[2] Thus theological anti-Judaism bore bitter fruit during the Holocaust both as ideological legacy and in some cases as grassroots motivation for deeply misguided Christians embedded in deeply distorted local expressions of the faith.

A second dimension of Christian failure during the Holocaust is found in the partial nazification of the German church during the Nazi era and its implications for Jewish survival. As Victoria Barnett and others have shown, the German churches, both Protestant and Catholic (though in different ways), allowed their moral witness, church practice, and at times their theology to be compromised by Nazism.[3] The admirable resistance of some church leaders is well documented, and by no means can it be said that the churches organized or endorsed mass murder. But as many have noted, most resistance, where it was offered, was not focused on the plight of Germany's Jews. Even those with the most acute theological sensitivity to the paganization of the church did not see

---

[2]For documentation, see my *Righteous Gentiles of the Holocaust* (Minneapolis: Fortress Press, 1994) esp. chaps. 3 and 6.

[3]Victoria Barnett, *For the Soul of the People* (New York: Oxford University Press, 1992).

that an assault on the Jews must be met by the church's determined resistance.

Looking beyond Germany, one also finds plenty of evidence of Christian failure. One must note the reticence of historically Christian Western nations, such as Great Britain and the United States, to act aggressively on behalf of the Jews, both before the war when emergency immigration could have saved hundreds of thousands of lives and during the war when efforts on behalf of the Jews were never high on the Great Powers' agenda. Meanwhile, throughout occupied Europe and among Germany's wartime allies, so-called Christians could be found who collaborated directly with the Nazis in murder. Baptized and sometimes deeply devout Christians from many European nations participated in the most atrocious acts of mass murder, as perpetrators, collaborators, bureaucrats, and all manner of "cogs in the wheel." To read the accounts of Holocaust survivors and other Europeans from that time is horrifying and heartbreaking on this point. The complacency and passivity of grassroots local bystanders all over occupied Europe as their Jewish neighbors were ghettoized, deported, shot, and gassed, must also be noted. In numerical terms bystanders were the majority, and in situations of moral crisis bystanders function as silent if unwitting allies of those who would do evil.[4]

Let us remind ourselves why we are reviewing this litany of moral failure. It is because Jesus taught his followers to do God's will and to bear good fruit. When we do the opposite, something is seriously wrong. It should force us back to our roots for a consideration of the reasons for the tragic gap between Christianity as taught by Jesus and lived by those who carry his name. Not responding to that gap is to sin further. We are not free to ignore it; neither are we free, I believe, to assume that the problem lies with the Christian faith itself, which must thus be abandoned or radically revised in ways that transgress the boundaries of scriptural revelation. Instead, after the needed analysis of what went wrong, we are called to explore the vast treasury of resources in Scripture in order to reclaim a morally fruitful version of the Christian faith that can once again constitute "Good News."

---

[4]For documentation and further analysis, see my *Righteous Gentiles of the Holocaust*, esp. chap. 3.

Sources of Christian Failure during the Holocaust

We are attempting to consider what kind of Christian faith produced murderers, bystanders, and a cultural climate conducive to the Holocaust. At the risk of overgeneralization, let me name several currents of Christian thought that at least arguably contributed in one way or another to this catastrophe.

Some Christians had been taught to hate Jews. We have already discussed this issue briefly above. The Christian faith, like any faith, stirs profound passions because it deals with ultimate questions. Jesus intended that his followers would be stirred to sublime trust in God, a commitment to advancing his Kingdom (Matthew 6:33) on a rebellious planet, and a life of obedience through the practice of his teachings (Matthew 7:21-27). Yet the origins of Christianity include a painful and protracted split from Judaism that created internecine rivalry and hostility and took the church far afield from its commission. Jesus was a Jew whom Christians (the earliest of whom were also Jews) considered the long-promised Messiah; most Jews did not accept this belief, and by the end of the first century Christianity was a predominantly Gentile religion. These sociological developments affected the trajectory of Christian theology, which from these earliest years forward wrestled with its "Jewish question/s"—Why did most Jews not believe in Jesus? What is God's current relation to the Jewish people? Will the Jewish people as a whole ever be reconciled with the world's Jewish Savior? These are difficult questions with which Christian thought cannot fail to wrestle, but over time their answers became the source of considerable hatred of the Jewish people. That hatred poisoned Christian consciousness to a considerable though uneven extent, and its impact was clearly felt during the Holocaust.

Many Christians were taught a privatized Christianity focused on a personal salvation transaction. Christian bystanders, and even some who participated directly in murder, were not necessarily motivated by hatred of Jews. Some were simply working from within the framework of a misconstrued privatized Christianity. The Christian faith had shrunk into a way to avoid eternal annihilation or punishment and to gain admission to heaven. "Christians" are on this view those who avoid eternal death and gain eternal life through Christian baptism, official membership in a Christian church, or assent to belief in Jesus rather than some other deity. They are baptized, married, and buried in the church rather than synagogue or mosque or no place at all, so that makes them Christians. It is possible to find New Testament passages that do emphasize the importance of these Christian practices, but they are not the heart of the

Christian experience. Nor did Jesus teach that admission to heaven is the central issue of the Christian life.

Christians were taught a tribal/ethnic Christianity as an identity/boundary marker. Especially in southern and eastern Europe, Christianity was all too frequently part and parcel of an overall ethnic/tribal identity rather than a way of life centered around following Jesus. We learned during the Bosnian war of the mid-1990s, for example, to speak of Bosnian Muslims, Croatian Catholics, and Orthodox Serbs, not to mention Jews and Roma. Here peoplehood and religious identity were joined at the hip, and when war broke out it was inflamed by religious fervor. Eastern Europe, where the great majority of Jews were actually murdered during the Holocaust, had for centuries been a melange of ethnic/tribal/religious groups, all of whom cherished their own sacred sites and rites, memories and dreams, the latter of which, if fulfilled, would require the subjugation or elimination of another people busy dreaming in the same space. The Nazis proved themselves able at times to inflame the religioethnic tribalism of Poles, Ukrainians, Latvians, Hungarians, Lithuanians, Croats, and Romanians, to name several groups from which large numbers of collaborators were recruited. Ethnic/tribal Christianity of this type is less familiar in Enlightenment-affected Western Europe and North America, but one sees examples of it in the Christian militia movement or the older Ku Klux Klan. It is a fundamental corruption of the Christian faith and has nothing to do with what Jesus intended.

Christians were taught an establishment Christianity of power and privilege. Despite the dramatic erosion of Christian dominance in Europe as of 1940 or so, the prevailing model of the relationship between Christianity and culture still was establishmentarian. German Protestant leaders, for example, were in the early days somewhat susceptible to Hitler's charms because he promised a restoration of "positive Christianity" to its rightful place in national life. It was possible to interpret Hitler as the leader of a conservative movement that would defeat the forces of modernity and secularization, and he made every effort to be thus interpreted when it served his interests. The Christian church in Europe had ascended to a position of cultural power with the conversion of Constantine and the Christianization of the Roman Empire in the fourth century. By the middle of the twentieth century, the church had weathered several centuries of attack on its truth-claims and on its centuries-old power, giving ground dramatically in some arenas while retaining considerable resources and power in others. The situation varied nation by nation, but it is fair to say that Hitler faced a church tempted to focus on self-interest rather than on those whose lives were threatened by the Nazi regime. It is also fair to say that the incorporation of the church into the power structure of a state inevitably makes costly obedience to the radical demands of Jesus very difficult indeed. There is too much to lose; too much embeddedness in structures of influence; too much of a tendency to accommodate to earthly powers and authorities.

Christians were taught a corrupted vision of Christian community. It is striking how constantly Scripture emphasizes the participation of believers in a distinctive and set-apart community of disciples (see, for example, 1 Peter 2:9-12). This community consists of men and women fully committed to loving God, obeying Jesus, and apprenticing one another in the life of discipleship. This kind of faith community was a rarity during the terrible days we are considering. Too often the churches in the regions where the Holocaust occurred were expressions of an established Christianity that included everyone in the realm (except those stubbornly committed, as minorities, to other cohesive faiths, like the Jews, or to secularist ideologies). Entry into the bonds of that community occurred, quite frequently, through the decision of others or simply by accident of birth. Instruction in the way of life of the Christian people was often sorely lacking. Accountability for a drift into heresy or sin was a rare thing. Church and nation were intertwined and in many ways indistinguishable.

I have identified antisemitic, privatized, tribalistic, and establishment Christianity as historical distortions of the Christian faith that, along with a very poorly developed concept of Christian community, were sources of Christian moral failure during the Holocaust. Let us turn now to a reclamation of a healthier and more faithfully biblical Christianity in response to these failures.

Reclaiming the Good News

Can there be Good News after Auschwitz? If so, what might its content be? Let us take each one of the five issues discussed above and reconsider it in the shadow of Auschwitz and the light of Scripture.

God has grafted authentic disciples of Jesus into the family tree of biblical faith—that is Good News. Biblical faith should be understood as the story of God's decisive effort to reclaim his rebellious creation. That God would continue to wrestle with human beings at all is gracious beyond measure, for, given the sinfulness to which we have abandoned ourselves, we are worthy of condemnation and destruction (Genesis 6:5-7). But God has chosen to relate to humanity, to work with us, to reclaim us. The means by which this reclamation occurs is through the election of a covenant people who will live out God's intention for human life before the world and will lead its reclamation. The Jewish people were the people God chose for this relationship (Romans 9:4). In Jesus Christ, God graciously opened the covenant to include any and all who would join with Jesus in reclaiming the world for God and in living out God's design for human life. The Apostle Paul's language of ingrafting (Romans 11:17-24) is rich with meaning in this regard. Christians should occupy themselves with gratitude to God for the undeserved opportunity to join the biblical family tree and participate in "the reconciliation of the world" (Romans 11:15).

A careful reading of this section of Romans reveals Paul's anguish over how to understand the place of the Jewish people in God's plan after Christ's coming. He affirms that God continues to love the Jewish people (Romans 11:28) and that their "gifts" and "calling" are "irrevocable" (Romans 11:29). He is also clear that "by no means" has God rejected his people (Romans 11:1). He strictly warns Christian believers against any "boasting" (Romans 11:18-24) or condescension toward those Jews who do not "confess . . . that Jesus Christ is Lord" (Romans 10:9). He envisions an ultimate consummation when "all Israel will be saved" (Romans 11:26) and ends with a doxology of wonder at the mystery of God's plan of redemption (Romans 11:33-36).

There are no grounds here for a hatred of the Jewish people in any form. A fair reading of this critical passage, on the contrary, should lead Christians to an awestruck sense of gratitude at inclusion into this holy covenantal relationship with God. Rather than linger over questions that belong to God to resolve, it is more than enough to be occupied with serving in the vineyard of the "reconciliation of the world." The Good News is that God's Kingdom is advancing, and we who are grafted into the covenant community have opportunity to participate in that great work. The informed Christian who knows of the horrendous history of Christian antisemitism will be especially sensitive to these issues and to the wounds we have inflicted on our aggrieved Elder Brother in the biblical family of faith, and should simply be grateful to God that, given our sordid history, God has decided to "spare" the church rather than "cut off" (Romans 11:21,22) a people who have so badly wronged the Jews, the apple of God's eye.

God, the source of love and life, makes abundant life available here and hereafter—that is Good News. Privatized faith must give way to a richer theology of the Christian experience and God's way with the world. God's purpose on earth is not solely, or even primarily, to rescue individual souls from eternal death. Instead, God is the loving source of life. As loving Creator, Redeemer, and Spirit, God's mission in relation to the world is that this world should not perish but live (John 10:10, 14:19).[5] God brings life into the world, "saves threatened and impaired life from the powers of annihilation"[6] both here and hereafter, and breathes renewal into the people of God, the human family generally, and all creation. Where the God who is characterized as "love" (1 John 4:16) is, there is life—and vigorous resistance to forces that bring death. Christians ought to see themselves as being in the life-preserving, life-cherishing, life-defending, and life-enhancing business, because that is what God does.

I argued above that baptism, church membership, and assent to belief in Jesus are all part of the Christian experience but not enough in themselves. The paradigm of a God of love and life helps us recast these elements: baptism is initiation into the love of God and into work to advance that love at every opportunity; church membership should mean participation in a local family of faith in which love and life are enjoyed and shared; and assent to belief in Jesus is not merely the embrace of a set of doctrines but of a particular vision of the God-man who is the loving source of life abundant and the one through whom all life was created (John 1).

Christ brings peace to warring peoples—that is Good News. That tribal/ethnic Christianity is a tragic corruption of Christian faith is not difficult to demonstrate. Indeed, a central theme running through the New Testament is that Christian community heals ancient racial, ethnic, and tribal divisions. The church is an interethnic, intertribal, international, interlinguistic, intergenerational family. This theme is foreshadowed—though not without ambiguity—in the Gospels as Jesus brings his ministry to a variety of non-Jews. Then it explodes into the forefront in Acts 2 as the Holy Spirit falls upon the disciples and enables them to speak the languages of the international assemblage gathered in Jerusalem at that time. The rest of Acts depicts the missionary travels of the apostles and their successes with a wide array of people groups. The epistles reflect not only on the crossing of the seemingly impassable Jew/Gentile divide but also upon the creation of a kind of new humanity, a new "household of God" (Ephesians 2:19). Paul writes: "For he is our peace; in his flesh he has made both groups into one and has broken down the dividing wall, that is, the hostility between us" (Ephesians 2:14). John's apocalyptic vision in Revelation completes the picture: "I saw another angel flying in midheaven, with an eternal gospel to proclaim to those who live on the earth—to every nation and tribe and language and people" (Revelation

---

[5]Jürgen Moltmann, *The Source of Life* (Minneapolis: Fortress, 1997) 19.
[6]Ibid., 21.

14:6). The shrinking of the Christian faith into a tribal identity marker—and one to kill for—is nauseating, and a fundamental negation of the New Testament message. The Good News is that we can, and often do, experience a miraculous boundary-crossing and reconciling community in the family of faith.

Christ modeled the power of suffering servanthood—that is Good News. An establishment Christianity of power and privilege is based on a misunderstanding of the fundamental way in which God's will gets done on this planet. The meaning of the life of Christ is found in the mysterious power of the Cross rather than the Crown. Martin Luther King, Jr. picked up this theme with his constant refrain that "unearned suffering is redemptive."[7] In doing so he drew on the entire Cross motif in New Testament theology, as well as the many references to the suffering of Christ and of his people. First Peter, a work clearly written to a suffering and persecuted community, consistently strikes this note. Peter writes:

> Beloved, do not be surprised at the fiery ordeal that is taking place among you to test you, as though something strange were happening to you. But rejoice insofar as you are sharing Christ's sufferings, so that you may also be glad and shout for joy when his glory is revealed. (1 Peter 4:12-13)

The sufferings of an innocent Redeemer saved the world, and the sufferings of the people belonging to that Redeemer will likewise advance the cause of the planet's redemption. A church that focuses on establishing, wielding, and preserving earthly privilege usually does so, it believes, in order to be as effective as possible in advancing Christ's cause. Meanwhile Christ's own example, as well as the literary witness of the entire New Testament, teach precisely the opposite principle. As Dietrich Bonhoeffer so well recognized, the church can only be the church of Jesus Christ when it is "for others" as he was "the man for others." Participation in the Christian family involves a prior commitment to die to self and live for Christ (Galatians 2:19-21). The Christian is to "look not to [one's] own interests, but to the interests of others" (Philippians 2:4). How much better prepared European Christendom would have been for the Nazi challenge if it had long before given up on the dream of temporal power and instead had committed to suffer with and for the vulnerable and victimized "other."

---

[7]See Martin Luther King, Jr., "Suffering and Faith," in James M. Washington, ed., *A Testament of Hope* (San Francisco: Harper & Row, 1986) 41.

The Holy Spirit creates an unmatched experience of human community—that is Good News. A sound New Testament theology of the church begins with the wonder of election into the family of faith; salvation is received as a matchless and unmerited gift. We are God's beloved (Romans 1:7). Our internal life as a community is to involve participation in the kind of joyful fellowship of souls that is every human being's dream if they dare to acknowledge it. Here one finds love, joy, mercy, forgiveness, kindness, peace, affection, companionship, hope, humility, hospitality, and a host of other virtues of community (see Romans 12). This quality of community is understood as a gift of the Holy Spirit of God. Here there is a pooling of resources so physical needs can be met; effectual prayer in times of sorrow and grief; accountability, challenge, and example all aimed at a life well lived. Here there is also a profound sense of shared mission and purpose, to wit, reclaiming the world for God in the name of Jesus Christ. The inner life of this community is characterized by a repertoire of biblical practices that build community and advance mission. Entry into the community, its doctrinal and moral integrity, and the effectiveness of its mission, are carefully guarded by community leaders and indeed by the body as a whole.

This vision of Christian community may sound impossibly dreamy and idealistic. Yet it was precisely this kind of community of faith that saved at least 5,000 Jews in the French village of Le Chambon sur Lignon. It was Christians like this who formed informal rescue networks like that in which the ten Boom family of Haarlem, Holland, was involved. And there are cohesive Christian congregations and networks of individuals in various spots around the globe making a transformative impact today.

Conclusion:
The Holocaust as Stimulus
for a Retrieval of a Deed-Oriented Faith

Elie Wiesel has said that Christianity died at Auschwitz. Wiesel, I think, would understand and appreciate a response that says both Yes and No to his assertion. I believe that what died at Auschwitz (and Babi Yar, and Treblinka, and Warsaw) was not the Gospel but the corrupt version of "Christianity" and "church" that helped pave the way for mass murder. What died, *and needed to die*, and must be renounced for all time, was a Christian rendering of salvation history that fomented theologically inspired hatred and moral corruption; a politics of domination and exclusion and the civil institutionalization of churchly power and authority; a missiology devoted to converting people to the Christian *religion* rather than inviting them into a rich experience of the love of God, source of abundant life; a morally impotent (at best), spiritless, undisciplined, and unrepentant experience of Christian community; and any kind of nominal, tribal, racial, or ethnic Christianity. What must be retrieved is the kind of Christianity that motivated rescuers of Jews during the Holocaust—and so many others both before (abolitionists, social gospelers, suffragists) and after (civil rights activists, humanitarian workers, crisis pregnancy interveners).

What must be recovered is a Christianity of deeds that conform to God's revealed moral will. Irving Greenberg once wrote that "Religion is as religion does: all the rest is talk."[8] This statement would be viewed as entirely unremarkable in the Jewish moral tradition but would raise eyebrows over on the Christian side, at least my branch of it. But if after the Holocaust we are genuinely open to reconsidering Christian faith through a fresh review of its biblical sources, we will discover the overwhelming evidence that backs this claim.

Let us briefly walk through the canon and consider the matter. Old Testament legal materials prescribe a range of deeds that conform to God's will in social, familial, cultic, political, military, civil, dietary, and every other area of life. The historical books narrate Israel's pilgrimage through the lens of covenant obedience or disobedience and their consequences. The prophets call Israel back to God's law but with special emphasis on deeds of justice and mercy—a strand that was always important in the law in any case (compare Exodus 23:19, for example, and Micah 6:6-8). The wisdom writings, especially Proverbs, contain hundreds of concrete moral exhortations.

Jesus does not set aside but instead intensifies and radicalizes the Hebrew Bible's moral demands (Matthew 5:17-20). He offers dozens of concrete moral exhortations and tells his listeners that following him and gaining admission into the Kingdom of heaven means building their lives upon the actual doing of his words (Matthew 7:21-27). He summarizes the law as love of God and love of neighbor (Matthew 22:34-40), and famously illustrates love of neighbor through a story enjoining compassion for the suffering (Luke 10:25-37). He routinely offers parables in which one's eternal condition hinges upon the deeds of one's lifetime (see Matthew 25:31-46).

Nearly every epistle emphasizes the centrality of love, not as a sentiment but as a practice. First John repeatedly claims that love is the

---

[8]Irving Greenberg, "The Third Great Cycle of Jewish History" (New York: CLAL, 1981) 19.

test of whether one "lives in the light" or in the darkness (1 John 2:10). John states flatly that "Whoever does not love abides in death" (1 John 3:14) and "Whoever does not love does not know God, for God is love" (1 John 4:8). And love is expressed "not in word or speech, but in truth and action" (1 John 3:18). James likewise emphasizes the moral practice of the Christian faith: "What good is it, my brothers and sisters, if you say you have faith but do not have works? Can faith save you? . . . [F]aith by itself, if it has no works, is dead" (James 2:14, 17).

Even Paul, author of the famous justification by grace through faith formula, routinely offers demanding calls to action and to a way of life that is clearly distinctive from the world. He consistently claims that the undisciplined and debauched life of the pagan dies and must die upon one's entry into the Christian community. "[O]ur old self was crucified with him so that the body of sin might be destroyed, and we might no longer be enslaved to sin. For whoever has died is freed from sin" (Romans 6:6-7). The Holy Spirit dwells in the Christian, thus bringing "life and peace" and an end to life "according to the flesh." He offers lists of vices that characterize the pagan (sexual immorality, greed, idolatry, drunkenness, robbery—1 Corinthians 5:11) and strictly forbids such a way of life among the people of faith.

I argued early in this essay that a real commitment to biblical authority requires us to cut through inherited patterns of interpretation and hermeneutical grids in order to see the Scripture afresh. After the Holocaust, as we are driven back to the biblical texts, we cannot fail to see that the major note struck by biblical faith conforms to the Greenberg formula: religion is as religion does. From one end of the canon to the other, a *way of life* is demanded. That does not exclude the significance of the content of Christian beliefs but does lift up orthopraxy to the place given to it in the canon. Perhaps the final aspect of that Good News we are wondering about in this volume is found just here: *the way of life God demands of those who would be his people is clearly revealed in Scripture and remains accessible, through the Holy Spirit's empowerment, to those who are committed to it.*

The abolitionist Frederick Douglass offers the right words with which to end this discussion:

> I love the religion of our blessed Savior. I love that religion that comes from above . . . that sends its votaries to bind up the wounds of him that has fallen among thieves. I love that religion that makes it the duty of its disciples to visit the fatherless and the widow in their affliction. I love that religion that is based upon the glorious principle, of love to God and love to man. . . .

> It is because I love this religion that I hate the slaveholding, the woman-whipping, the mind-darkening, the soul-destroying religion that exists in the Southern states of America. . . . Loving the one I must hate the other, holding to the one I must reject the other.[9]

There are many versions of Christian faith. Many are unrecognizably different from the faith taught by Jesus Christ, some so vicious as to bring far more harm than good. Such corruptions of Christian faith can and must be utterly rejected. The question is not whether "Christianity" has survived, or whether there can be Good News after Auschwitz. The real question is whether more of the world's two billion confessed Christians can be persuaded to practice the religion taught by their Savior. That, indeed, would be Good News.

---

[9]Frederick Douglass, *Life and Writings*, in J. Philip Wogaman and Douglas M. Strong, eds., *Readings in Christian Ethics* (Louisville: Westminster/John Knox Press, 1996) 209.

Chapter 13

Good News after Auschwitz: Does Christianity Have Any?

John K. Roth

And the Word became flesh and dwelt among us, full of grace
and truth. . . . (John 1:14)

When attention is paid to the Holocaust, the news about Christianity is
scarcely good. So the question is: *Why be a Christian after Auschwitz?* Post
Holocaust Christians—people who identify themselves as Christians and
insist that the Holocaust requires fundamental revision of Christian self-
understanding—must respond credibly to that question. If we post-Holocaust Christians cannot do more than lament Christianity's sin, which has
been catastrophically destructive in its anti-Jewish manifestations, the
tradition will ultimately be left with little to affirm. A credible post-Holocaust Christian response to the question "Why be a Christian after
Auschwitz?" should go beyond confessing the tradition's faults and
acknowledging the shame those faults should make us Christians feel.
The importance of such acts of confession and acknowledgment cannot
be underestimated, but those acts are insufficient. A credible post-Holocaust Christian response should also affirm that "this tradition is mine,
and I want to make it better." Unless post-Holocaust Christians are
indifferent about or despairing over the future of Christianity, we need
to make our tradition better in ways that enable us to emphasize Christianity's good news and the positive difference that post-Holocaust
versions of it can make.

To address that challenge, I want to go to what I take to be the heart
of traditional Christianity. I even want to draw out that theme by
reference to the Gospel of John, which is often rightly cited as a major
source of the Christian anti-Judaism that helped set the stage for the
Holocaust.[1] As I hope to make clear, the move I shall make is one that

---

[1] For an excellent and succinct overview of scholarship about the anti-Jewish
polemics in the Gospel of John, see Norman A. Beck, *Mature Christianity in the
21st Century: The Recognition and Repudiation of the Anti-Jewish Polemic in the New*

will affirm "good news" in part by using Christianity against itself, a step that must always remain in play for post-Holocaust Christianity. To cut to the chase, then, I want to advance the thesis that the post-Holocaust good news of Christianity is stated in John 1:14: "And the Word became flesh, and dwelt among us, full of grace and truth." That New Testament claim says something fundamental about the nature of reality, especially in the teeth of the Holocaust. Particularly by emphasizing grace and truth, that claim announces good news.

Such an announcement should never be regarded as compelling anyone to be a Christian. Nor, in particular, should it ever be a pretext for anti-Jewish exclusiveness. History already contains the sorry record of such obsessions and compulsions. Yet it is still the case that the goodness of Christianity's message—goodness that deserves to be expressed *in spite of* the Holocaust—can be a persuasive reason for being a post-Holocaust Christian. To make that case, more needs to be said about four topics: (1) the fundamental claim about reality made in John 1:14; (2) the goodness of the news that claim contains; (3) the importance of grace; and (4) the centrality of truth. To be sure that none of those themes loses touch with the Holocaust's deadly particularity, including ways in which Christianity's anti-Jewish attitudes—the Gospel of John's among them—helped to set Jews up for the kill, I will begin my discussion of each one by recalling a moment of Holocaust history. These recollections will help to draw out the key elements that post-Holocaust Christianity should proclaim self-critically for the mending of the world.

The Fundamental Claim

Theo Richmond, a Jewish journalist and scholar, spent years studying the history of Konin, the Polish town 120 miles west of Warsaw from which his parents emigrated to England just before World War I. Many of Richmond's relatives were not so lucky. Among the approximately 3,000 Jews in Konin's population of some 13,000, they witnessed the German occupation of the town on 14 September 1939. Richmond's research revealed that perhaps two hundred of Konin's Jews survived the subsequent Holocaust.

It came to Richmond's attention that a postwar trial in Konin included the deposition of a Polish Catholic who had been imprisoned by the Gestapo. Early one mid-November morning in 1941, F. Z. (as Richmond identifies him) was removed from his cell, driven to a forest

---

Testament, rev. ed. (New York: Crossroad, 1994) 285-312.

clearing, and, along with about thirty other Poles, ordered to collect clothing, shoes, and valuables from Jews who were stripped before they entered the killing pits that would become their unmarked, mass graves. Specifically, F. Z. remembered the following episode.

A layer of quick lime covered the larger of the two pits. Naked Jews—children, women, men—were forced into that pit until it was full. "Two Gestapo men," F. Z. continued, "began to pour some liquid, like water, on the Jews. But I am not sure what that liquid was. . . . Apparently, because of the slaking of the lime, people in the pit were boiling alive. The cries were so terrible that we who were sitting by the piles of clothing began to tear pieces off the stuff to stop our ears. The crying of those boiling in the pit was joined by the wailing and lamentation of the Jews waiting for their perdition. All this lasted perhaps two hours, perhaps longer."[2]

Why were those Jews from Konin lime-boiled to a hideous death? Good answers for that question do not exist, but no credible response can avoid the Gospel of John. In particular, John 8:42-45 is one of the most virulent sources of Christianity's anti-Jewish tendencies, which helped to set Jews up for the kill during the Holocaust. That text puts into Jesus' mouth damning words about Jews who apparently challenged his authority: "You are of your father the devil," Jesus tells them, "and your will is to do your father's desires."

Jesus and his disciples were profoundly Jewish. The community that produced the Gospel of John in the 80s or 90s CE consisted of Jewish-Christians or Jews become Christians. More than sixty times, however, far more than the first three gospels (Matthew, Mark, and Luke) taken together, John uses οἱ Ἰουδαῖοι *hoi Ioudaioi*—"the Jews," as that Greek phrase has typically been translated—and often "the Jews" are vilified as benighted disbelievers who are hostile to God's grace and truth. Biblical scholars—Christians and Jews alike—have been working diligently to produce translations that are both more accurate and less destructive, but the Gospel of John's negative references to "the Jews" have by no means been removed from Christian consciousness. Much remains to be done in that regard.

Thanks to recent biblical scholarship, the context of those polemics is better understood today than it was for almost nineteen centuries. The Gospel of John reflects the Christian side—one side—of a disputatious competition between Jewish Christians and Jews who were reconstituting

---

[2]Theo Richmond, *Konin: A Quest* (New York: Vintage Books, 1996) 480.

Judaism in the wake of a disastrous revolt against Roman rule (66–70 CE) that left Jerusalem and its sacred temple in ruins. In that situation, Jewish Christians—especially those of the Johannine community—seemed an internal threat to Jewish tradition, and they took offense when they were treated accordingly in the synagogue. The Gospel of John, including its polemics against "the Jews," reflected and emerged from this family fight. Those polemics, in short, say more about developments late in the first century CE than they do about the Jesus of history. By the end of that century, the split between the early church and the synagogue had become wide and deep. As Christianity spread in the predominantly non-Jewish, Mediterranean world, John's gospel was read in ways that lost sight of the details of that Jewish family fight and the divorce it produced, but that reading still pitted Christians against "the Jews" in an "us" versus "them" schism. That estrangement had disastrous consequences.

Historical understanding helps to clarify that the fundamental claim of Christianity expressed in the Gospel of John is *not*—must not be— about Christian-Jewish rivalry. First, the Jewishness of Jesus and his followers, the family nature of the quarrel in the Gospel of John, John's emphasis on God's love and on Jesus' commandment that "you love one another as I have loved you" (John 15:12) show that this Gospel is badly misinterpreted unless its negative rhetoric about "the Jews" is relativized by (1) an accurate understanding of that rhetoric's context and (2) an emphasis on God's love and the compassion for others that it enjoins. Second, although the Gospel of John has been disastrously misunderstood as inviting Christian hostility toward Jews, Christianity must be used against itself to change that interpretation. Especially after Auschwitz, one cannot avoid reading the Gospel of John in terms of Christian-Jewish relations, and the point of such reading must be to recognize how much harm John's anti-Jewish polemics have done to the Jewish people and to the vitality of both religious traditions. At the same time, a post-Holocaust reading of the Gospel of John should involve more than repudiation of its destructive side. As far as possible, it should also include a reclaiming of its positive themes. Such interpretation is not easy, because the two aspects mix and mingle in the text. But let us try and see what can helpfully be done.

The Gospel of John makes clear that there are differences, fundamental ones, between Christian and Jewish traditions. None is more fundamental than their disagreement about God's incarnation in Jesus, the Jewish teacher from Nazareth. Even within that disagreement, however, there is much that Christians and Jews can mutually affirm without sacrificing their particularity or insisting that their particularity is exclusively true. Judaism never depends on Christianity as Christianity does on Judaism, but the differences between them cannot be understood without taking into account what they share—first and foremost, the Hebrew Bible.

That said, Christian particularity resides in the fact that vast numbers of people profess that they have encountered God in life-transforming ways through the life and teachings of the Jew named Jesus. When the Gospel of John has Jesus say, "salvation is from the Jews" (John 4:22), Christians will think of Jesus in particular and interpret his words self-referentially. But a post-Holocaust reading of that claim will be broader and more in keeping with awareness that *Christian* particularity makes no sense apart from *Jewish* particularity. The point, moreover, is not that these traditions must meet each other primarily as the disconfirming other, but that they discern related, though not identical, insights and hopes that Christians experience and express in relation to Jesus, the one through whom they have come to know the God of Abraham, Isaac, and Jacob.[3]

By professing that "the Word became flesh and dwelt among us," post-Holocaust Christians testify that the world is not only God's creation but also that God has neither abandoned the world nor given up on humanity in particular, even though history provides abundant reasons to do so. Furthermore, the claim is that God's embodied presence in the world constitutes light that shines in the world's darkness. Unrelenting though it may be, that darkness does not overcome the light. Even more than that, the light brings warmth that the Holocaust's ice-cold night has not destroyed. That warmth is love that will not leave us completely alone or let us go absolutely. In spite of the Holocaust, God abides.

Such claims are not made everywhere. Newscasts, philosophies, politics, the buying and selling of everyday life, let alone the Holocaust's

---

[3]When I write "come to know," I mean to take at least two factors into account. First, I regard Christian faith in God as a kind of grafting onto Jewish faith. Not only do Christians properly affirm that the God they worship is the same God whom Jews worship, but also Christian understanding of that point is correct just to the extent that it grasps Christian dependence on Jewish understandings of God and respects those Jewish understandings accordingly. Second, to a large degree Jewish understandings of God were both spread and modified in the Western world by missionizing Christians. Absent Christianity, faith in God might have spread far and wide through Jewish practice and commitment, but there is no question that the spread of Christianity became the primary historical path through which the God of Israel became known to vast numbers of people.

destruction, do not contain them. They emerge, if at all, in special circumstances and traditions. Christians find these claims about reality revealed particularly in the life, death, and resurrection of Jesus. Post-Holocaust Christians share that affirmation but not in exclusivistic ways. Specifically, we see our perspective as one that depends upon a preceding and coexisting Jewish tradition, which Christianity ought to complement even as it differs from Jewish ways.

The proclamation that "the Word became flesh and dwelt among us" is not the only way that enables people to live in the hope that darkness does not extinguish the light, but it is one of the relatively few options that keeps such hope alive. It does so, moreover, in a way that can be particularly powerful because of the claim that God's enduring Word comes to us face to face, in a personal form, in a particular life so that God does not identify with human life abstractly but in its utter particularity. God is with us.

The Goodness of the News

"It's hard to recognize," said Simon Srebnik, "but it was here. They burned people here." Srebnik, forty-seven, had returned to Chelmno, a place he first saw in the spring of 1944 when he was sent there from the Jewish ghetto in Lodz, Poland, at the age of thirteen. The Nazi SS assigned Srebnik to a work detail. Shot and left for dead by the fleeing Nazis as Soviet troops approached in January 1945, he was one of the very few Jews who survived this killing center.

Situated in Poland, about fifty miles west of Lodz, Chelmno was the first Nazi extermination camp. More than 150,000 Jews and about 5,000 Gypsies were murdered there. Chelmno's victims perished in special mobile gas vans that piped deadly engine exhaust fumes into the trucks' interior compartments. Chelmno operated from December 1941 to March 1943. It reopened in the spring of 1944 during the liquidation of the Lodz ghetto. That summer the Germans tried to obliterate the evidence of mass murder by exhuming the mass graves and burning the remains. "A lot of people were burned here," Srebnik recalled. "Yes, this is the place. No one ever left here again."[4]

---

[4]My account of Chelmno is drawn from material I prepared for John K. Roth et al., *The Holocaust Chronicle* (Lincolnwood IL: Publications International, 2000). See also Claude Lanzmann, *Shoah: An Oral History of the Holocaust* (New York: Pantheon, 1985) 5.

Simon Srebnik's Holocaust recollections contain no good news. Nothing that any religious tradition can say should minimize, let alone justify or legitimate, the evil and despair evoked by memories such as his. But when Srebnik says "they burned people here," that fact raises questions that should not be minimized, either, for they express heartfelt yearnings. Does evil win? Does despair prevail? Is suffering eliminated only by death? Is death the end of our personal existence and of those we love?

To such questions, the Gospel of John says *No!* Its ways of doing so involve detail about what it means to say that "the Word became flesh and dwelt among us." In John's narrative that meaning is revealed in actions—things that Jesus does or that happen to him—as well as by his words, which frequently provide assurance that death is not the end. In the Gospel of John, Jesus, the Word made flesh, is active: he heals the sick, restores sight to the blind, feeds the hungry, and raises Lazarus from the dead. Whether one takes those reports as factual accounts or as symbolic narratives, their message—underscored by Jesus' resurrection— is clearly that evil, despair, suffering, and death do not have the last word. That message does nothing to explain Chelmno, but nonetheless it responds powerfully to the conviction that Chelmno deserves no victory.

For post-Holocaust Christians, the goodness of the claim that "the Word became flesh and dwelt among us" is found in the fact that the claim persists *in spite of* the Holocaust. No doubt the Holocaust stands as a mighty objection against the claim that God's light, let alone God's love, persists in the world's darkness. And yet the promise that such claims are true has power because it protests against evil and injustice, and thus the promise corresponds to what the New Testament calls a hunger and thirst for righteousness. Such hunger yearns for Auschwitz not to be the last word in a cosmic as well as in a historical sense. The yearning and the promise are both *in spite of* the Holocaust—they persist even though the Holocaust took place, and, in doing so, they refuse to succumb to its despair.

The yearning and the promise understand, moreover, that unless there is a real, not just a symbolic, way in which darkness is subservient to light, then the darkness of death ultimately consumes the light of every human life, and the Holocaust's dead—remembered and memorialized for a time though they may be—are nevertheless dead and gone forever. The goodness of the news that Christians, perhaps especially post-Holocaust Christians, have to tell is that history—even Holocaust history—is not all there is. Light, love, life—these are not confined to history, where they so often seem to be trumped by darkness, hatred, and death. Light, love, and life abide beyond the forgetfulness of earthly memory. They outlast injustice. They survive death. They remain sources of hope that set people free to resist injustice and to show compassion. To affirm that "the Word became flesh" is a refusal to grant the Holocaust a victory it does not deserve. Post-Holocaust Christianity has news that is good because it exists *in spite of* Auschwitz.

The Importance of Grace

"One wants to live," wrote Salmen Lewental. Those words were found in a clandestine notebook buried near the ruins of Crematorium III in Auschwitz-Birkenau, the main extermination center in the Auschwitz network of camps.[5] "Selected" for labor when he entered Auschwitz on 10 December 1942, Lewental was put in the *Sonderkommando*[6] a month later and condemned to work in the gas chambers. He lasted long enough to join the *Sonderkommando* uprising on 7 October 1944. The date of his death is unknown.

At one point in Lewental's notebook, he imagines someone asking him: "Why do you do such ignoble work?" Beyond answering that "One wants to live," there is no good reply, for what choices did Lewental have?

Nazi power repeatedly forced defenseless people to make what the Holocaust scholar Lawrence L. Langer calls "choiceless choices." Such choices, he says, do not reflect "options between life and death, but between one form of 'abnormal' response and another, both imposed by

---

[5]See Jadwiga Bezwińska and Danuta Czech, eds., *Amidst a Nightmare of Crime: Manuscripts of Members of Sonderkommando* (Oświęcim: Publications of State Museum at Oświęcim, 1973) 125-78, and esp. 139. My account of "choiceless choices" draws on material I prepared for Roth et al., *The Holocaust Chronicle*.

[6][Editors' note.] The German *Sonderkommando*—"special commando" or "special squad"—was a group of Jewish prisoners in extermination camps who supervised the herding of inmates into gassing chambers and then the disposal (burning, grinding remains, and scattering the ashes) of the bodies. The actual labor of herding the victims into the gas chambers ("showers") and disposing of the bodies, after removing every useful item on the bodies—clothing, shoes, even gold teeth—was done by inmates involuntarily enlisted. For the inmates, work as a *Sonderkommando* was short-lived: after a short stint as a *Sonderkommando*, an inmate would himself be taken to the "showers," in order, of course, to remove that witness.

a situation that was in no way of the victim's own choosing."[7] Such was Lewental's miserable situation. He did not volunteer for the *Sonderkomm-ando* any more than he chose deportation. In Auschwitz his "choices"— dying by suicide, dying by resisting, or dying as a *Sonderkommando*—were essentially "choiceless."

Lewental was like millions of Holocaust victims. He wanted to live, but his "choices" were "choiceless." They were devoid of grace. Death pervaded them all.

No choices anyone makes now can undo what happened to Salmen Lewental then. Nevertheless, people today do have choices about how to respond to the fact that the Holocaust happened. Those choices range far and wide. They can reflect indifference or Holocaust denial. They can also resist forgetfulness, protest against denial, encourage memory and memorialization, and insist that the Holocaust is remembered well only to the extent that such memory provokes us to relieve suffering and to combat injustice in our own times and places. In sum, post-Holocaust choices involve priorities: What most deserves to be affirmed, resisted, and encouraged?

Trusting that light, love, and life—not darkness, hate, and death—are the fundamental and ultimately lasting realities, post-Holocaust Christians testify that Jesus embodies that message not only as a proclamation about reality but also as a call that we need to hear and heed. The Gospel of John sounds this call in variations on a central theme. Repeatedly, the Gospel of John has Jesus identifying himself by using the phrase "I am." That phrase recalls a crucial narrative in the Hebrew Bible (Exodus 3). Facing a burning bush that was not consumed, Moses encountered God, who commissioned Moses to deliver the people of Israel from Egyptian slavery. What should I say, Moses asked God, when the people want to know the name of the God who has sent me to them? "Say this to the people of Israel," God said, " 'I AM has sent me to you' " (Exodus 3:14).

In Greek, the expression "I Am" was the way "Yahweh," the sacred name of God, was translated from the Hebrew. The Gospel of John echoes that phrase in relation to Jesus, who says, for example, "I am the bread of life" (John 6:35, 48) or "I am the light of the world" (John 8:12; 9:5). The message is that Jesus embodies God. When one discerns how John portrays this incarnation, the message gets fleshed out in greater detail, and the importance of grace is clarified.

---

[7]Lawrence L. Langer, "The Dilemma of Choice in the Deathcamps," in John K. Roth and Michael Berenbaum, eds., *Holocaust: Religious and Philosophical Implications* (St. Paul MN: Paragon House, 1989) 224.

The Word made flesh, says John, shows itself to be full of grace. As Christians understand it, grace refers to unmerited gifts from God—life itself but also time to spend, health to enjoy, strength to do what is right, courage to persevere against injustice, and love to show compassion and to heal wounds. When Jesus says "I Am," the descriptions that follow indicate gifts of that kind. "I am the bread of life" identifies Jesus with the One who gives and sustains life. "I am the light of the world" identifies Jesus with the One who does not permit darkness to prevail. "I am the good shepherd" (John 10:11) identifies Jesus with the One who cares. "I am the resurrection and the life" (John 11:25) identifies Jesus with the One who will not let death win. "I am the way, and the truth, and the life" (John 14:6)—summed up in "I am he" (John 18:6)—identifies Jesus with the One who shows us how to "choose life, that you and your descendants may live" (Deuteronomy 30:19).[8]

When the Gospel of John has Jesus say "I Am," the words assert that "the Word was made flesh," but the assertion is also a call to make a decision about their truth. More than one decision about their truth—including Jewish rejection of Christian claims about Jesus—can be made authentically and with integrity, and Christians should respect such differences accordingly. It is also true that both the assertion and the call have power to be heard far and wide because their appeal is so basically in tune with deeply felt human needs. Living "full of grace," Jesus helps the helpless, intercedes for those in need, feeds the hungry, defends the defenseless, heals the sick, and condemns oppression. He mends the world and calls others to follow him and to do the same by loving our neighbors as ourselves. In these acts of service and compassion, our love for God becomes incarnate as God's love for humankind enters the world visibly, though not only, through Jesus.

An essential part of the good news that post-Holocaust Christians have to tell is that Jesus, full of grace as he is, can help humankind to be more grace-full and thereby to mend the world. That task calls out to leaders and followers in the most poignant ways after Auschwitz. Acting on that call will not take the Holocaust away—nothing can do that—but it can make post-Holocaust life meaningful in ways that very little else is likely to do.

---

[8]Reflecting the Gospel of John's contentious origins, John 14:6 also attributes to Jesus the claim that "no one comes to the Father except through me." The Holocaust shows how harmful such exclusive, supersessionist language has been. Post-Holocaust Christianity should reject it.

The Centrality of Truth

During the winter of 1940–1941, Magda Trocmé answered a knock at her door. There stood a frightened woman who identified herself as a German Jew. She had heard that help might be found in Le Chambon. Magda Trocmé said, "Come in."[9]

Le Chambon sur Lignon is a mountain village in south-central France. Many of the villagers are descendants of Huguenots who fled to that high plateau so they could practice their Protestant Christianity without fear of punishment. But Roman Catholic persecution persisted. Some people and pastors of Le Chambon were hanged or burned at the stake for fidelity to the biblical principles that gave their lives meaning. The memory of that persecution gave Le Chambon solidarity when Nazi Germany occupied France.

Five thousand persecuted Jews found refuge in Le Chambon, but the village's response did not take place overnight. For years, André Trocmé, the community's Protestant minister, had preached Christianity's basic lessons—peace, understanding, love—in a church whose doorway-arch inscription came from the Gospel of John: "Love one another." Trocmé's was a message of nonviolence, but a nonviolence that rejected inaction and deplored complicity with injustice. The people of Le Chambon responded.

Le Chambon's resistance to the Holocaust started with small gestures—with Magda Trocmé's opening her door and welcoming a Jewish refugee. She and everyone else in Le Chambon were well aware of the danger, but that did not deter them. "None of us thought that we were heroes," Magda Trocmé observed. "We were just people trying to do our best."

The people of Le Chambon made their village an ark of hope in a sea of flame and ash. But the full truth is that the people of Le Chambon were far from typical Christians during the Holocaust years. Much more typical was a pattern of betrayal, denial, and abandonment that can be found in the Gospel of John's account of the arrest, trial, and crucifixion of Jesus. In language contrasting with Jesus' "I am," his disciple, Simon Peter, denies knowing Jesus three times, saying, "I am not" when asked if he is one of Jesus' followers. The difference during the Holocaust was

---

[9]My account of Le Chambon is drawn from material I prepared for John K. Roth et al., *The Holocaust Chronicle*. See also Carol Rittner and John K. Roth, eds., *Different Voices: Women and the Holocaust* (St. Paul: Paragon House, 1993) 309-16.

that Christian denial was less explicit but still immensely destructive in its abandonment of the Jews. Christian words still professed fidelity to Jesus during those dark times, but Christian practice typically did not do so when it came to honoring the truth that Jesus taught, namely, that the friends of Jesus are those who "do what I command you," which means to "love one another as I have loved you" (John 15:12, 14).

Post-Holocaust Christians proclaim that the Word is "full of truth." Too often, of course, the truth is not good news. The Holocaust happened; Auschwitz was real. Such truths repudiate goodness. They do not set anyone free. Instead they choke us with despair, shatter hope, mock morality, and reveal the shallowness of conventional optimism—or at least they should. Such truths also judge Christianity and find it wanting. They may even judge God and find God wanting. They leave post-Holocaust Christians with immense responsibilities—or at least they should.

At the same time, and in spite of truth's all-too-frequent bad news, the Gospel of John affirms—and it is a basic Christian affirmation—that "the truth will make you free" (8:32). If we pursue, respect, and live by what is true—confessing sin, acknowledging shame, loving one another first and foremost—then we will save life and not destroy it. We will protest against injustice and not be indifferent to or complicit with it. In unprecedented ways, the Holocaust shows us what is evil and what is good, what is right and what is wrong. Such revelatory power does nothing to justify the Holocaust or to confer any special religious status upon it. The Holocaust ought not to have been—period. But given that the Holocaust did take place, and that life continues in its wake, those truths leave us to respond to them.

Cynicism is inviting. Despair is tempting. Resignation appeals. Gloom and discouragement await our embrace. Few have encountered the Holocaust and not fallen prey—however momentarily—to any or all of those moods. But if we go deep down, the truth is that those dispositions will not strike us as the best ones for a post-Holocaust existence. If we go deep down, the truth will set us free—not to be untouched by melancholy and despair but to find strength that post-Holocaust Christianity can encourage, strength to resist despair, to refuse to allow melancholy to crush the joy that can still be found when people serve and love one another.

Post-Holocaust Christians have this good news to share. If you sincerely abhor the Holocaust, if you wholeheartedly regret it, if you refuse to let Auschwitz-night prevail, if you hunger and thirst for righteousness in a world scarred by the Holocaust, the good news of post-Holocaust Christianity is a good place to start and to stand. In that place, there is room to protest what humankind has done, what God has not done (and that list is long and hard), and what Christians in particular have failed to do as followers of Jesus. But at the end of the day, the claim that "the Word was made flesh and dwelt among us, full of grace and truth" is one that affirms good news that the world badly needs. That news will not silence every question. It will not settle everything. Much has happened that deserves to remain unsettled and unsettling forever. But in ways that penetrate to the very core of existence, a post-Holocaust profession that "the light shines in the darkness, and the darkness has not overcome it" still offers good news full of grace and truth.

Postscript

The Courage to Try

Carol Rittner and John K. Roth

Charlotte Delbo was not Jewish, but her arrest for resisting the Nazi occupation of her native France made her experience the Holocaust when she was deported to Auschwitz in January 1943. Witnessing what happened to European Jewry, Delbo survived the Nazi onslaught. In 1946, she began to write the trilogy that came to be called *Auschwitz and After*. Her work's anguished visual descriptions, profound reflections on memory, and diverse writing styles make it an unrivaled Holocaust testimony.

Delbo called the second part of her trilogy *Useless Knowledge*. Normally we think that knowledge is useful, and it certainly can be, but Delbo showed how the Holocaust produced knowledge about hunger and disease, brutality and suffering, degradation and death that did nothing to unify, edify, or dignify life. "The sound of fifty blows on a man's back is interminable," she recounted. "Fifty strokes of a club on a man's back is an endless number."[1] This was only one example of what Delbo called useless knowledge. Its vast accumulation drove home her point: for the most part, what happened in the Holocaust divided, besieged, and diminished life forever.

As her trilogy drew to a close, Delbo wrote:

I do not know
if you can still
make something of me
If you have the courage to try . . . [2]

She was not optimistic about fresh starts and new beginnings, let alone redemption and salvation. By no means is it clear that she would have been very hopeful about post-Holocaust Christianity, either. Nevertheless, a key passage in *Auschwitz and After* makes a poignant reminder for post-Holocaust Christians, the faith that they profess, and the responsibility for the Christian tradition that they bear. Delbo said:

---

[1]Charlotte Delbo, *Auschwitz and After*, trans. Rosette C. Lamont (New Haven: Yale University Press, 1995) 58-59.

[2]Ibid., 352.

> I beg you, do something
> learn a dance step
> something to justify your existence
> something that gives you the right
> to be dressed in your skin in your body hair
> learn to walk and to laugh
> because it would be too senseless
> after all
> for so many to have died
> while you live
> doing nothing with your life.[3]

The effort can be lonely, and it takes courage, but the contributors to this book are trying to do something worthwhile to justify their existence as post-Holocaust Christians. Surrounded by the Holocaust's darkness, they strive to teach themselves and others the new steps that need to be taken after Auschwitz to preach and bring good news about the kingdom of God. A word from each of them can help to sum up what they have found thus far about the precautions, practices, proclamations that such work involves.

1. From Stephen Haynes: "Is there good news for Christians after Auschwitz? How this question is answered depends on how well Christians do their homework. . . . Attention to the fallacies of authenticity, superficial engagement, and theological retrieval will cause post-Holocaust Christians to proceed carefully."
2. From Stephen Smith: "Christians still need to face the fact that the metamorphosis of Christian theology and practice was nothing short of the *rejection* of Jesus as a practicing Jew. Every time Christianity misconstrued or poured contempt on Judaism or the Jewish people, so too it poured contempt on Jesus, its source."
3. From Bev. Allen Asbury: "To repent is to turn back. I turn away and then back, post-Auschwitz-wary, vigilant, cautious, skeptical; conscious, informed, sensible, affirming. I turn back to life out of a confrontation with death, with a passion remaining to seek a renewal and reordering of human life and society."
4. From Hubert Locke: "Rather than the God who is active in human history—leading, redeeming, judging, saving, proclaiming—perhaps we for whom conversation and communication are almost constants

---

[3]Ibid., 230.

have instead to confront and learn to grapple with a God who is silent when we most expect God to speak and act, and thus—in the moments of God's silence—leaves us to come to terms with the consequences of our own human failings."

5. From Eloise Rosenblatt: "Acknowledging and reforming an internal culture which fosters antisemitism is a continuing task facing all Catholic orders of men and women. . . . The canonization in 1998 of Edith Stein is a signal to engage in a new stage of communal repentance for Christianity's history of antisemitic racism."

6. From Robert Bullock: "The purpose of the Liturgy of the Word is the proclamation of the Lord Jesus Christ. But how can this be a true proclamation of the Lord when the text is misused and the structure is supersessionist?"

7. From Jolene Chu and James Pellechia: "The Christian gospel of the first century CE opened to all, Jew and non-Jew alike, the opportunity to reap the blessings of the Kingdom—this was good news indeed. But citizenship in the Kingdom brought with it responsibilities, requiring faithful obedience to God as Sovereign Ruler, along with an unbreakable commitment to God's law of neighbor love and to human brotherhood."

8. From Henry Knight: "Hospitality, when understood as making room for the other in one's life and in one's worlds of relation and significance, holds an important key for rethinking Christian expressions of good news after Auschwitz. Radical hospitality becomes the counter-testimony to the radical inhospitality of the Shoah."

9. From Carol Rittner: "The prophet Ezekiel, common to both our religious traditions, reminds us that God can and does give life to even our dead, dry bones (Ezek. 37:1-14). Should we not ask, therefore, Is there no overriding mercy to which guilt-tormented souls can entrust themselves? Will human beings have to learn to live with eternal guilt? What is the purpose of religion? (Is it to escape the just consequences of our actions?) Again and again, alone and together, we Christians and Jews must explore these questions, and we must try to expose 'our arguments to each other' so that we can gain 'a better understanding of [each] other's views.' "

10. From Victoria Barnett: "We as Christians must rethink our interpretation of scripture. We must rethink our Christology. We must rethink our ethics. And we must engage in other acts of faith—such as genuine repentance and remorse at our weakness and complicity in acts of real evil—that acknowledge that the Holocaust was an event that occurred within the realm of Christian history, not just world history.

Only in this way can we lay the theological foundation that enables us to conceive of a 'good news after Auschwitz.' "

11. From Douglas Huneke: "Rescuers want to know if lessons will be learned from their actions and applied to the crises of contemporary times. Theirs is not a wistful quest for validation—a surprising fact given the absence of notice by the churches—but an insistent, genuine concern for the world they are leaving behind that can only be addressed by a Christendom that is truly "post-Shoah."

12. From David Gushee: "The question is not whether 'Christianity' in the abstract has survived, or whether there can be Good News after Auschwitz. The real question is whether more of the world's two billion confessed Christians can be persuaded to practice the religion taught by their Savior. That, indeed, would be good news."

13. From John Roth: "At the end of the day, the claim that 'the Word was made flesh and dwelt among us, full of grace and truth' is one that affirms good news that the world badly needs. That news will not silence every question. It will not settle everything. Much has happened that deserves to remain unsettled and unsettling forever. But in ways that penetrate to the very core of existence, a post-Holocaust profession that 'the light shines in the darkness, and the darkness has not overcome it' still offers good news full of grace and truth."

When Charlotte Delbo said that "it would be too senseless / after all / for so many to have died / while you live / doing nothing with your life," she did not mean that anything one can do *now* would take away the senselessness of what took place *then*. Her words suggest, however, that a failure to change could make the Holocaust even more senseless than it was. If that failure persists, then senselessness would be compounded, because it will pervade our present and future lives as well.

Its anti-Jewish past leaves Christianity "credibility-challenged." As post-Holocaust Christianity sincerely faces that challenge, there are important contributions it has to offer. This book suggests that they include at least the following.

- Repentant honesty about Christianity's anti-Jewish history.
- New appreciation for the Jewish origins of Christianity, the Jewish identity of Jesus, and the continuing vitality of the Jewish people and their traditions.
- Welcome liberation from liturgies and biblical interpretations that promote harmful Christian exclusivism.

- Deepened understanding that the core of Christian practice is to love—inclusively and hospitably—one's neighbors as oneself.
- Intensified awareness that faithfulness to God entails human responsibility.
- Determined commitment that the darkness of injustice, evil, and death will not overcome the light of justice, goodness, and life itself.

Post-Holocaust Christianity cannot make the Holocaust less hideous than it was. But post-Holocaust Christians can be changed Christians. If we seek to walk in Christian faith anew, if we have the courage to learn our proper versions of Charlotte Delbo's "dance step," then in spite of the Holocaust, we may yet make something of ourselves—and of our tradition—that will proclaim good news.

Select Bibliography

The writings listed below, which include many that have influenced the contributions to this book, contain some of the most important reflections on post-Holocaust Christianity.

A Blessing to Each Other: Cardinal Joseph Bernadin and the Jewish Catholic Dialogue. Chicago: Liturgy Training Publications, 1996.

Abbott, Walter, ed. *The Documents of Vatican II.* New York: Herder and Herder, 1986.

Altizer, Thomas J. J. *The Descent into Hell: A Study of the Radical Reversal of the Christian Consciousness.* Philadelphia: Lippincott, 1970.

Altizer, Thomas J. J., and William Hamilton, eds. *Radical Theology and the Death of God.* Indianapolis: Bobbs-Merrill, 1966.

Barnett, Victoria J. *Bystanders: Conscience and Complicity during the Holocaust.* Westport CT: Greenwood Press, 1999.

_____. *For the Soul of the People: Protestant Protest against Hitler.* New York: Oxford University Press, 1992.

Baum, Gregory. *Is the New Testament Anti-Semitic? A Reexamination of the New Testament.* Revised edition. Glen Rock NJ: Paulist Press, 1965.

_____. *Protestant Theology in Communist East Germany.* Grand Rapids: Eerdmans, 1996.

_____. *Religion and Alienation: A Theological Reading of Sociology.* New York: Paulist Press, 1975.

_____. *The Social Imperative: Essays on the Critical Issues That Confront the Christian Churches.* New York: Paulist Press, 1979.

_____. *Theology and Society.* Mahwah NJ: Paulist Press, 1987.

Bea, Augustin. *The Church and the Jewish People.* New York: Harper & Row, 1966.

Beck, Norman A. *Mature Christianity in the 21st Century: The Recognition and Repudiation of the Anti-Jewish Polemic of the New Testament.* Revised edition. New York: Crossroad, 1994.

Bergen, Doris. *Twisted Cross: The German Christian Movement in the Third Reich.* Chapel Hill: University of North Carolina Press, 1996.

Blumenthal, David R. *Facing the Abusing God: A Theology of Protest.* Louisville: Westminster/John Knox Press, 1993.

Bonhoeffer, Dietrich. *Letters and Papers from Prison.* New York: Macmillan, 1972.

Bratton, Fred. *The Crime of Christendom: the Theological Sources of Christian Anti-Semitism.* Boston: Beacon Press, 1969.

Bristow, Edward, ed. *No Religion Is an Island: The Nostra Aetate Dialogues.* New York: Fordham University Press, 1998.

Brown, Robert McAfee. *Creative Dislocation—The Movement of Grace.* Nashville: Abingdon Press, 1980.

————. *Elie Wiesel: Messenger to All Humanity.* Revised edition. Notre Dame: University of Notre Dame Press, 1989.

————. *Saying Yes and Saying No: On Rendering to God and Caesar.* Philadelphia: Westminster, 1986.

————. *Speaking of Christianity: Practical Compassion, Social Justice, and Other Wonders.* Louisville: Westminster/John Knox Press, 1997.

————. *Spirituality and Liberation: Overcoming the Great Fallacy.* Philadelphia: Westminster, 1988.

Cargas, Harry James. *A Christian Response to the Holocaust.* Denver: Stonehenge Books, 1981.

————. *Reflections of a Post-Auschwitz Christian.* Detroit: Wayne State University Press, 1989.

————. *Shadows of Auschwitz: A Christian Response to the Holocaust.* New York: Crossroad, 1990.

Cargas, Harry James, ed. *Holocaust Scholars Write to the Vatican.* Westport, CT: Greenwood Press, 1998.

————. *The Unnecessary Problem of Edith Stein.* Lanham MD: University Press of America, 1994.

————. *When God and Man Failed: Non-Jewish Views of the Holocaust.* New York: Macmillan, 1981.

Crollius, A. R. ed. *Good and Evil after Auschwitz: Ethical Implications for Today.* Rome: Gregorian University Press, 1998.

Croner, Helga, ed. *Stepping Stones to Further Christian-Jewish Relations.* London: Stimulus Books, 1977.

————, ed. *More Stepping Stones to Jewish-Christian Relations: An Unabridged Collection of Christian Documents, 1975–1983.* New York: Paulist Press, 1985.

Danielou, Jean. *Dialogue with Israel.* Baltimore: Helicon Press, 1968.

Davies, Alan. *Anti-Semitism and the Christian Mind: The Crisis of Conscience after Auschwitz.* New York: Herder and Herder, 1969.

Davies, Alan, ed. *Anti-Semitism and the Foundations of Christianity*. New York: Paulist Press, 1979.

Davis, Stephen T., ed. *Encountering Evil: Live Options in Theodicy*. Second edition. Louisville: Westminster/John Knox Press, 2001.

de Gruchy, John W., ed. *The Cambridge Companion to Dietrich Bonhoeffer*. Cambridge: Cambridge University Press, 1999.

de Lubac, Henri. *Christian Resistance to Antisemitism: Memories from 1940–1944*. San Francisco: Ignatius Press, 1990.

Dietrich, Donald J. *God and Humanity in Auschwitz: Jewish-Christian Relations and Sanctioned Murder*. New Brunswick NJ: Transaction Publishers, 1995.

Dillard, Annie. *For the Time Being*. New York: Alfred A. Knopf, 1999.

Eakin, Frank E., Jr. *What Price Prejudice?: Christian Antisemitism in America*. Mahwah NJ: Paulist Press, 1998.

Eckardt, A. Roy. *For Righteousness' Sake: Contemporary Moral Philosophies*. Bloomington: Indiana University Press, 1987.

————. *Jews and Christians: The Contemporary Meeting*. Bloomington: Indiana University Press, 1986.

————. *Reclaiming the Jesus of History: Christology Today*. Minneapolis: Fortress Press, 1986

Eckardt, A. Roy, and Alice L. Eckardt. *Long Night's Journey into Day*. Detroit: Wayne State University Press, 1988.

Ellis, Marc. *Ending Auschwitz: The Future of Jewish and Christian Life*. Louisville: Westminster/John Knox Press, 1994.

Ellul, Jacques. *The Ethics of Freedom*. Translated and edited by Geoffrey W. Bromiley. Grand Rapids: Eerdmans, 1976.

————. *Hope in a Time of Abandonment*. Trans. C. Edward Hopkin. New York: Seabury, 1973.

————. *Prayer and Modern Man*. Trans. C. Edward Hopkin. New York: Seabury, 1970.

Ericksen, Robert P. *Theologians under Hitler: Gerhard Kittel, Paul Althaus, and Emanuel Hirsch*. New Haven: Yale University Press, 1985.

Ericksen, Robert P., and Susannah Heschel, eds. *Betrayal: German Churches and the Holocaust*. Minneapolis: Fortress Press, 1999.

Farmer, William R., ed. *Anti-Judaism and the Gospels*. Philadelphia: Trinity Press International, 1999.

Fasching, Darrell J. *The Ethical Challenge of Auschwitz and Hiroshima—Apocalypse or Utopia?* Albany: SUNY Press, 1993.

————. *Narrative Theology after Auschwitz: From Alienation to Ethics*. Minneapolis: Augsburg/Fortress Press, 1992.

Fasching, Darrell J., ed. *The Jewish People in Christian Preaching*. New York and Toronto: Edwin Mellen Press, 1984.

Ferrucci, Franco. *The Life of God (as Told by Himself)*. Chicago: University of Chicago Press, 1996.

Fisher, Eugene J. *Faith without Prejudice: Rebuilding Christian Attitudes toward Judaism*. New York: Crossroad, 1993.

Fisher, Eugene J., ed. *Visions of the Other: Jewish and Christian Theologians Assess the Dialogue*. New York: Paulist Press, 1994.

Fiorenza, Elisabeth, and David Tracy, eds. *The Holocaust as Interruption*. London: T.&T. Clark Ltd., 1984.

Flannery, Edward. *The Anguish of the Jews*. New York: Paulist Press, 1985.

Fleischner, Eva. *Judaism in German Christian Theology since 1945: Christianity and Israel Considered in Terms of Mission*. Metuchen NJ: Scarecrow Press, 1975.

Fleischner, Eva, ed. *Auschwitz: Beginning of a New Era?* New York: KTAV, 1977.

Forstman, Jack. *Christian Faith in Dark Times: Theological Conflicts in the Shadow of Hitler*. Louisville: Westminster/John Knox Press, 1992.

Fuchs, Josef. *Human Values and Christian Morality*. Dublin: Gill and Macmillan, 1970.

Gager, John G. *The Origins of Anti-Semitism: Attitudes toward Judaism in Pagan and Christian Antiquity*. New York: Oxford University Press, 1983.

Gerlach, Wolfgang. *And the Witnesses Were Silent: The Confessing Church and the Persecution of the Jews*. Translated and edited by Victoria Barnett. Lincoln: University of Nebraska Press, 1999.

Gilbert, Arthur. *The Vatican Council and the Jews*. Cleveland: World Publishing Co., 1968.

Godsey, John D., and Geoffrey B. Kelly, eds. *Ethical Responsibility: Bonhoeffer's Legacy to the Churches*. New York and Toronto: Edwin Mellen Press, 1981.

Greeley, Andrew, and Jacob Neusner. *Common Ground: A Priest and a Rabbi Read Scripture Together*. Cleveland OH: Pilgrim Press, 1996.

Gushee, David P. *The Righteous Gentiles of the Holocaust: A Christian Interpretation*. Minneapolis: Fortress Press, 1994.

Hall, Sidney G. III. *Christian Anti-Semitism and Paul's Theology*. Minneapolis: Fortress Press, 1993.

Hallie, Philip. *Lest Innocent Blood Be Shed: The Story of the Village of Le Chambon and How Goodness Happened There*. New York: Harper & Row, 1979.

_____. *Tales of Good and Evil, Help and Harm.* New York: HarperCollins, 1997.

Hargrove, Katharine T., ed. *Seeds of Reconciliation: Essays on Jewish-Christian Understanding.* Bible Alert Publications, 1996.

Häring, Bernard. *Embattled Witness: Memories of a Time of War.* New York: Seabury Press, 1976.

_____. *Free and Faithful: My Life in the Catholic Church.* Liguori MO: Liguori/Triumph, 1998.

_____. *My Hope for the Church: Critical Encouragement for the Twenty-First Century.* Liguori MO: Liguori/Triumph, 1997.

_____. *My Witness for the Church.* Introduction by Leonard Swidler. New York: Paulist Press, 1992.

Harrelson, Walter, and Randall M. Falk. *Jews and Christians: A Troubled Family.* Nashville: Abingdon Press, 1990.

Harris, Maria. *Proclaim Jubilee! A Spirituality for the Twenty-First Century.* Foreword by Walter Brueggemann. Louisville: Westminster/John Knox Press, 1996.

Hauerwas, Stanley, Richard Bondi, and David Burrell. *Truthfulness and Tragedy: Further Investigations in Christian Ethics.* Notre Dame: University of Notre Dame Press, 1977.

Haynes, Stephen R. *Prospects for Post-Holocaust Theology.* Atlanta: American Academy of Religion, 1992.

_____. *Reluctant Witnesses: Jews and the Christian Imagination.* Louisville: Westminster/John Knox Press, 1995.

_____. *Holocaust Education and the Church-Related College: Restoring Ruptured Traditions.* Westport CT: Greenwood Press, 1997.

Haynes, Stephen R., and John K. Roth, eds. *The Death of God Movement and the Holocaust: Radical Theology Encounters the Shoah.* Westport CT: Greenwood Press, 1999.

Herbstrith, Waltraud, ed. *Never Forget: Christian and Jewish Perspectives on Edith Stein.* Trans. Susanne Batzdorff. Washington DC: Institute of Carmelite Studies, 1998.

Huneke, Douglas K. *The Stones Will Cry Out: Pastoral Reflections on the Shoah (With Liturgical Resources).* Westport CT: Greenwood Press, 1995.

Jacobs, Steven L., ed. *Contemporary Christian Religious Responses to the Shoah.* Lanham MD: University Press of America, 1993.

_____. *Holocaust Now: Contemporary Christian and Jewish Thought.* East Rockaway NY: Cummings and Hathaway, 1996.

Jones, L. Gregory. *Embodying Forgiveness: A Theological Analysis.* Grand Rapids: Eerdmans, 1995.

Kasper, Walter, and Hans Küng, eds. *Christians and Jews*. New York: Seabury Press, 1974.

Kee, Howard Clark. *What Can We Know about Jesus?* Cambridge: Cambridge University Press, 1990.

Kee, Howard Clark, and Irvin J. Borowsky, eds. *Removing Anti-Judaism from the Pulpit*. New York: Continuum, 1996.

Klein, Charlotte. *Anti-Judaism in Christian Theology*. Philadelphia: Fortress Press, 1978.

Knight, Henry F. *Confessing Christ in a Post-Holocaust World: A Midrashic Experiment*. Westport CT: Greenwood Press, 2000.

Küng, Hans. *Judaism*. London: SCM Press, 1992.

Leddy, Mary Jo. *At the Border Called Hope: Where Refugees Are Neighbours*. Toronto: HarperCollins, 1997.

_____. *Memories of War, Promises of Peace*. Toronto: Lester & Orphen Dennys Ltd., 1989.

_____. *Say to the Darkness, We Beg to Differ*. Toronto: Lester & Orphen Dennys Ltd., 1990.

Littell, Franklin H. *The Crucifixion of the Jews: The Failure of Christians to Understand the Jewish Experience*. New York: Harper & Row, 1975. Reprint with a preface by the author: ROSE 12. Macon GA: Mercer University Press, 1986, 1996.

Littell, Franklin H., and Hubert G. Locke, eds., *The German Church Struggle and the Holocaust*. San Francisco: Mellen Research University Press, 1990.

Littell, Marcia Sachs, and Sharon Weissman Gutman, eds. *Liturgies on the Holocaust: An Interfaith Anthology*. Valley Forge PA: Trinity International Press, 1996.

Locke, Hubert. *Learning from History: A Black Christian's Perspective on the Holocaust*. Westport CT: Greenwood Press, 2000.

Marcus, Joel. *Jesus and the Holocaust: Reflections on Suffering and Hope*. New York: Doubleday, 1997.

McFadyen, Alistair I. *Bound to Sin: Abuse, the Holocaust, and the Christian Doctrine of Sin*. Cambridge: Cambridge University Press, 2000.

McGarry, C.S.P., Michael B. *Christology after Auschwitz*. New York: Paulist Press, 1977.

Metz, Johann Baptist. *A Passion for God: The Mystical-Political Dimension of Christianity*. Trans. J. Matthew Ashley. New York: Paulist Press, 1998.

Miller-Fahrenholz, Geiko. *The Art of Forgiveness*. Geneva: WCC Publications, 1997.

Minow, Martha. *Between Vengeance and Forgiveness: Facing History after Genocide*. Boston: Beacon Press, 1999.

Moltmann, Jurgen. *The Source of Life*. Minneapolis: Fortress Press, 1997.

Moore, James F. *Christian Theology After the Shoah: A Reinterpretation of the Passion Narratives*. Lanham MD: University Press of America, 1993.

Ottati, Douglas F. *Jesus Christ and Christian Vision*. Minneapolis: Fortress Press, 1989.

Pawlikowski, John T. *Christ in the Light of Christian-Jewish Dialogue*. New York: Paulist Press, 1982.

_____. *Jesus and the Theology of Israel*. Wilmington DE: Michael Glazier, 1989.

Peck, Abraham J., ed. Foreword by Elie Wiesel. *Jews and Christians after the Holocaust*. Philadelphia: Fortress Press, 1982.

Plank, Karl A. *Mother of the Wire Fence: Inside and Outside the Holocaust*. Louisville: Westminster/John Knox Press, 1994.

Pollefeyt, Didier. *Jews and Christians: Rivals or Partners for the Kingdom of God?* Grand Rapids: Eerdmans, 1997.

Rahner, Karl, and Pinchas Lapide. *Encountering Jesus—Encountering Judaism: A Dialogue*. New York: Crossroad, 1987.

Rausch, David A. *A Legacy of Hatred: Why Christians Must Not Forget the Holocaust*. Chicago: Moody Press, 1984.

Riches, John. *The World of Jesus: First-Century Judaism in Crisis*. Cambridge: Cambridge University Press, 1990.

Rittner, Carol, and John K. Roth, eds. *From the Unthinkable to the Unavoidable: American Christian and Jewish Scholars Encounter the Holocaust*. Westport CT: Greenwood Press, 1997.

_____. *Memory Offended: The Auschwitz Convent Controversy*. Westport CT: Praeger, 1991.

Rittner, Carol, Stephen Smith, and Irena Steinfeldt, eds. *The Holocaust and the Christian World*. New York: Continuum, 2000.

Roth, John K. *A Consuming Fire: Encounters with Elie Wiesel and the Holocaust*. Atlanta GA: John Knox Press, 1979.

Roth, John K., ed. *Ethics After the Holocaust: Perspectives, Critiques, and Responses*. St. Paul: Paragon House, 1999.

Roth, John K. and Michael Berenbaum, eds. *Holocaust: Religious and Philosophical Implications*. New York: Paragon House, 1989.

Rubenstein, Betty Rogers, and Michael Berenbaum, eds. *What Kind of God? Essays in Honor of Richard L. Rubenstein*. Lanham MD: University Press of America, 1995.

Rubenstein, Richard L., and John K. Roth. *Approaches to Auschwitz*. Atlanta: John Knox Press, 1987.

Ruether, Rosemary Radford. *Disputed Questions: On Being a Christian*. Nashville: Abingdon, 1982.

_____. *Faith and Fratricide: The Theological Roots of Anti-Semitism*. With an Introduction by Gregory Baum. New York: Seabury Press, 1974.

Saramago, José. *The Gospel according to Jesus Christ*. San Diego: Harcourt Brace, 1994.

Schuster, Ekkehard, and Reinhold Boschert-Kimmig, eds. *Hope Against Hope: Johann Baptist Metz and Elie Wiesel Speak Out on the Holocaust*. New York: Paulist Press, 1999.

Schwartz, Regina. *The Curse of Cain: The Violent Legacy of Monotheism*. Chicago: University of Chicago Press, 1997.

Shriver, Donald. *An Ethic for Enemies*. New York: Oxford University Press, 1995.

Siker, Jeffrey S. *Disinheriting the Jews: Abraham in Early Christian Controversy*. Louisville: Westminster/John Knox Press, 1991.

Smiga, George M. *Pain and Polemic: Anti-Judaism in the Gospels*. New York: Paulist Press, 1992.

Soelle, Dorothee. *Against the Wind: Memoir of a Radical Christian*. Minneapolis: Augsburg Fortress Press, 1999.

_____. *Beyond Mere Obedience*. New York: Pilgrim Press, 1982.

_____. *Theology for Skeptics: Reflections on God*. Minneapolis: Fortress Press, 1995.

Soulen, Kendall. *The God of Israel and Christian Theology*. Minneapolis: Augsburg/Fortress Press, 1996.

Spong, John Shelby. *Liberating the Gospels: Reading the Bible with Jewish Eyes*. San Francisco: HarperCollins, 1996.

Steele, Michael R. *Christianity, Tragedy, and Holocaust Literature*. Westport CT: Greenwood Press, 1995.

Thoma, Clemens. *A Christian Theology of Judaism*. New York: Paulist, 1980.

van Beeck, Franz Josef. *Loving the Torah More than God?: Towards a Catholic Appreciation of Judaism*. Chicago: Loyola Press, 1989.

van Buren, Paul. *A Theology of the Jewish-Christian Reality*. Part 1. *Discerning the Way*. New York: Seabury, 1980.

_____. *A Theology of the Jewish-Christian Reality*. Part 2. *A Christian Theology of the People Israel*. New York: Seabury, 1983.

_____. *A Theology of the Jewish-Christian Reality*. Part 3. *Christ in Context*. New York: Harper & Row, 1988.

Volf, Miroslav. *Exclusion and Embrace: A Theological Exploration of Identity, Otherness, and Reconciliation*. Nashville: Abingdon Press, 1996.

Wallis, James H. *Post-Holocaust Christianity: Paul van Buren's Theology of the Jewish-Christian Reality*. Lanham MD: University Press of America, 1997.

Wiesenthal, Simon. *The Sunflower: On the Possibilities and Limits of Forgiveness.* Revised and expanded edition. Ed. Harry James Cargas and Bonny V. Fetterman. New York: Schocken Books, 1998.

Willebrands, Johannes Cardinal. *Church & Jewish People: New Considerations.* New York: Paulist Press, 1992.

Williamson, Clark. *A Guest in the House of Israel: Post-Holocaust Church Theology.* Louisville: Westminster/John Knox Press, 1993.

_____. *Has God Rejected His People? Anti-Judaism in the Christian Church.* Nashville: Abingdon Press, 1982.

_____. *When Jews and Christians Meet: A Guide for Christian Preaching and Teaching.* St. Louis: CBP Press, 1989.

Williamson, Clark, ed. *A Mutual Witness: Toward Critical Solidarity between Jews & Christians.* St. Louis: Chalice Press, 1992.

Williamson, Clark M., and Ronald J. Allen. *Interpreting Difficult Texts: Anti-Judaism and Christian Preaching.* Philadelphia: Trinity Press, 1989.

Wink, Walter. *Engaging the Powers: Discernment and Resistance in a World of Domination.* Minneapolis: Fortress Press, 1992.

_____. *When the Powers Fall: Reconciliation in the Healing of Nations.* Minneapolis: Fortress Press, 1998.

Wistrich, Robert S. *Antisemitism: The Longest Hatred.* New York: Schocken, 1991.

About the Editors
and Contributors

Carol Rittner, is Distinguished Professor of Holocaust Studies at the Richard Stockton College of New Jersey. She has been actively involved in teaching about the Holocaust for many years. In addition to her publications, including *The Courage to Care: Rescuers of Jews During the Holocaust* (edited with Sondra Myers), *Memory Offended: The Auschwitz Convent Controversy* (edited with John K. Roth), and *The Holocaust in the Christian World* (edited with Stephen Smith and Irena Steinfeldt), she has contributed to several books of essays and written numerous essays about the Holocaust. Beyond her projects in the United States, Rittner is actively involved in community work around the topic of "living with differences" in Northern Ireland (with Holywell Trust, Derry, Northern Ireland), where she also encourages education about the Holocaust and about Jews and Judaism in the schools in that part of the world.

John K. Roth is the Russell K. Pitzer Professor of Philosophy at Claremont McKenna College, where he has taught since 1966. He has published numerous books and articles about the Holocaust and Jewish-Christian relations, including *Approaches to Auschwitz: The Holocaust and Its Legacy* (with Richard L. Rubenstein), *Different Voices: Women and the Holocaust* (edited with Carol Rittner), *Ethics after the Holocaust*, and major contributions to *The Holocaust Chronicle*. One of his recent books, *Private Needs, Public Selves*, concentrates on public discourse about religion in the United States. Roth has served on the United States Holocaust Memorial Council, Washington, where he has been on the Church Relations Committee. He is an active member of the Claremont Presbyterian Church in Claremont, California.

Bev. Allen Asbury retired from Vanderbilt University in 1996 after thirty years as university chaplain, senior lecturer in Religious Studies, and adjunct professor in the Divinity School. At Vanderbilt, he founded the Holocaust Lecture Series, now the longest-sustained series about the

Holocaust on a college campus in the United States. Asbury was a founding member of the Tennessee Holocaust Commission and served as its chair for twelve years. He is a member of both the Education and Church Relations Committees of the United States Holocaust Memorial Museum and served on the executive board of the Association of Holocaust Organizations. He has published numerous articles on the Holocaust and its implications for Christianity.

Victoria J. Barnett is an independent scholar, translator, and writer. She has been a consultant to the Church Relations Department of the United States Holocaust Memorial Museum, Washington, since 1994. She is the author of *For the Soul of the People: Protestant Protest against Hitler* and *Bystanders: Conscience and Complicity in the Holocaust.* In addition, she is the editor and translator of Wolfgang Gerlach's *And the Witnesses Were Silent: The Confessing Church and the Jews.* An authority on the German theologian and resistance figure Dietrich Bonhoeffer, she serves on the editorial board for the new English edition of Bonhoeffer's complete works, and she is the editor of the new revised English edition of Eberhard Bethge, *Dietrich Bonhoeffer: A Biography.*

Robert W. Bullock, a priest of the Roman Catholic Archdiocese of Boston, is pastor of the Our Lady of Sorrows Parish in Sharon, Massachusetts. The town has a unique demography. It is seventy-five percent Jewish; is the site of the Islamic Center of New England; and is home for seven Christian congregations. Prior to this assignment, Bullock was for twelve years the director of campus ministry for the archdiocese and was for nine years the Catholic chaplain at Brandeis University. He has been involved in Facing History and Ourselves: The Holocaust and Human Behavior since the founding of that organization in 1975 and serves as the chairperson of its National Board of Scholars. He is a panelist on "Talking Religion," a Sunday morning interreligious conversation program that is broadcast in New England. Bullock has been a member of the Archdiocesan Liturgical and Ecumenical Commissions, and he is a founding member of the Catholic-Jewish Committee of the Archdiocese.

Jolene Chu, a researcher, archivist, and lecturer at the Watch Tower Society, specializes in the history of Jehovah's Witnesses during the Nazi era. In this capacity, she is the project coordinator for Holocaust-related education programs and cooperative efforts with schools, universities, and Holocaust education and research facilities. Her past projects include educational conferences at Tulane University, the University of Texas at

Austin, Rice University, San Diego State University, Appalachian State University, and the University of Toronto, as well as the documentary film *Jehovah's Witnesses Stand Firm against Nazi Assault* and its accompanying study guide.

David P. Gushee is the Graves Professor of Moral Philosophy at Union University and a senior fellow at the university's Center for Christian Leadership. The author of *The Righteous Gentiles of the Holocaust: A Christian Interpretation,* he is a Christian ethicist whose numerous articles about the Holocaust and Christian-Jewish relations have appeared in *Holocaust and Genocide Studies, Annals of the American Academy of Political and Social Science,* and *Christianity Today.*

Stephen R. Haynes is the Albert B. Curry Professor of Religious Studies at Rhodes College. He has written or edited five books: *Prospects for Post-Holocaust Theology, To Each Its Own Meaning: An Introduction to Biblical Criticisms and Their Application* (edited with Steven L. McKenzie), *Reluctant Witnesses: Jews and the Christian Imagination, Holocaust Education and the Church-Related College: Restoring Ruptured Traditions,* and *The Death of God and the Holocaust: Radical Theology Encounters the Shoah* (edited with John K. Roth). Haynes is cochair of the American Academy of Religion's Religion, Holocaust, and Genocide Group. He has served on the Regional Advisory Council of Facing History and Ourselves since 1993, and in 1996 was appointed to the Tennessee Holocaust Commission.

Douglas K. Huneke is the senior minister of Westminster Presbyterian Church, Tiburon, California. He served as Presbyterian University pastor and as a member of the Honors College faculty at the University of Oregon. In 1980 he received the Faculty Research Award from the Oregon Committee for the Humanities. With that award, he began a twenty-year systematic study of the moral and spiritual development of Christians who rescued Jews during the Shoah. He is the author of *The Moses of Rovno,* the biography of the German rescuer Herman Graebe, and *The Stones Will Cry Out: Pastoral Reflections on the Shoah.* He has contributed chapters to six volumes and is completing a young adult book about a teenager in Poland who rescued a Jewish girl and her father.

Henry F. ("Hank") Knight is university chaplain and associate professor of Religion at the University of Tulsa, where his teaching specializes in Holocaust studies and, in particular, post-Shoah Christian Theology. An active participant in the Annual Scholars' Conference on the Holocaust and the Churches, Knight chaired that group's 1993 meeting in Tulsa. He is the author or editor of several Holocaust-related books and essays, including *Confessing Christ in a Post-Holocaust World: A Midrashic Experiment* and *The Uses and Abuses of Knowledge: Proceedings of the 23rd Annual Scholars' Conference on the Holocaust and the German Church Struggle* (edited with Marcia Sachs Littell).

Hubert G. Locke is the John and Marguerite Corbally Professor at the University of Washington, where he holds appointments on the faculties of the Graduate School of Public Affairs, the Program in Jewish Studies, the Program in Comparative Religion, and the Department of Sociology. He is a member of the Committee on Conscience, the Education Committee, and the Committee on Church Relations of the United States Holocaust Memorial Museum. Locke is associate editor of *Holocaust and Genocide Studies* and a member of the editorial board of *Shoah*. He is also the author or editor of numerous works about the Holocaust, including *Exile in the Fatherland: The Prison Letters of Martin Niemoeller*, *The Black Anti-Semitism Controversy*, and *Learning from History: A Black Christian's Perspective on the Holocaust*.

James N. Pellechia directs the public affairs office of the Watchtower Society, where he is also the associate editor for Watch Tower publications. A lecturer on the modern history of Jehovah's Witnesses, he coordinates Holocaust-related academic programs and produces films, including the award-winning documentary *Jehovah's Witnesses Stand Firm against Nazi Assault*.

Eloise Rosenblatt, is associate dean of the faculty at the Graduate Theological Union in Berkeley, California, and is a law student at Santa Clara University Law School. She has been a Sister of Mercy since 1967, and a classroom teacher of New Testament studies for twenty-five years at secondary, college, university, and seminary levels. She has lived and studied in Jerusalem and was twice a fellow at the Shalom Hartman Institute in Jerusalem, where she participated in projects sponsored by the National Conference of Christians and Jews and under the leadership of David Hartman and the late Paul van Buren. The author of *Paul the Accused: His Portrait in Acts of the Apostles*, which argues that Paul did not reject his Jewish heritage, and that the reading of Acts should get beyond the conventional rejectionist paradigm of Christians as the New Israel, Rosenblatt is also interested in the political and religious debate about who should "own" Edith Stein, the Jewish philosopher who converted to Roman Catholicism, entered the Carmelites, and died at Auschwitz.

Stephen D. Smith is cofounder and director of Beth Shalom Holocaust Memorial Centre, Great Britain's first Holocaust education institute. He is editor of the "Witness Series," a collection of Holocaust survivor testimonies, and is actively engaged in the creation of education texts and resources. He is project advisor and trustee for the Cape Town Holocaust Centre. He frequently lectures on Holocaust education in the United Kingdom and abroad. Among his publications are *Forgotten Places*, a photographic essay on the remnants of Holocaust destruction in Poland, and *The Holocaust in the Christian World* (edited with Carol Rittner and Irena Steinfeldt).

Index

"Good News" after Auschwitz?
Christian Faith within a Post-Holocaust World.
   edited and introduced by Carol Rittner and John K. Roth

Mercer University Press, Macon, Georgia 31210-3960 USA.
ISBN 0-86554-701-7. Catalog and warehouse pick number: MUP/H520.
Text, interior, and title-page design, composition, and layout
    by Edmon L. Rowell, Jr.
Text font: Palatino 10/12. Interior titles font: PalatinoBF.
Title-page font: PeignotDemi.
Cover and dust jacket design, composition, and execution
    by Jim Burt, Burt&Burt.

June 2001.

[23 March 2001]